by R C McDonald

Ca

How To Ke...   aries

with a chapter by Sharon Klueber

Dig deep into the mysteries of Canariculture with this collection of Robirda's canary-care articles, newly edited and updated, including an article by Sharon Klueber and never-before-published material by Robirda.

Part One covers canary caging, care, and feeding, while Part Two delves into health and health issues, especially preventative health maintenance. Part Three expands on the ins and outs of breeding canaries, from preparing for the breeding season, to how to deal with commonly encountered problems, and even offers ideas on what to do with the resulting flock of youngsters.

This book is not intended to replace the advice of a qualified avian veterinarian, but rather is meant to offer insight and assistance in learning to understand the life processes of pet and show canaries. You'll find practical canariculture skills, along with information garnered from years of experience and a wide variety of sources.

For basic canary care, refer to Robirda's book, *'Brats in Feathers'*; when you're ready for more, read *'Canary Crazy'*.

Reader's reviews; *"Robirda, I received your signed book, thank you very much. It is just as the reviews stated, bursting with practical information and ready to implement tips. Again many thanks..."* C. Walter, ON

"I thoroughly enjoy Flock Talk! Yours is the first pet bird publication that actually offers useful advice, and provides correct information! As a biologist and self-proclaimed bird nut, I really appreciate that! Keep up the great work!" D. Lahaise, GA

Dedicated to those who work to bring peace and harmony to the world and all its beings, & especially to Sharon Klueber; we love & miss you.

Many of these articles were first published in Flock Talk ezine, between the years of 2000 and 2006. Most of the rest were published by Bird Talk or in Birds USA, in 1996, 1997, 2009, 2010, and 2011. Cover photos of Robirda's canaries are by Michael deFreitas, used with his permission, and copyright © by him. Articles are copyright © by their author, and may not be used without specific permission of author or editor.

ISBN-13: 978-1479363520

ISBN-10: 1479363529

Author's note: Any information related to medicinal or health care for sick or injured canaries in this book is drawn directly from personal experience and studies, and is not intended to replace the advice or services of an accredited avian veterinarian. If you think your bird is ill, consult a professional avian veterinarian as soon as you possibly can; there will be no time to waste!

No part of this book may be copied, edited, or reproduced (electronically or in print), translated, or arranged without written permission of the author, with the exception of brief passages quoted in a review.

by R C McDonald

Canary Crazy

How to Keep, Breed, & Care For Canaries

by Robirda McDonald,
with a chapter by Sharon Klueber

Canary Crazy

by R C McDonald

Part 1
Care, Cages, & Feeding

Wild Canary Habitat	pg 09
Should I Buy a Pet Store Bird?	pg 16
Getting a Gift Canary	pg 20
Song Canaries	pg 26
Colour & Type Canaries	pg 33
The Best Possible Pet Canary	pg 46
Understanding Territoriality	pg 51
Canary Cage Set-Up	pg 56
Can Canaries Share Cages?	pg 60
Flight Cages Are For The Birds	pg 65
Home Free	pg 71
Gardening For Your Birds	pg 76
Chickweed, the Bird's Choice	pg 84
Glorious Greens	pg 88
Why Soak Seed?	pg 99
Complete Nutrition?	pg 104
Enter The Moult	pg 109
Colour-Fed or Colour-Bred?	pg 113
Colourfeeding	pg 117
Building an Indoor Aviary	pg 124
Aviary Management Considerations	pg 131
Moving With Your Birds	pg 136
Translating 'Birdspeak'	pg 141
Pet Bird Communication	pg 145

Part 2
Canary Health Care

Photosensitivity	pg 153
Troubleshooting Problems	pg 157
The Treatment Quandary	pg 165
Air Quality	pg 170
Supplemental Lighting	pg 175
Bird's First Aid Kit	pg 180
Encouraging Beneficials	pg 187
Overgrown Beak	pg 192
Mites!	pg 198
Pet Birds & the Avian Flu	pg 204
Avian Gastric Yeast (Megabacteria)	pg 209
Metal Toxicity	pg 215
The Non-Stick Issue	pg 220
Bald Spots & Tatty Feathers	pg 224
Feather Lumps	pg 230
Bird Keeper's Lung	pg 237
Air Sac Mites	pg 242
Quarantine	pg 248
Unseasonal Moult	pg 253
Beat The Heat	pg 258

Part 3
Breeding Canaries

The Breeding Quandary	pg 267
The Controversy of Diversity	pg 273
A Hen's Gotta Lay	pg 278
An Ethical Breeder	pg 284
Gender-Specific Canary Behaviour	pg 288
Wintering Canaries	pg 294
Conditioning Canaries	pg 300
Pairing Canaries	pg 306
Egg-Binding	pg 310
Infertile Eggs	pg 318
Non-Feeding	pg 324
Banding Babies	pg 332
What Now?	pg 340
Unseasonal Breeding	pg 346
To Breed or Not?	pg 352
Shipping Birds	pg 358
Sharing the Dream	pg 363
About The Author	pg 369

Canary Crazy

by R C McDonald

Wild Canary Habitats

Some of the best advice that I've ever heard given on keeping birds consists of only two words; *emulate nature*. It sounds simple, but these two short words encompass an entire world of ideas.

In order to do this, it's first necessary to learn about the environment where the species evolved; the climate, the seasonal variations, other plants and animals that live there, and how together they interact to form a complete ecosystem. With this thought in mind, let's spend a little time examining the original wild canary habitat.

Mankind has kept canaries for over 500 years. During that time we have assisted in the creation of a broad spectrum of breeds. But whatever their colour or kind, canaries everywhere share one thing in common: they all descended from a family of little green songsters originally found in the wild in only one place in the world; the Canary Islands.

It's said that if you stand on the beach at the furthest north-western point of the continent of Africa, on a clear day you can see the peak of Tenerife rising above the mists of the sea. This volcanic island has an area of 795 square miles, and is the largest of the island group known as the Canary Islands.

It is situated roughly 200 miles west of the Moroccan coastline, at approximately 28 degrees latitude and 16.5 degrees longitude. This modest-sized island just happens to possess the tallest volcano in Europe. This peak forms a key element in the wide range of micro-climates and the extreme variety of weather patterns seen across this small group of islands.

The entire island group consists of seven larger islands: Tenerife, Fuertenventura, Gran Canaria, Lanzarote, La Palma, La Gomera and Hierro, and four smaller islands: La Graciosa, Alegreza, Lobos and Montafla Clara.

It's thought that these islands formed during the movements of the continental plates of Africa and Europe during the middle of the Cretaceous period, about the same time the Alps were formed.

The islands closest to the African coast are the most ancient. As you move toward the open ocean, they become younger. These changes are echoed underwater; moving from east to west the sounds around the individual islands get deeper, from about 3000 feet between the African coast and Lanzarote to more than 12,000 feet around La Palma.

The islands were originally inhabited by a wide variety of indigenous peoples. The people of the island of Tenerife were known as Guanches, while the inhabitants of Fuerteventura and Lanzarote were referred to as Maxos. Gran Canaria was inhabited by a tribe known as the Canarii, while El Hierro supported the Bimbaches. On La Palma lived the Auaritas, and on La Gomera were found the Gomeros. Evidence suggests that interaction between these groups was relatively low, with each island populated by its own distinct socio-cultural group.

In general, wildlife found in the Canary Islands differs little from that found in Europe, with two exceptions; the dromedary and the canary, often known locally as the 'thistle-finch'.

Plant life found on the islands is in many ways a reservoir of history; species which vanished from the nearby continents hundreds of years ago or more can easily be found. These islands contain a world's worth of genetic

by R C McDonald

history that becomes more fascinating and unique the more it is examined.

The climate of the islands ranges widely from near-desert conditions, to icy alpine ranges, and just about everything in between. Snow and fire are the characterizing extremes, highlighting the almost two-sided nature of the local weather.

The volcanoes with their awesome heights are the origin of this variety of climatic contrast. The Trade Winds bring humidity and fresh air from the west and northwest and establish a typical oceanic humid climate on the windward sides. This results in a great luxuriance of plant growth. The effects of these winds is the most obvious between 900 and 3400 feet; under this zone the effect can hardly been felt, while above it is an arid climate of hot dry summers and icy cold winters.

On the other hand, the sides of the islands that face towards Africa are influenced by the hot, dry winds blowing from the Sahara, resulting in a dry, arid climate. The contrasts between these two extremes have spawned an amazing array of plant-life.

Geologists and ecologists recognize six distinct micro-climates on the islands (some add two more human-created zones, termed 'ruin' and 'artificial', to create eight). These are Coastal, Arid, Laurel-like Forest, Pine Forest, High Mountain, and Rocky.

The coastal zone is similar in nature to that found around the Mediterranean, but more rocky, with small areas of sand and salt water. These provide a home for those species able to withstand both the salt and the aridity, many of which are found only in these tiny coastal island habitats.

This arid zone forms a fairly even strip between the coast and the first slopes of the mountains, up to a height of 2000 feet or so. It is characterized by a hot, arid sub-desert climate. Rainfall fluctuates between 50 and 100 inches per year, while the annual average temperature is almost always above freezing. The vegetation compares with that of the arid areas of Sudan, Ethiopia, Arabia and Iran and is typical of the steppes in the African continent. Plant life is dominated by cactus-like plants and small creeping lianas.

The Laurel-like forested zone is found in the humid areas and on the mountain slopes, and is characterized by luxurious groups of evergreen trees with laurel-like leaves. The trade winds bring a constant supply of moist air from the northwest, which climbs up the slopes of the mountains and condenses into thick fogs, seen in varying densities for most of the year. This fog belt allows optimal conditions for sub-tropical evergreen forests to develop on slopes that face north or north-west.

These forests range upwards from an average of 1500 feet above the ocean, although on occasion they will dip as low as 300 feet above sea level. The upper range can often extend as high as 4,800 feet above sea level.

These forests are widely regarded as a kind of living Paleo-flora, relics of sub-tropical humid vegetation which, until the end of the Tertiary period (late Miocene and early Pliocene), could be found in large parts of South Europe and North Africa. In fact, fossils of plants belonging to genera still living in the Canary Islands have fairly recently been discovered in many countries around the Mediterranean: Spain, France, Italy and Georgia. These forests have diminished greatly in the past few decades, and now cover less than 7% of the islands.

The pine forest zone is found directly above the laurel-like forests, and harbours a wide variety of bird life. It is here that wild canaries can often be most easily found, although apparently the canary is one of the few birds native to the islands that does not restrict its ranges to only one zone, but is in fact found in all areas of the islands. However, it is said that wild canaries do seem to be a bit more frequently seen on the island of Gran Canaria, the

by R C McDonald

second largest island of the group.

Vegetation in the pine zone is dominated by the tree 'Pinus Canariensis', a species of pine whose closest living relative is native to the Himalayas. In general these forests range from approximately 3000 feet to 6000 feet above sea level, but on occasion they can be found ranging as high as 8000 feet before giving way to the high mountain habitats.

The high-mountain zone is characterized by hot, arid summers and very cold winters, and is subject to frequent hard frosts between October and April. These high mountain areas provide little water and much sun, and are dominated by low-growing plants adapted to withstand the extremes of temperature, consisting mostly of shrubby and under-shrubby legumes.

The final zone (unless you consider the man-made 'ruin' and 'artificial' zones) is simply known as 'Rocky'. This may seem an odd name for a microclimate, but in this case the name fits well. The irregular topography of the mountains frequently favours the development of a community of plants living entirely on rock. These are characterized by a large number of local plantlife, sometimes found in very restricted areas.

Typical species in this zone belong to genera in the family of Crassulaceae. Their usual appearance is that of small shrubs or perennial herbs, often with succulent leaves held in basal rosettes.

Rosettes of these plants will take root on dry, perpendicular rocky areas and persist all the year. Some will trail floral scapes (on occasion very long and narrow) that will branch off and hang down the cliffs or walls. These can easily be seen on both natural rocks and on artificial structures such as man-made rock walls, unless they are made with concrete.

It's difficult to determine quite where the canary fits, in all this; although found on all the islands, and often regarded as a symbolic representative to the rest of the world for the island group, canaries themselves don't ever seem to be a subject of much interest to those who study the islands and their unique species. Rarer avian species under threat of extinction are studied intensely, but the sturdy, hardy, thrifty and tuneful little birds who originally brought the world's attention to these islands, rarely earn much more than a passing comment.

There seems to have been no studies conducted on just what canaries eat in the wild, but given the widely varying climactic conditions and the fact that these little birds can be found in all areas of the islands, suspicion arises that the canary has become a specialist in the same trait that humans historically rely on for survival; adaptability.

Wild canaries are about 5 inches or so long, and are coloured yellow-green, with darker, very obvious striations on their backs. They are larger, longer and less contrasted than their relative the European Serin, with more grey and brown in their plumage. They are thought to be primarily seed-eaters, and are often found in semi-open areas near mankind, such as orchards. These bold little birds nest in bushes or trees, and have a kind of silvery twittering call, more varied although less refined than the songs of many domestic canaries.

One often-observed trait of the canary is their inclination to gain much of the water needed by their body from foods, rather than through direct intake of water. Looking at the islands, it is easy to imagine how a species known for ranging through the various island microclimates could develop such a habit as a survival trait; in the areas where free-running waters are rare to nonexistent, the ability to get water by consuming plant life could mean the difference between living well or extreme suffering. One visitor to the islands spoke of seeing canaries running their beaks along leaves, grasses, and branches in the early mornings. When this was mentioned to his innkeeper, he was informed that they were drinking the dew.

Another easily observable canary trait is the species'

apparent tolerance for relatively high levels of salt. This is accompanied by a need for more iodine than a species that evolved further away from the ocean usually seems to require. Domestic canaries living inland are often found to require supplemental iodine, an element which is provided simply through breathing the salt air when living in an island environment.

Likewise, the widely varying temperatures and difference of climates found on this island group shows how these hardy little birds developed their ability to tolerate such wide-ranging extremes. As long as they are allowed to adapt at their own rate, canaries can easily tolerate temperatures ranging from well below freezing, to sizzling hot. Indeed, stories abound among canary breeders of canaries freely playing in snow-drifts, or happily bouncing about in baking hot sunshine that would send most humans running for cover.

This scenario also makes it easy to understand the entire canary species' love of water for bathing. When pools of water are not always easy to find, the discovery of one such pool will be instantly taken advantage of. This instinct seems to have been inherited by most domestic canaries, even those who are 500 generations away from their wild cousins.

While much remains to be learned about the wild canary and how they live, one thing is certain; our fascination with the canary species has only just begun, in evolutionary terms, yet already their domesticated cousins have earned their place in our languages, our homes and in our hearts, forever.

Should I Buy a Pet Store Bird?

Time and again one issue in particular arises wherever pet bird owners gather to talk. To call it controversial is an understatement! Specific factors may change dramatically from area to area, which means that every ethical pet bird owner needs to learn the facts pertinent to his or her local situation before deciding what is the best answer for them.

We've all seen it, time and time again. We walk into a pet store, looking for supplies for our treasured birds, and our eye is caught by a too-familiar scenario.

There sits a bird (or maybe there's more than one) who looks at you dully, with misery and suffering in his eyes. He's in a tiny cage, with one perch, a seed dish full of husks, and a cup with a layer of slimy-looking water in the bottom. Period. His feathers are thin, ratty and mussed, and he looks as if he feels he is living in hell.

What loving, caring human wouldn't want to rescue any creature found in such a situation? Yet, you will hear time and time again from those who spend their lives working with birds, that if you are planning on keeping it as a pet, buying a bird like this may not be a very good idea.

It is important to realize that buying any bird from a store that is not taking proper care of their birds (or that does not take sufficient care to see that their stock comes only from reliable sources), will only encourage them to continue the misery.

by R C McDonald

You may be able to save one bird or two, or in some cases a few more than that, but by giving these companies your money, you are letting them know that it is in their fiscal interest to replace the bird/s you buy with others, using your money to help continue the chain of misery.

The *only* way to permanently stop horrors such as this is to refuse to offer these companies your support— especially financial support.

Remember, every bird rescued will promptly be replaced with another, and another, and another... to an operation like this, any living things that are not human, including birds, are nothing but inventory, and, similarly to the rest of their stock, as long as the 'item' is selling, they will continue to restock, usually from the cheapest source.

It is important to let such stores know that you will not buy any live animals from them, and why. In fact, one reason there are so many more pet supply stores than there are stores that sell the pets themselves, is that there is often much more profit (and far less expense) involved in selling pet supplies than there is in keeping and selling live animals or birds.

After all, sacks of seed or kibble don't need anything like the level of care and attention live animals require. This helps keep costs low, allowing for higher profits.

There are, of course, other factors to consider. For example, if a bird is being offered for sale at $100, it is likely that half of that or less was paid to the breeder, depending on whether it was sold directly to the store by the breeder, or second-hand via a wholesaler.

The sad fact is, it is impossible to make much (if any) profit raising properly cared for birds if you plan to supply the pet trade. This applies to most of the smaller species such as budgies and finches, and is doubly true of canaries, whatever the breed, since they take so much longer to mature. This is even more true of the so-popular exotic species, rumoured to become the perfect pet if hand-raised.

Hand-raising properly socialized bird-babies takes an incredible amount of time and money. The only way to make a profit yet still offer competitive prices is to operate under the kind of factory-line conditions that allow no time for any social interaction. Youngsters who would be given several years of teaching and close training by their elders in the wild are treated as if they have no feelings or needs what-soever. No attention is given to the youngsters' mental state, nor is any thought devoted to the eventual resulting adult.

Such babies rarely get any human attention at all, other than having a gavage-tube full of food shoved down their throats several times a day. Many are raised in complete isolation, with no contact whatsoever with any living thing. Such birds may become permanently psychotic long before maturity is reached.

If a young bird is to be properly socialized, (and this is doubly true of hand-fed youngsters), the time spent will mean that the selling price will almost certainly fall well below the break-even point, if the breeder is to make anything like what would normally be considered a moderately fair wage.

The time and expense of proper care can also mean that when such birds are meant for the commercial trade, corners may be cut in the diet or the living environments provided, in the effort to prevent fiscal loss. While this may show no obvious ill effects on the youngsters' health in the short term, it can and often is a major factor behind many longer-term avian health issues.

Aside from potential health problems, this sad series of events means that too many of the young birds currently being marketed as 'handfed' (and/or 'handtame'), may actually have very little idea how to interact with another living being of *any* species, including their own.

A young bird lacking proper socialization skills already has serious psychological problems. Even worse, this lack of social balance also affects the levels of general health

by R C McDonald

such a bird can achieve; a bird who understands and is secure and happy in his environment will achieve a much more stable and sustainable level of health than a bird who is constantly nervous, worried, or insecure.

That combination can mean a lot of trouble for a pet-owner, including far too many vet bills and eventually perhaps even heart-break for a new bird owner. Too often such scenarios can occur within only a few short months of the bird's arrival.

Good pet stores do exist— but they tend to be quite rare. Such stores buy their stock only from ethical breeders, and keep them in clean, spacious quarters, offering ongoing social interaction, a variety of fresh healthy foods, and plenty of entertaining toys.

If you should happen to find such a store, please give them all the support you possibly can—they are fighting an uphill battle, and can use all the help you can offer.

Is it not better to try to stop the carnage while we can, and let pet stores everywhere know that we require that they treat their stock as the living, feeling beings that they are?

Is it not better to inform any company we see refusing to care for their stock adequately, that we will NOT support their attempt to profit from the suffering of these helpless creatures, and that is the reason why we will refuse to buy anything from them?

Is it not better to continue to attempt to educate anybody interested in birds, in what is *really* required for a pet bird's comfort, happiness, and long-term health?

After too many years, and too many pet-store horror stories, this is my own conclusion. I have offered here only a few of the most important reasons behind it.

The horror must stop, and we are the only ones able to do it. Each of us must make up our own mind about this. What will *your* decision be?

Getting a Gift Canary

I can't recall just how many times I've heard the story; somebody in the family has decided that they want a singing canary, and because you own or have owned a canary, you've volunteered (or been volunteered) to arrange the process. You want to find a healthy, well-raised canary who is not too old or too young, and, most importantly, one who sings.

Canaries are seasonal birds, and can seem mighty scarce indeed if you are looking for one during the spring or early summer; the reason being that most adult canaries are breeding just then, while the youngsters they've hatched are barely weaned, probably in the middle of their juvenile moult, and are not yet old enough to have begun much development of their true song. Soon afterwards, the youngsters will begin to undergo their first moult, while the adults will want to continue to breed until midsummer or so, before beginning their annual moult.

The length of any given canary's actual moult will vary, but most average eight to twelve weeks or so. Once canaries are adult, about a year old or more, this should happen annually, during mid- to late summer.

The moult is a highly stressful time for any bird, and this is especially the case for canaries. All birds are at their worst when moulting. They are in the weakest physical condition of the year, and are quite unable to cope with any kind of stress, especially changes in their environments or routines.

This means that it is quite important that a moulting canary never be moved to a new home, if at all possible— it is just too stressful to have to adapt to new conditions while in the midst of undergoing a moult. Besides that, moulting canaries rarely sing much if at all, and they will take quite a lot longer to adapt to a new situation well enough to begin singing— if indeed they don't actually get sick!— if they are required to adapt to a new home during their moult. This kind of forced change can increase the duration of the moult dramatically, in some cases meaning it could be a year or more before you will actually hear such a canary singing freely.

Finally, if a singing canary is what you are after, then the person he will be living with should really hear him sing before he is purchased. After all, what if it turns out that his song is too loud, or too soft, or for that matter— what if he never sings at all? If you have heard him singing, you will know for certain that he *does* sing, and you will also know just what his song sounds like. Regardless of what you have been told by the seller, your own ears will still be the best and most reliable judge, when it comes to buying a singing canary.

What all this means is that the best time of year to buy a singing canary begins sometime during the fall, running through to late winter. This ensures the youngsters will have plenty of time to finish their juvenile moult and develop their full adult songs. With canaries, this also makes it possible to guess a little more accurately what gender each youngster really is.

You see, many young canary hens sing quite as well and every bit as much as the young males. This can be true until they are more mature, and in some cases, the hens will continue to sing even when they have become fully adult. This is fairly rare in the canary population at large, but can be a fairly common occurrence in some strains, especially in some of the canaries bred for their songs.

So whether a canary (especially if that canary is a youngster) sings or not is rarely an accurate way to tell gender; although it *is* usually true that most (if not always all) of the best adult singers will turn out to be male.

So unless you are lucky enough to find yourself hunting for that special canary during the right time of year for canaries to be available, you might want to consider getting that special person a 'voucher' as a promise that you will get him or her a healthy, singing canary, when the youngsters of that year become available.

Then all you need to do is find a good place to buy said youngster.

Rather than looking in pet stores, your best bet is to find a reliable breeder. You will also want to put some thought into considering that it is often best (once you have actually found a good breeder) to arrange to take your special person to visit, and allow him or her to choose their own bird.

Buying a bird for somebody else is rather like adopting a child for somebody else... everything just seems to work out better if the person who will be keeping the pet gets to choose their pet.

That's not to say that you won't have anything to offer, though! There is a lot of room for gift-giving in such a scenario. You can do the legwork of finding a breeder who raises healthy, well-socialized stock, along with offering transport, a good sized cage, supplies of fresh, good quality foods, etc... these are thoughtful details to include in such a gift, and will help ensure that the chosen canary will be cared for properly and will remain happy and healthy enough to sing for many years to come.

One of the more reliable methods for finding a good breeder is to look for a bird club near you. A great place to start is at the A.F.A. website's 'affiliated clubs' listings. You will find a link to this site and more in the 'Clubs and

Organizations' area of the 'Links' area at *www.robirda.com*. You will also find a great many bird clubs listed, with their contact info, at *www.upatsix.com*.

You may notice that some breeders advertise online and will promise to ship your birds to you. I do *not* recommend purchasing a canary this way, as shipping is highly stressful for canaries. If anything should go wrong in transit and the bird becomes ill or dies (which *can* happen, all too easily!) you will be out-of-pocket for both the shipping expenses *and* the cost of the bird. Rarely if ever will either be cheap.

Some breeders will offer to ship UPS. The problem with this is that it is illegal to do so in many states, and some post offices may reject the parcel, or not handle it properly. Worse, it might take longer than planned in transit. This last can mean that you might find a very weak, suffering canary when your package finally arrives— or even a dead one.

So, you're back to locating a local breeder, via your local bird clubs. Do note that no matter which species the local clubs focus on, they may still be able to help you; bird people tend to know other bird people near them, no matter what species they keep. So don't limit yourself to looking for canary clubs— talk to somebody from every bird club in your area, if you can, and you may just find a good breeder faster than if you limited yourself to canary clubs only.

Once you've found a club, ask various members who they think the best local canary breeders are, and why. Then see if you can arrange to visit any of them. Your goal is to learn a little about which breeds they keep and how they care for their birds— some breeders are more reliable than others, and a good breeder is more likely to supply you with a healthy bird who will live a long life.

Here's some of what I look for when visiting a canary breeder (from here on out, I will refer to the breeder as 'he', even though it is just as likely 'he' could be 'she').

Will he allow you to see the kind of set-up he has? Even if you are not allowed too close to some areas, he should be willing to allow you to give the premises a quick look-see. If not, he could have something to hide— and I would not buy a bird there.

Are his birds bright-eyed, tight-feathered, healthy and active, with clean vents, and bright colours? Or are the birds dull, scraggly-looking, and lethargic? If I see the latter, I don't buy.

What kind of condition are the cages and general premises in? All birds can be rather messy, but this is quite different from just plain dirty— it should be obvious that the premises are cleaned thoroughly on a regular basis.

Is he interested in what kind of home you will provide for his youngster, or does he just want you to buy and scram? I find good breeders care quite passionately that their youngsters will be properly cared for.

Less often seen, but a habit which earns a big plus mark in my estimation— are there toys for the birds to play with? Canaries are quite intelligent for their size, and stimulation which encourages plenty of activity and play is a healthy part of a good environment for developing young canaries. Most will manage to play even without toys, with whatever they have— paper, seed, greens, water— but if there's safe toys around, you know the breeder cares about his birds' state of mind, as well as their beauty and song.

Another consideration; do the birds have easy access to greens and/or vegetables, as well as seed and water? This earns the breeder a big plus in my mind, as feeding greens takes more trouble and time than just tossing some dry feed into a cup.

These are just general guidelines, and of course there are differing variables in any situation. But if these basics are met, you can feel sure that you've found a canary breeder who should have strong, healthy youngsters when the time comes to sell.

by R C McDonald

    Once you find a breeder you like, you may need to reserve a bird until he is ready to sell. It's usually possible to request that your name be put on a waiting list. Then just get a nice card stating that your giftee has a top-quality canary on reserve. Add a cage and a ride out to the breeder's to choose their canary when the time comes, and you will have a very impressive gift indeed. Finally, don't forget to recommend learning more about the basics of caring for a pet canary. A good book is always a great way to go, or you can get them started reading the articles linked to *www.robirda.com/basicpg.html*

    This kind of approach can make the process of giving a gift canary a fun and easy one for everybody involved— even the canary! Have fun, and enjoy your gift of 'Cheep Trills'.

Song Canaries

There are three general kinds of canaries; these are, song canaries, colour canaries, and type canaries. Within each kind of canary exists, in most cases, a multitude of different breeds.

While you can find good songsters in just about any breed of canary, rarely will those bred for colour or type have the refined songs of those canaries bred for many generations specifically for the best qualities of their song.

I have discussed a few of the more common song breeds here, but this is by no means a complete list— new breeds are in development every day. The real goal of this chapter is to give you an idea of the variety available in the world of song canaries.

The German Roller

The German Roller Canary, originally known to many as the 'Hartz Mountain Roller', is the bird most people think of when they speak of a singing canary. This is one of the older and best-known of the distinct breeds of canaries, having been in development for hundreds of years. The history of the Roller Canary goes back to the beginning of canariculture. It has a quiet, highly refined song, singing its songs, or 'tours', with the beak almost fully closed.

These birds are trained to sing on cue for shows, but this does not mean that they require training to sing, as you will sometimes hear said. In fact, all canaries sing naturally. Training can help to refine the sound of the song to a certain extent, and will help to teach the canary to sing when he is expected to, but it does not teach him *how* to sing; he knew that already.

A few breeders worked on developing red German Rollers some years back, but none of these attempts seem to have been successful at producing red or bronze roller canaries with a pure song for their breed. In general, red or bronze colouring should not occur in any of the song breeds; if it does, it usually means one of two things, either the bird is not purebred, or it has been artificially colourfed.

Some fanciers of the German Roller endorse feeding a diet rich in oily seeds such as canola. It is claimed that such a diet improves the song. What it actually does is coat the syrinx (the canary's voice box) with a layer of fat, which mellows the sound of the tones the bird is able to emit. The fact that such a diet renders a canary susceptible to heart and liver disease is not always taken into consideration. There is another fact to consider here too; such a practice can help to mask song faults which would otherwise be very noticeable. This in turn might encourage a novice breeder to attempt to work with inferior stock.

In my experience, it is not necessary to feed a well bred song canary any special diet to hear beautiful songs. I recommend that anybody wanting to buy a roller should make a point of inquiring about the diet the bird has been given, before considering a purchase.

Finally, it should be noted that nowadays there *is* a breed of canary known as the Hartz; however although it is probable that Hartz Mountain Roller canaries were among its ancestors, the modern American Hartz canary is *not* a song breed but a type canary, one of the breeds bred for their looks rather than their song.

The Waterslager Canary

Waterslager canaries, like most of the other song-breed canaries, are an old breed. They originated in Belgium, where records indicated their presence as early as 1733, when a French traveller noted the beauty of the songs emitted by the otherwise rather plain-looking little yellow canaries raised by people living in the town of Mechelen, which the French called Malinois. This is why you will sometimes, to this day, still find the Waterslager being referred to as a 'Malinois' canary.

Waterslagers were bred for the 'water' sounds of their songs, rather than the 'rolls' typified by the German Roller. This trait led to the name they are most commonly known by, 'Waterslager', from the Flemish term 'waterslag', meaning, 'water sounds'.

Rumor has it that this unique song was taught to the ancestors of the breed through 'tutoring' the young canaries by allowing them to listen to a nightingale, in order to encourage the canaries to mimic the nightingale's bubbling, cheerful song. Whether this is actually true is not known, but the fact remains that this breed of canaries has song elements that can be heard in no other breed.

The reason for their unique songs may be simpler than the choice of song tutors used for the ancestors of the breed, however; scientists have recently discovered this breed has a genetically inherited difference from other breeds of canary; their inner ear lacks certain sensory hairs, so that the birds hear (or don't hear) a different range of sounds than do other breeds of canaries. Perhaps this altered hearing also affects how their songs are altered? We are still learning.

There is something else about Waterslager canaries. Most breeds of canary show a fairly wide range of basic colours, from greens and browns similar to wild canaries, to the clear bright yellows and whites. This is not true of the Waterslagers. You will never see a dark Waterslager canary; they don't exist. It is rare to see even a small dark tick on one of these birds; some say that such a tick is an indication of impure blood. Most Waterslagers are pure yellow, with an occasional white bird occurring. Red or orange should never be seen. If they are, they indicate that

by R C McDonald

the bird cannot be purebred.

White Waterslagers, while not yellow, are considered acceptable by most, yet visit a show and you will find groups of fanciers engaged in intense discussions over whether white birds should be allowed to be shown on an equal basis as the yellows, it being argued that the white is a mutation from the original yellow stock, and so is not pure. (A note for colour enthusiasts; the mutation that produced white Waterslagers, while not specifically bred for, appears to be recessive.)

The American Singer Canary

This breed is one of the three breeds of canary developed in the United States, the others being the American Hartz Canary and the Columbus Fancy. The latter two breeds are type canaries, which leaves the American Singer as the sole contender for a song canary from North America.

The American Singer originally came from a planned cross between the Roller Canary and the Border Canary as it existed earlier in the 20th century. The goal was to breed a canary who had the bright active personality and freely offered song of the Border Canary, a popular type breed, but with the overly loud, often harsh song of the Border Canary modified by the singing skills bred for so long into the German Roller.

The American Singer Canary Club records show that it took an average of six generations to produce a canary that would consistently reproduce itself with each new generation. The final result is a average-sized canary who sings more loudly than a Roller, but is nowhere near as loud as a Border. The American Singer also displays that quality so admired in Border and Fife canaries, that has made these breeds so popular; as well as having charming and friendly personalities, they are all very free with their songs, offering them willingly and frequently.

Many American Singers are known to be inventive little

birds, with the ability to mimic sounds they hear in their environment. This means that breeders need to be careful what their birds hear; if any member of the flock decides they like a certain sound, they are liable to keep repeating it, and teach it to the whole flock!

When this happens, it is usually known as 'song contamination'— except in the case where the added sound enhances rather than detracts from the overall quality of the song.

The way American Singer Canaries are judged at shows reflects this philosophy, and has led to some fanciers of the older song breeds, who are judged much less freely, to be heard to state the opinion that the American Singer is not a 'real' singing canary.

Occasionally you will find a seller who believes that, because they are situated in America, they have the right to term any singing canary they sell as an 'American Singer', due apparently only to their geographic location, and because the bird sings!

This is a rather blatant invention, and the truth is, that if a bird is going to be sold as an American Singer, it should be wearing the certified American Singer closed bands, marked with the club's initials, on its leg. These bands are registered with and obtainable only through the AS clubs, and must be put on when the chicks are still in the nest, helping to serve as proof of the bird's lineage.

Last but not least, the American Singer Club is legally incorporated; that means any seller incorrectly using this terminology to describe their birds is actually conducting business illegally. What it comes down to is that a canary not close-banded with the proper leg rings— no matter what kind of lineage it has— cannot legally be called an American Singer Canary.

The Timbrado Canary

Although new to most of the rest of the world, the

by R C McDonald

Timbrado Canary has a long history in the land of its origin, Spain, where it was known for centuries as the 'Canary of the Country'. The Spanish breeders who developed this breed kept only two goals in mind, that the bird's song must be attractive and freely offered, and that no use must be made of other songbirds, whether other breeds or other species, either in breeding or in song training. Instead, the songs considered the most desirable were fixed to the repertoire of the breed through strict selection of the breeding stock.

The Spanish Timbrado Canary is similar in appearance to the wild canary, but tends to be a little larger. In principle, all colours are accepted in the Timbrado, however, it should be stressed that the pure bloodlines of the Timbrado do not include the Red Factor, which derives its red colouration from genes inherited from the South American Red Siskin.

Beware when looking to buy a Timbrado, of people who will try to take advantage of its rarity by trying to sell you any dark-coloured canary as a Timbrado, which will usually sell for a much higher price than a bird of a more ordinary breed.

The Timbrado's song is often called 'metallic', being freely offered, bright and cheery, full of bell tones. A good songster will have a great richness and variety in his songs, a trait the breed is famous for. This new breed of canary was not officially recognized as a song breed until 1962, when, after several failed attempts, the breed was finally recognized during the celebrated General Convention in Brussels. This was a triumph to many Spanish breeders, for whom it was the first great honour of Spanish canary keeping.

The Russian Canary

This breed has reportedly been in existence for more than three hundred years, but suffered severe declines through the political climates of the last century or so in its homeland. Nonetheless, the breed persisted here and there, due mostly to the efforts of the people who loved them and were unable to give them up, despite the label given this canary as being a symbol of everything bourgeois. Although they kept the breed alive, it is still in a state of severe decline, with few dedicated fanciers remaining.

Ironically, at the same time it has recently begun to gain more notice throughout the world for the uniqueness of its song, known in its homeland as 'ovsyanochnevo'. These days very few people know much about this unique and historic canary, but recently a society was created to support and educate interested fanciers, as well as planning contests, creating record libraries, etc, so it is hoped that in the future more will be heard of this unique and interesting breed of song canary.

The Future of Song Canaries

Raising and training song canaries requires dedication, skill, and much time. The art of training canaries in the delivery of their song is a long and involved process, requiring not only interest and a natural talent and ability for working with birds, but also specific skills developed laboriously through much practice, along a good ear; not to mention a fairly hefty material investment in equipment and other related costs.

In these days of fast food, fast travel, and fast living, such arts can drop by the wayside with little notice, and few ever seem to realize what is being lost until it is already gone. Will our beloved song canaries, who left their mark on so many ears, take the same route, in the end? Or will there be enough interested and dedicated fanciers to maintain their presence in an ever-more-rapidly changing world?

Only time will tell; time, and our own efforts.

by R C McDonald

Colour & Type Canaries

While song canaries are among the oldest and best known of canary breeds, there is in actuality far more breeds of canary in existence, some of whom display extremes of plumage, posture, or size when compared to the original wild canary.

Some of these birds, in fact, don't look much like the popular notion of a canary anymore, and it's not uncommon to see someone unfamiliar with these breeds to exclaim in surprise when told that this unusual-looking bird is indeed a living example of a 'common' canary.

In reality most canaries these days are anything but common. There is a wide variety of breeds that present an almost bewildering array of shapes, colours, and sizes.

Generally there are three different kinds of canary, with a variety of breeds being found in each kind. Song canaries, bred for specific qualities in their song, are perhaps the best known, but equally popular, although less well recognized, are the variety of breeds belonging to the other two kinds of canary; Colour and Type canaries.

Colour Canaries are bred, as their name implies, for the colour of their feathers, while on the other hand, Type Canaries are bred for their body size and shape as well as, in many cases, their posture.

Most Colour Canaries retain a body shape quite similar to the original wild canary, if a little larger, but the Type

Canary breeds cover a huge range of size, shape, and stance, from the large, curly-feathered Parisian Frill to the hunchbacked Scots Fancy or the tiny but popular Gloster Canary.

Some of the Type Canary breeds, such as the Gibber Italicus, a frilled posture canary, have such thin feathering that it is possible to see quite a lot of the bird's skin. Other breeds, such as the Border Canaries, have such a thick coat of feathers that even when they are soaking wet, it is almost impossible to see the skin.

A few of these breeds have reached world-wide status and are popularly recognized even by those who know nothing of canaries; chief among these are the small but popular Gloster Canaries, most usually known as the 'birds with the Beatle hair-dos'.

This title refers to the crest of feathers worn by these diminutive birds, but in fact they are far from the only crested breed of canary, and are actually one of the newer crested breeds. The crest itself has been known in canaries since the 1700's or earlier, and can be found in at least a dozen or more breeds of canary around the world, from the tiny Japanese Hoso, a crested posture canary, to the relatively huge Crested Canary, a relative as well as ancestor of the giant Norwich Canary.

Colour canaries, on the other hand, are bred simply for the colour (and in some cases the pattern) of their feathers. Little to no attention is paid to the quality of song these birds produce, while the only attention paid to shape is to ensure the birds retain an average canary shape and size.

These canaries can be found in an almost bewildering range of colours, in almost all shades except sky blue and black. (This may change, as enthusiast canary breeders have been working on both challenges for a good number of years now. So it *is* possible that one day we may yet see a true black canary, or, even more difficult, a sky blue canary.)

by R C McDonald

Many of the breeders involved in these projects are motivated by the fact that canary breeders of the early 20th century created the first genetically engineered creature on our planet. The resulting bird was no fluke, but rather was documented to have been produced intentionally by design rather than haphazardly by nature; the Red Canary.

These results were produced by hybridization and carefully documented breeding over long years of study and research, rather than by using the 'test-tube' methods most people think of on hearing the phrase 'genetic engineering', however the accomplishment is and will remain a marvel of achievement, a hallmark of historic importance.

Here is a brief list of a few of the more popular breeds of Type and Colour Canary available today;

Type Canaries;

Border Canary;

This canary is fairly large, with a well- rounded body and head, averaging 16 to 17 cm tall, or 6 ½ inches. These birds have heavy, dense feathering, tend to have a lovely personality, are well known for their tendency to tame easily, and can be quite sociable even amongst other canaries. They sing freely and often, but may have quite a loud and occasionally even harsh song that can be a little overwhelming indoors.

Fife Canary

Popularly known as the 'Wee Gem', this breed of canary is a smaller version of the modern Border Canary, bred to resemble the older, much smaller (some say original) size of Border Canary, with similar shape and attributes but a much smaller size, as well as a quieter, although still very enthusiastic, song. Like their larger cousins, Fife Canaries tend to be very personable and are usually easily tamed, making this breed a great choice for those wanting a pet canary.

Raza Español

One of the smallest and newest breeds of type canary, this tiny canary tends to be a very active and busy little bird, showing little of the laid-back kind of personality seen in so many other breeds. This recent breed originated in Spain, and is descended from the same 'canaries of the country' which produced the Timbrado song canary, with it's distinctive bell-toned songs.

The Raza, however, unlike it's larger relative, is bred for its tiny size rather than its song. According to some owners, many Raza canaries possess a lovely twittering song, higher and with more 'silvery' tones than their larger cousins. They are still quite rare in North America, although they are rapidly gaining popularity and interest, for their out-going personalities and active, busy natures as well as for their easy care and free-breeding style.

Gloster Canary

Known by people the world over as 'the little birds with the Beatle's hairdo', this breed of canary is one of the few known and recognized by the general population. The best known of the crested breeds of canaries, this popular breed is most often described as 'diminutive'.

I feel this to be a bit misleading, since these short, stocky little birds are actually quite sturdy; they may not stand very tall, but they are strong and thickly built. Like all breeds of Type Canary, Glosters are not bred for their song, yet a good many individuals are known to have attractive songs. Moreover, this breed produces a good many individuals showing a great deal of personality and character, making it very popular with pet owners as well as show-breeders.

Scotch Fancy

This breed shows one of the more unusual stances seen in canary breeds, and is probably the best known of the breeds usually termed as 'hunch-back' or 'posture' canaries. The Scotch Fancy is one of the older breeds of posture canary, but although highly popular in earlier centuries, it has dwindled and become rarer. However it has retained a loyal following through the years, and is today beginning to stage a comeback in popularity. This breed is of a medium size, with a thick coat of feathers and a posture that most resembles the letter 'C'.

Gibber Italicus

This breed combines the unusual stance of the posture canaries with the curly feathers of the frilled canaries. This breed is the Italian version of the hunch-backed canary, and it has a unique quality rarely seen in any of the other breeds of canary; rather than the varying feather types seen in other breeds, this canary is seen only with the thin hard feathers usually known as 'intensive' or 'hard'.

This gives this breed of canary such thin feathering that the skin of the thighs and chest can often be easily seen. Such thin feathering would be considered a fault in most other breeds of canary, but, in this breed, it is normal.

Belgian Fancy

This canary, like the other hunchbacked breeds of canary, is known as a 'bird of position'. It is larger than the other hump-backed breeds, being first established in the middle of the 19th Century. It has had a very difficult time becoming re-established as a breed due to the war in Europe decimating much of the original breeding stock.

Unlike most of the posture breeds, Belgian Fancy chicks hatch with a visibly humped back. Also unlike most of the other breeds of posture canary, when adult the Belgian's build and stance assumes more of the shape of a backwards 7, rather than the 'C' shape seen in most of the other posture canary breeds.

Parisian Frill

There are several breeds of canary who show curly feathers, but most canary fanciers will agree that of them all, the Parisian Frill is the best known. A giant in size by comparison with most other breeds, this canary usually averages 18 centimetres or almost 7 inches tall in size, with some individuals being known to reach 22 cm, just over 8½ inches tall. This breed has long, curly feathers all over its body, along with an attribute considered to be a fault in any other breed of show canary; the Parisian Frill normally displays long, curled toenails.

Dutch Frill

The Dutch Frill Canary is similar to the Parisian in many ways, but tends to be a little smaller, standing only 14 to 16 cm tall, with a smooth, normally-feathered head, rather than the curly head feathers seen on the Parisian. Although there are several other breeds of Frilled canary, such as the Padovan (or crested Frill), or the Milinais, (a red-coloured Frill), the Parisian and the Dutch Frill Canaries are probably the best known of the Frill Canaries.

Lizard Canary

This breed is one of the oldest known canary breeds still in existence today. The Lizard Canary is one of the few breeds of Type Canary that exists only in a dark form; all Lizard canaries display quite a lot of melanin in their feathers, with the only allowable clear patch being on the head. This clear patch of feathers without any melanin is not found on all Lizard canaries, but when it is present it is known as a *cap*, and can be seen in *broken, extended,* and *clear* forms.

The Lizard canary's dark feathers display a mutation seen in no other canary; the feathers are spangled with melanin rather than striped, as is seen in all other canaries showing melanin in their feathers. This spangling offers an unusual visual effect, making the feathers appear almost as if the bird is wearing a lizard's scales, rather than the more usual striations seen in other dark canaries.

Like many of the older breeds, Lizard canaries are quite rare, and some lines are rumoured to have difficulty with fertility and inbreeding, due to poor selection. Luckily, this is changing over the last few years as they have begun, once again, to grow in popularity as appreciation for their unique qualities grows.

Norwich Canary

This is another of the very old breeds of canary, having been around since the 16th century. Originally, the Norwich and the equally ancient Crested Canary were considered to be the same breed; the crest is a dominant mutation, which was recognized early on when crest-to-crest breeding was seen to regularly produce high rates of dead-in-shell chicks, along with a higher-than-normal rate of mutation in the chicks that did hatch.

Experimentation soon showed that the best and most reliable method of breeding more crested canaries was to breed a crested individual to a non-crested partner.

The non-crested birds were at first considered to be nothing more than a means to breeding more crested canaries, similarly to the non-crested Gloster or Stafford canaries of today, but as the general public began to first recognize then appreciate the non-crested members of this large-breed canary, they began more and more to be bred for themselves.

As they became more common, the question of what to call them arose. After all, the breed name was 'Crested Canary', which these canaries, though used to produce more Crested Canaries, couldn't really be called, not being crested. Eventually it was agreed to recognize the county where a good many members of the breed were developed, and they came to be known as the Norwich Canary.

The Norwich is a large, rather stout-looking canary, and due to its thick head and stocky body has often been called the 'Bulldog' or 'John Bull' canary. It averages 6½ inches or 17 centimetres in length, as well as being stout for their length of body. Usually exhibiting a laid-back approach to life, this 'gentle giant' of canaries often has a sweet song, and is popular as a pet as well as for show.

Yorkshire Canary

The Yorkshire canary is often known as the 'gentleman canary' or sometimes the 'soldier canary', for its upright posture. The ideal stance for this breed of canary is said to be '5 after 7', referring to the hands of a clock. It is a little larger than most other breeds of canary, with most members of the breed averaging at least 17 centimetres or 6½ inches in length.

This is yet another of the older breeds of canary, originating in (you guessed it) Yorkshire County, Britain, however the breed as it exists today has undergone quite a few changes from the original Yorkshire canaries, who had, not just an upright stance, but a body so slender it was said to be able to pass through a gentleman's ring.

This ideal was thought to be unrealistic by many breeders, and in the 1960's an updated standard allowing the bird to be somewhat deeper in the chest was drawn up and agreed upon, and has been maintained to this day. Like its distant ancestors, though, the Yorkshire Canary has retained its upright stance, and has today begun to regain much of its lost popularity.

Stafford Canary

The Stafford or Staffordshire Canary is a newcomer to the world of canaries, having been officially recognized as a new breed only as late as 1990, the first breed of type canary to be so recognized since the Fife canary in the 1950's. This breed is rare among type canaries in that it is bred for three specific traits; the colour (red or rose-

by R C McDonald

ground); the type, or body shape; and the crest. In the case of the non-crested members of this breed, the standard specifies the required shape of head. This is meant to show that the genetics of the bird will, when bred with a crested member of the breed, allow the resulting youngsters to carry and show the right shape, colour, and kind of crest.

Other Type Canary Breeds

The breeds discussed above are just a few of the many breeds of type canary available today. There is, quite simply, just not enough space to discuss them all here, but I have tried to include most of the more popular breeds in this summary.

I would encourage anyone who is interested in learning more about this fascinating group of canary breeds to take a little time and do some research on the internet, where just about every breed of canary is represented by its own group of admirers.

Most of these sites offer all the detail anyone could wish to know about these breeds, and even better for any researcher, most list contact information for people who will be only too glad to discuss their favourite breed with any interested party. You just might find yourself with a hobby that will keep you busy for the rest of your life!

Colour Canaries

Entire books have been written about the wide variety of colour canaries being bred today, and if it is your intention to learn as much as possible about them, it is my recommendation that you consider consulting one of these books. Probably the best published on the subject to date is Geoff Walker and Dennis Avon's book '*Colour, Type, & Song Canaries*'.

Although currently out of print, it is usually possible to find a copy for a reasonable price, if you are persistent. It will provide you with answers to any questions you may still wish answered after reading this article, which, in contrast to the above-mentioned book, offers only a relatively simple, brief synopsis of just what colour canaries are all about, along with a rough outline of how to understand the various colours, and a little about what you are seeing when looking at one of them.

Colour canaries exhibit two different kinds of colours, that is, *lipochrome* colours, which are created from deposits of naturally occurring fatty acids within the feathers while they are growing, and *melanins*, which are inherited genetically and are a natural expression of dark feather colours such as blacks, greys, and browns.

All the colours found to date in canaries result from various combinations found in a feather's expression of the lipochromes or melanins it contains.

Lipochrome colours are also known as *ground* colours, because they affect the entire underlying web of the feather, whether or not any melanin is expressed. The two most commonly occurring lipochrome (or ground) colours are *yellow* and *red*.

White is usually considered a ground colour as well. Technically, white is not a true lipochrome colour, since both the dominant and the recessive white mutations act to suppress the feather's ability to express lipochrome, however it is simpler for everybody to just treat *white* as a ground colour too.

It should be mentioned that for most of the canary's history with humanity, there was only two ground colours, white and yellow. Red coloured canaries are relatively recent additions to the field, true red canaries having been finally produced by dedicated breeders in the late 1950's, after several decades of interbreeding with the south american black-capped red siskin.

Twenty-five percent of the resulting hybrid male offspring proved fertile, and eventually breeders were able to fix the gene for red feather colouration into canaries, producing the first genetically modified animal in human history.

by R C McDonald

The final lipochrome colour is *ivory*. Like red, ivory is a relatively recent mutation, with the first known occurrence being in the mid 1950's in Holland, when a pale youngster was spotted in the midst of a nest of red canaries. This young canary grew up to become a pinkish colour rather than the red of its nest-mates. This new colour eventually became known as '*ivory rose*'.

Several years of experimental breeding determined and fixed its traits into the breeder's stock, and in time other breeders managed to transfer the mutation to yellow-ground canaries, where it changed the normal lipochrome yellow to a lovely shade of pale ivory. This new ground colour became known as '*ivory gold*'.

Melanin introduces several more combinations of colour into our canaries. There are three kinds of melanin found normally in the original dark canary's feathers; black, dark brown, and a lighter brown.

The original normal canary had yellow lipochrome and all three shades of melanin in the feathers. These layers of colour made this canary appear to the human eye to be green, and so it was originally known. Many type and song breeders still use the term *green* for a normal dark canary, but in colour canary circles these days this colour is known as *yellow-black*.

Keep all three shades of melanin and change the ground colour, and you have another colour. Canaries with a red lipochrome and all three melanins were originally known as *bronze*, but today are termed *red-black*.

Similarly, the dark white-ground canaries were first known as *blue* canaries, but are now called *white-black* canaries. Rose-ground dark canaries, similarly to their red-ground cousins, were first known as *rose-bronze* canaries, but today the accepted term is *rose-black*.

These four colours (yellow-black, white-black, red-black and rose-black) are known as the *classic* canary colours. From them spring most of the multitude and variety of canary colours available today, as various mutations arise and are fixed by breeders.

Perhaps the first mutation to occur to canary melanin was the *agate* mutation, originally known as the *dilute* because of the way it appeared to dilute the black melanin in the bird's feathers. This mutation acted to suppress the two shades of brown melanin, and also made changes to the black melanin. In the agate canary, the normal dark canary's heavy black striations became a faint black striping over a pale dove-grey.

As with the normal dark canary, when the lipochrome or ground colour changed, the colour of the canary changes. So we have the *white agate,* the *yellow agate,* the *red agate* and the *rose agate*.

The next mutation to occur was probably the *brown* mutation; much is guessed at, but we don't really know for sure, since both mutations have been around for centuries. The brown colour mutation has quite a simple effect, on the surface at least; it acts to suppress all black melanin in the dark canary, allowing only the two shades of brown melanin to be visible over the lipochrome colour.

Again, the ground colour changes the bird's appearance somewhat, giving us the *white-brown* canary (known in type and song canary circles as *fawn*), the *yellow-brown* canary (known by many as *cinnamon*), the *red-brown* canary, and the *rose brown* canary.

These are just the basic canary colours. There are many more colours of canary to be found these days, and more are being added on a regular basis.

Mosaic (actually due to a feather type mutation), Ino, Isabel, Onyx, and many more, collectively known as New Colour Canaries, are just a few among the many colours that have been added over the years to the international inventory of canary colours. More seem to arrive each year, while others still wait in the wings, their breeders working toward reliability and eventual acceptance.

by R C McDonald

The following table is simplified a little, but hopefully will help to clarify the relationships between the lipochrome or 'ground colour' and the various melanin colours, to produce the more commonly seen canary colours. Note too that feather type can change the visual appearance to a degree, depending on whether the feather is intensive, non-intensive, or dimorphic.

Basic Canary Colours

Lipochrome Colour with;	All Melanins	Black Melanins (no brown)	Brown Melanins (no black)	No Melanin
White	White-Black, or, Blue	White Agate	White-Brown, or, Fawn	(Dominant or Recessive) White
Yellow	Yellow-Black, or, Green	Yellow Agate	Yellow-Brown, or, Cinnamon	Yellow
Ivory	Ivory-Black	Ivory Agate	Ivory-Brown, or Cinnamon Ivory	Ivory
Red	Red-Black, a.k.a. Bronze	Red Agate	Red-Brown, or Cinnamon Red	Red
Rose	Rose-Black, or, Rose-Bronze	Rose Agate	Rose-Brown, or, Cinnamon Rose	Rose

The Best Possible Pet Canary

Over the years, breeding canaries has been many things to me. It is always a challenge, very often mysterious, continuously amusing and amazing, and constantly both confounding and enlightening. Out of all the projects which have grown out of my joint interests in canaries and genetic inheritance, none have been more challenging than the quest for breeding the best possible pet canary.

People demand many things of their pets. One of the more common conceptions of the canary involves a bird who sits in a tiny cage and sings his heart out all day. But these days many people are becoming aware that more possibilities exist for a pet canary, and accordingly are looking for different traits when they shop for a songster.

While no canary will ever learn to enjoy being petted– this is just not done if you are a canary– it is often possible to win their trust to the degree that they will willingly sit on your hand to accept treats, or ride about on your shoulder, 'snooper-vising'. A treat no bird lover should miss is having one of these beauties sitting on your shoulder singing 'sweet nothings' into your ear.

In order to achieve this you want a calm, intelligent, observant and curious bird. How the birds are treated during their weaning and baby moult seems to have a partial influence on the eventual personalities, but it has been my experience that many of the more desirable traits

by R C McDonald

for a pet canary are capable of being passed on from parent to chick.

Curiosity is a good example. My first pet canary was as curious as a cat. He came to me at quite a young age, three weeks old, and I was surprised to find that he explored everything in his new home environment with a thoroughness which smacked of logical progression. You could give the little brat a maze to solve, with a treat for the reward, and sit back and watch him solve the puzzle.

This ability fascinated me. I'd had no idea that there were any canaries capable of exhibiting such behaviour. With a brain pan that was (maybe) the size of half a pea, there shouldn't be physical room for such thought, or so I reasoned.

I began reading everything I could lay my hands on about canaries, and soon discovered that apparently I had a rather unusual specimen on my hands, as canaries went; in fact, he seemed to be about as far from being a 'normal' canary as it would be possible to get.

Intrigued, I went out and bought another canary. And, a few weeks later, another. I took the time to tame each, with quite widely varying results, and finally, a dozen canaries or so later, I had to admit that my little puzzle-solver was indeed quite an extraordinary canary. But the range and expression of the personalities I was discovering in my new flock had me thoroughly captivated. I just *had* to find out what their babies would be like!

My initial goal was to breed just a few pairs, finding ways to offer the youngsters a stimulating environment to grow up in, and see which families made the best pets.

Interestingly enough, my first canary's offspring proved to be as unusual as I had found my first little prodigy to be, when compared with the youngsters I from my other pairs of canaries. To me, this meant that my assumption that at least some of these traits could be genetically transmitted was quite likely correct. In the meantime, I was learning that the environment that the birds grew up in seemed to set a pattern which they would follow the rest of their lives.

To my surprise, I discovered that birds raised and kept only in the box-type breeding cages and the small flights used by many breeders, resulted in birds who were fixed in their habits. None showed much if any curiosity towards new objects or food in their environment– in fact the usual response to any kind of unexpected occurrence was fear. As a result, these canaries were easily stressed and had difficulty adapting to any unexpected changes in their life.

Four of these canaries were a year or so old when I first purchased them. They had been bred and raised in a three foot long flight cage about two feet tall and sixteen inches deep. This cage contained two perches, a gravel dish, and a seed dish. A dish of soft food such as egg, greens, or a little fruit was added daily. This routine was all they had ever known.

I quickly found, upon placing them in a larger cage, that their food and water must be placed within the bounds formerly covered by their older, smaller cage, or they would not find it. Although they could fly, each flew only in a tight loop which described perfectly the bounds of their previous cage.

It took all four of these birds close to a year and a half to begin to learn to use the extra space I'd provided for them. Not one ever learned to use the swings and toys which the rest of the flock so enjoyed playing with. I quickly discovered that once these birds were used to something I had best not change it, as it would take them a long time to adapt to even the smallest change, in the meantime causing them great stress and upset.

In complete contrast, youngsters raised in the home by myself or other hobby breeders seemed to be much more interactive and aware. In every case, it turned out that such canaries had been weaned in an environment offering plenty of variety and change. In such an environment, they were constantly faced with new experiences, and grew up used to seeing and exploring new and different additions to their lifestyle.

To these youngsters, change was not at all frightening. In fact, in a direct reversal of attitudes, changes and new experiences were instead greeted as a reliable and necessary source of stimulation and amusement. Further, when one of these canaries was placed in a relatively sterile environment such as the one the four birds formerly discussed came from, they usually exhibited one of two reactions; either shock and stress, or lassitude and 'the sulks'. If not removed from this non-stimulating environment, they began, every one of them, to display a lack of interest in living that clearly indicated a severe depression.

As I learned more about the habits and personalities of my canaries, I slowly began to learn how to begin to achieve my goal.

Outside of breeding season, most of my birds live in a group of large interconnecting flight cages. Each has a variety of differing types of swings, perches, and toys on which they bounce, tug, push, pull, poke, munch, and swing. Most of these flights are inter-accessible through pop-holes, small 'doorways' between the cages through which the birds can 'pop'. This kind of set-up serves to help reduce the arguments over territory so commonly engaged in by male canaries in particular. As long as there are at least two territories available, birds who don't get along will usually end up 'agreeing' to each play in different areas. The number of birds in each area at any given time constantly changes as the day progresses and the flock structure shifts.

Most of these flight cages have smaller pet-style cages attached here and there, hanging so that the smaller cage door opens into a pop-hole into the larger flight. These 'play' cages are very popular with the birds, and it is not unusual to see a dozen or so birds busily playing about in the same space which would be cramped for a single canary with nowhere else to go.

About once a month each bird is caught, examined for health, and has his or her toenails clipped as necessary. I try to see, too, that each bird spends about a week or so out of each month alone in varying sizes and styles of pet cages (except round ones, which should never be used for a canary), with a variety of different perch and feeder set-ups.

With all these fun things to play with and do, I suppose it is not surprising that most of the birds I raise turn out to be healthy, adaptable pets. It has become unmistakable over the generations that certain personality traits, particularly those such as friendliness, curiosity, calmness, and even a willingness to interact with people, are definitely handed down to a bird's descendants.

Every breeding season is a new series of adventures and discoveries with these birds. I hope to be able to continue learning from them for years yet in pursuit of my quest for the best possible pet canary.

After all, who knows what the future may bring? For me, as long as it contains canaries, it cannot help but be bright.

by R C McDonald

Understanding Territoriality

We've all seen them, and some of us even have them, for part of every year; aviaries filled with groups of canaries who appear to get along beautifully. For a new pet owner, it can be very confusing to see this, and then be told that their new pet canary does not need or even like to have any kind of company in his cage.

Like many small birds, canaries display obvious flocking instincts, particularly when feeding, that can seem to indicate that they enjoy and even rely on having company nearby. For a youngster or (for most of the year) a hen— and occasionally even a male— that is true, for part of the year at least. Yet those same canaries are demonstrably territorial the rest of the time, especially during the spring. Some have even been known to kill each other, when required to share a pet cage. Learn to understand how these two apparently opposed facts work together to produce the basic nature of the canary (and most other species of songbird), and you will have made a good step towards understanding the basics of canary territoriality.

It's easy to see how a new canary owner can think that their new pet would prefer company in his cage— it's a very common and easily made mistake, for a social creature such as a human. Yet the number one cause for premature death in pet canaries is due to owners thinking their pet canary needs company, and requiring him to share a cage.

It's important to remember that appearances can often be deceiving, especially when it comes to canaries! Ask any experienced canary breeder if he keeps his canaries together in the same flight cage year round, and if he is honest, he will tell you that he does not, because he cannot. Some breeds will tolerate crowding a little better than others, but in general, most canaries quite simply just don't share at all well.

Generally, three or more male canaries can share a large cage for about half a year or so, perhaps a little more, as long as there is plenty of individual perching space and several sources of food and water. Two canaries should never be allowed to share a cage, unless they are a breeding pair— and even then, they both need to be in full breeding condition before being placed together. Before and after pairing and breeding, each needs to live in a separate cage.

Another fact that can confuse new pet owners, is that the environment within a large walk-in flight cage containing ten or twenty birds is rather different than that of a smaller cage with the same number of birds.

It is not too difficult to find somebody who keeps multiple canaries in an aviary all year, and they often tend to pooh-pooh the idea that canaries should not share such a cage year-round. Yet experience has shown that the average lifespan of canaries who live this way will be three years or less— often as little as a year.

Many breeding birds have a average lifespan of from three to five years or so; yet a pet canary living in his own cage may live for 10, or even 15 or 20 years. Why? The answer is simple— stress! Breeding, and living in shared aviaries, causes stress; the more stress a canary is required to deal with, the shorter his lifespan will be.

It's true, though, that canaries *do* like company—but they like their company to be nearby, rather than inside the area they consider their own. 'Company' is a rather loose term, in this context; it can be as simple as a radio playing, or it could be another bird in a nearby cage—or it could be

by R C McDonald

you. Generally most canaries tend to be fairly easy-going and adaptable, as long as they don't have to share their private space with another canary. To put it in slightly more human terms; a similar scenario might be, you inviting a stranger in off the streets to share your bedroom.

An old canary breeder's joke shows a picture of a family in their living room looking at a canary in his cage, thinking "Poor thing, he must be so lonely in there all by himself," while the canary, in turn, is looking back at them, thinking, "Poor things, they must feel so harassed, packed in all together like that!"

People are social creatures, and often find it difficult to understand that a canary can be both friendly and territorial. It may sound odd to us, but it is true nonetheless.

Another problem with keeping multiple canaries in the same cage is not usually thought of, even those who have a fair bit of experience working with these charming little birds. I can't tell you how many times I've been told, "Oh, my birds get along beautifully in the aviary, I never see any signs of trouble at all!"

That can so easily appear to be the case, yet if you know canaries well enough to be able to see beneath the surface appearance of things, it is often possible to spot the signs of developing trouble.

The problem lies in the canaries themselves, and their instincts; the so-territorial canary has yet another instinctive behaviour that we people, thanks to our own instincts, just don't tend to notice or understand. This instinct tells a sick or weak canary that he *Must Not* let any other living thing know that he is not feeling top-notch.

When an ill bird doesn't think it is being watched, it will act the way it feels. But should a human or another bird be nearby, that self-same bird will expend as much energy as it can, to try to appear normal. In the wild, this is a protective instinct, helping the species to survive predation.

In an aviary what this more often means is we humans will miss seeing the small indicators that could tell us of developing problems in the aviary; a weak bird sitting on the floor would probably get attention, for example, but if that same bird, on seeing you, flies up and chirps cheerfully, how are you to know just how it is feeling? Another canary may be sitting around with his or her feathers fluffed up, another sign of possible trouble; but if that same bird, upon seeing you, shakes out his feathers and comes over to greet you, what are you to think?

It is all too easy, in this kind of scenario, to decide that your bird was just preening or some such, and that everything is fine. This is exactly the reaction that the canary is looking for, too. Until it is on death's door, any canary that is feeling even the slightest bit ill, will expend every last drop of the energy they have left, trying to act as normal as possible.

This protective canary instinct, shared by so many other species of birds, is why it is necessary to regularly handle any canaries who are living in an aviary. The best way to ensure the ongoing good health of your birds is to catch them up every once in awhile for a thorough physical exam.

It's not necessary to visit an avian vet to do this, unless you are uncomfortable handling your canary. Even if you are, I recommend you learn how, especially if you plan to keep your birds in an aviary for part of the year or more. If all else fails, have your vet or the breeder you bought your birds from teach you how to safely handle your canary, or use the instructions we have posted online; you will find them at *robirda.com/howto.html*.

Once you are comfortable picking up and holding your canary, checking his general level of health is quite easy; besides the usual things to look for, good, tight feathering, bright eyes, and clean rear, you will want to run a finger down the middle of the chest, where the keel-bone is. You should be able to just feel it; there should not be too much flesh covering the ridge of the bone, if there is, your bird is getting fat. You should not be able to feel the keelbone too easily, either; if the bone is sharp to the touch, or rises above the level of the flesh of the chest, then you will know that your bird is losing weight. This is an indicator that something is going wrong; no healthy bird should be so skinny that the keelbone sticks out. When the bird is living in an aviary, finding such a symptom means that it has not been able to eat enough for several days at least. This in turn means that the other aviary inhabitants will have been harassing it, unknown to you.

This is so often the case with aviaries or large cages holding multiple birds. Any arguments or harassment that is going to occur between the inhabitants, will rarely happen when you are around. Rather, the birds will deliberately act as normally as they know how, whenever they spot you, and will wait until you are gone before going back to whatever they were doing.

Some serious territorialism could be enacted when you are not watching, and you would never know. If you don't regularly catch and check your birds physically, the first sign of trouble you may find could be a dying bird sitting on the floor, with no strength left to try to keep on living.

I can't tell you how many 'unexpected' deaths I've heard of occurring in an aviary where 'everybody gets along just fine'. In actual fact, these deaths are quite predictable– *if* you know and understand canary territoriality.

Canary Cage Set-Up

One of the most basic facts in bird-keeping, is that the size, layout, and design of the cage a bird lives in, will establish a baseline for the quality of life that bird lives. Yet as obvious as this fact may seem, it often misses being properly considered by new canary owners. It can be so difficult to realize just how thoroughly these little creatures of the air can use their space in all its dimensions. Even experienced bird keepers sometimes allow their canaries to be kept in too-small or incorrectly set-up cages, whether for the sake of convenience or budget. While there may be short-term savings, such budgeting may have unforeseen long-term effects, if left in place too long.

It's difficult to say exactly how much limiting a canary's ability to fly and exercise will affect his longer-term life, but a look at data from studies on humans and other species tells us that inability to exercise properly is liable to have a rather strong impact on overall health and eventual lifespan.

Most retailers will tell you to get as large a cage as possible for your avian companion(s). While in general this is true, larger may not always be better. For example, a smaller but properly set-up rectangular cage will almost always offer more useable space to a canary, than a larger and incorrectly set up round cage.

Why? How useable the cage will actually be to the canary

depends on three factors; the volume of space the cage encloses, the shape of the cage, and how the perches are arranged within it.

Before you consider all that, though, you need to look at the cage bars. They need to be spaced closely enough together to ensure that the bird can't get his head between them; usually about a half inch or so is about right for canaries. Try to see that the bars are arranged horizontally rather than vertically; sometimes a canary will cling to the cage bars, and vertical bars will cause him to slide down them, potentially catching and trapping toes or worse.

Because of the way canaries prefer to move (back and forth), it's nice to have something as wide as possible, that allows for a little room to fly. Less than thirty inches in width will not do, simply because most canaries can easily hop that far with-out once needing to spread their wings. In other words, it's quite simply impossible to get much of any kind of flying exercise, in such a small space.

Ideally, perches should be placed across the narrow ends of each side of the cage, roughly parallel to each other, allowing the bird to travel back and forth between them easily. If the cage is tall enough, you can hang a swing in the center, making sure that the middle of the swing's perch hangs at about the same point you would find if you drew an equilateral triangle between the middles of the two lower opposing perches and the bottom of the swing.

The perches should be far enough away from the ends of the cage that the bird's tail won't touch the bars when he turns around. Unfortunately that perch arrangement may put the perches right over the food and water dishes, which are often centred in the lower right and left hand sides of the cage front.

If that's the case with your cage, I recommend throwing the food dishes away. If necessary, wire over the holes they leave behind. Get a few easily cleaned feed cups that can be hung anywhere in the cage, and go ahead and arrange your bird's cage to suit him, rather than requiring him to adapt to a poor cage design for a canary.

It's nice if you can also have a little height to a cage, without having it so tall that it requires a bird to enter 'helicopter mode' to reach the top perches. This kind of flight requires a lot of effort and is quite tiring, so make sure your bird is healthy and strong before you try him in a tall cage.

On the other hand, lots of upward flight will help to strengthen a healthy bird's wings and overall physique, and can be very useful exercise to be able to offer, especially for a group of hens during the winter season. Just try to see that the cage is at least as wide as it is tall.

During breeding season, canaries don't share well, and because of this most canary-keepers won't try to house their flock in an aviary through the spring and early summer. But the rest of the year, many canaries can and do share larger aviaries and flight cages. Attempting this can receive widely varying results, depending on— you guessed it— cage set-up.

No matter how large the cage, all the canaries will want to perch at the top level. That means that you will need a minimum of six inches of perch at that height, for every bird in the flight. That figure is just an average; depending on the breed, some canaries will require quite a lot more perch space. You need to have plenty of food dishes and drinkers in a shared canary flight, too. They are best spaced around the area, rather than near each other where one bird can dominate many dishes or drinkers.

Care and judgement always need to be exercised when providing canaries with larger-sized flying areas, because the energy required to use such a space can make a critical difference in a big hurry, should a bird become even the slightest bit ill. Keep a close eye on any canaries kept in larger aviaries or flights, and be prepared to pull any bird who looks even the slightest bit under the weather.

I always worry on hearing someone say they are looking

by R C McDonald

for a cage 'with some style'— because often this means they have something highly ornamental in mind. While many of these kinds of cages can be quite lovely, unfortunately very few are actually suitable for canaries to actually live in.

When you house your bird in a fancy cage, you will find that it can be difficult to see your bird clearly through all the fancy wire-work; with these cages, the eye is drawn to look at the cage, rather than the bird inside it.

Worse— most ornamental cages are quite a lot more difficult to keep clean than a simply designed cage. This may not sound like much at first, but can lead to problems faster than most of us like to think. Another factor is the fact that so many of these cages are finished in pastel colours. These look pretty, but in actual fact, lighter-coloured bars tend to 'grab' the eye, and so will wind up detracting some of your attention from the bird itself— unless, that is, you happen to own a dark-coloured canary.

In order to be able to see a lighter coloured canary easily, the best colour for the cage bars is black. This may sound dark and dismal, but in actual fact, the human eye tends to ignore the black bars, and look right through them to focus on the bird inside.

So spend a little time considering all these factors before you purchase your next canary cage. Make plans to rearrange it as necessary, in order to make it as suitable as possible for your canary. You never know, you just might find yourself reaping the rewards of your thoughtfulness for longer than you'd ever expected!

Can Canaries Share Cages?

This must be the second-most asked canary question, ranking close behind the ever-popular *"Why won't my canary sing?!?"* It seems we humans are fairly predictable when it comes to keeping a pet canary— we get one, and soon find we are thinking of getting another.

"Just one, to keep him company," we say, wanting the best for this tiny enchanting creature who has generally managed to wriggle his way into our affections much faster than we'd anticipated.

During the late summer, fall, and most of the winter, it *is* possible for some male canaries to share a cage relatively amicably. But no matter how well they get along, only the more dominant canaries will sing much— or even at all— in a shared-cage situation. You will get a little more song in a large shared-cage than a smaller one, but not as much song as you will hear if each bird has his own well-defined territory.

If you got your birds at a youngish age— say, 6 months or so old— the gender will be uncertain, since with very little exception it's impossible to accurately tell the gender of a young canary until it is both physically mature and in full breeding condition. Even song is not really a reliable indicator, as some canary hens will sing quite a bit when young. A smaller sub-group of singing hens even exists that can sing every bit as well as most males, even when adult, although such hens are fairly rare. Still, they do exist, so the fact remains that just because you saw a young canary singing, it doesn't necessarily mean that it is a male.

In general, hens are a little more social than the males, and some breeds are more apt to be sociable than others. Perhaps the most common breeds in this category are the Fife, Border, and American Singer canaries; but sometimes trouble can arise even within the most sociable group of canaries.

Two canaries in one cage is the worst possible mix, so it's one to avoid whenever possible, except during breeding season. Even then, pairing should be done carefully, using dividable cages; the canary breeder's most useful accessory. Pairing should never be done outside of breeding season, as the usual result is extreme antagonism.

If the cage is large enough and a variety of food and water sources are available in widely separated locations, three or more canaries will usually do quite well; the presence of the third canary is often enough to keep the balance of peace in the cage from tilting to extreme enmity between two of the three birds. This kind of thing works best if the birds are all the same gender.

Younger canaries are more sociable than older canaries. In the wild young canaries must learn 'flock manners'. As the youngsters wean the older hens will provide discipline as needed within the group, ensuring that peace is kept and everybody gets a fair share of food and water. In time, the youngsters learn what's needed in order to get along.

Part of these lessons often include pacification rituals such as feeding or begging to be fed; this kind of thing is often seen as a gender or age indicator, but in a mixed flock of canaries, such gestures are often used to pacify another, more aggressive canary, being intended to divert actual out-and-out aggression.

As the youngsters grow and mature, in the wild each would normally wander off, looking for his or her own best territory, but in a shared aviary this is not possible. So while allowing your youngsters to share an aviary with your older hens after weaning can be beneficial for their social skills, it is needful to keep in mind that as they mature, the males will require their own quarters, for part of the year at least, and as the season extends towards spring, so will any hens.

A gender-mixed grouping of canaries sharing an aviary is likelier to get along better than a group of all-males, during the winter months at least— but no matter what the actual genders, trouble can easily happen when the days begin to get longer, and the birds start preparing for the arrival of breeding season.

Sometimes (rarely, but it *can* happen) everything goes smoothly— but more often than not, canaries in the same cage will come into breeding condition at different times, and when this occurs the bird who is in 'higher' breeding condition will almost always harass the bird (or birds) who are not.

Given these facts, what many of us who have had plenty of experience keeping multiple canaries will do, knowing both the benefits for the birds of being able to fly, and the potential for trouble when canaries are housed in groups (especially during the breeding season) is keep our canaries in flight cages during the summer moult, on through the fall and early winter until mid-winter or so, when the males especially begin to get more antagonistic. At this point they are are separated into individual cages for the rest of the spring and early summer.

Once midsummer has come and gone and the summer moult is well underway for each bird, ensuring that they won't have a lot of spare energy to spend harassing each other, they can usually be returned to the flight cage for the rest of the year. Not always— some adult male canaries seem to live just to pick fights— but often.

What all this adds up to, is that the odds are greatly against keeping any group of canaries in a cage successfully all year round, especially when you have multiple male canaries involved. Younger males are more likely to get along with each other than adults, and some male canaries, once adult, will never willingly share a cage with another male. On the other hand, you will find others who don't seem to mind sharing much, and a few can be found who will quite happily socialize.

But male canaries that fall into the latter group are not all that common, and usually, the more pugnacious males also tend to be the best and most constant of singers. Such a canary will definitely benefit from having a clear territory to call his own, which will encourage his song as well as his peace of mind.

I have seen some experiments at setting up a situation where the birds had individual areas opening off a large shared flight area, which actually did work reasonably well. They were rather a nuisance to set up and clean, though, and setting up such a jury-rigged arrangement in a way that allows easy access to all the areas for easy cleaning and servicing is none too simple. Many such designs involve putting cage doors together to create 'pop-holes', or cutting some small access doors (pop-holes) into the sides of two adjacent cages.

The best design I've seen consisted of three large cages arranged around each other— one large cage in the middle with two longer but less tall cages attached to two sides of the larger cage, with small pop-holes connecting all three. It also had a half dozen smaller cages that could be attached to the larger cages. Each was hung off a side of the larger cages, with the smaller cage's doorway opening into a pop-hole cut into the side of the larger flight.

If you can manage such an arrangement, it might work well for your birds too; results will vary depending on the personalities of the individual birds involved. But this kind of aviary set-up has a better chance of working than most, with canaries, simply because given the chance to claim a distinct territory of his own, most male canaries will prefer to choose one and stake it out for their own.

As long as this 'privately owned' territories are clearly separated, many male canaries have no problem with amicably sharing a common feeding-and-foraging area with the rest of the birds in the aviary. Just be aware that even then, there will usually be a fair bit of squabbling among the males, and in most cases you will hear less song than you would if the birds were caged separately.

Once breeding season approaches, everything changes. This is the season— late winter until early summer— when it can be actually dangerous to keep two canaries in the same cage, with one exception; you have a true pair, and both were in full breeding condition before being allowed to share their cage.

Successful breeding of your canaries is quite a complex affair. For now, suffice it to say, if you have more than one canary and aren't planning to breed, don't plan on being able to keep your canaries together during the late winter through early summer or so, no matter what gender they are.

Within a few weeks after the passing of Midsummer's Day on June 21st, most canaries who are exposed to natural lighting will stop trying to breed and within a few weeks or so will instead begin their annual moult. Once the moult is underway, there is a lot less energy to spare for squabbling, and many canaries will once again share a large flight or aviary reasonably well.

What this all means is that in the end, the real answer to the question of whether or not canaries can successfully share a cage, is, "It depends." On the birds, on the exact situation, on the time of year— and most importantly, on the time the birdkeeper is willing to devote to his or her birds.

by R C McDonald

Flight Cages Are For The Birds

It is a cool, crisp morning, and I lean back contentedly into the chair in the corner of my birdroom, sipping coffee. In front of me is a series of interconnecting flight cages, filled with crowds of busy, happy young red canaries. The air is filled with the sound of their songs, squabbles, and chirps, while they themselves zip about their home feeding and playing. They look very like a drift of autumn leaves tossed by a playful wind as they alternately rise and spin madly about for sheer fun, or descend in a series of spiralling curves to feed. Many of the bolder birds seem to almost throw themselves where they want to go, they fly with such force and enthusiasm.

I think of the smaller cages and flights so many young birds are restricted to growing up in and sigh. Too many of these youngsters go on to spend most or all of their lives in similarly small cages. Many owners cite convenience, lack of money, or lack of room for the reason. I have even heard, "Well, I tried a larger cage, but he/she/they just sat there and didn't *use* the space when they had it, so I got rid of the great unwieldy thing."

In my opinion, these people have drawn their conclusions prematurely. The fact is, a jump from a small cage to a flight cage is scarey to many birds, particularly at first, and most especially if the bird is already adult and has never seen such a space before.

In order to use, and allow your bird to use, a flight cage, first you must properly understand just what a flight cage is, and how it differs in care and function from a regular cage.

Generally speaking, a flight cage is simply a cage large enough to allow the occupants to achieve flight; therefore the name, flight cage. A small flight cage can be as little as two feet or so cubed; with 3/16" spacing of the bars a cage like this is known as a 'finch flight'.

Myself, I don't think the designers of such a cage ever really watched a finch of any sort fly; although tiny, they are masters of the air. Their speed and agility make a much larger space look barely adequate for the gyrations they are capable of performing.

In all honesty, most of the larger birds are capable of some rather amazing aerial antics as well, but the requirements of a four or five foot wingspan demands an area in proportion to the size of the bird; a macaw needs to flap his wings very few times to fly twenty feet, after all!

Occasionally the term 'flight cage' becomes confused with the cages used by dog or cat owners for their pets to travel the airlines in. I feel it is my duty as a bird person to insist that these terms should change. Birds have *flight* cages, while dogs and cats have *travel* cages. Much simpler!

Usually flight cages are used to allow the birds access to exercise. The larger the area, (relative to the size of the bird, of course) the more exercise the inhabitants receive as long as the interior of the cage is arranged to allow the birds maximum use of the space. This is the single most important aspect of cage design, and it is too often the one first sacrificed to human convenience.

Another often over-looked fact, especially with respect to breeding birds, is that hens *need* to exercise the muscles they will use in laying the eggs. Even hens kept only as pets have this need, as they can and often will lay eggs whether or not a male is present. These muscles run the length of the bird, from the keelbone to the sternum, and are the same muscles which power the wings.

For this reason, I make my hen flights as tall and as wide as possible, reasoning that the higher the hens are encouraged to fly, the more exercise they will get. After all, it take much more effort to fly up six feet than it does to fly across the same six feet. Since canaries aren't built like helicopters, the wide horizontal space is necessary along with the height, to allow them to use the space properly.

Some species of birds *need* to live in flight cages or they will not live long. Many of the more exotic finches, such as the lavender breasted waxbill and the red-cheeked cordon bleus are included in this category, as are most softbills, such as the shama thrush and the Pekin Robins.

One thing it is important to remember; there are times when putting a bird into a flight cage is the *last* thing you should do. For example, if you take a finch or canary that was raised and kept solely in a small cage, particularly if it is more than a couple of years old, and put it straight into a large flight cage, you risk losing it to confusion, stress, and exhaustion. This is especially true if there are other birds already living in the flight who are used to and comfortable with the cage's arrangements.

If, on the other hand, you gradually acclimatize the same bird to the idea of more space by moving it gradually up the scale to ever larger cages, it will usually adapt readily and easily.

It is extremely important never to release a single bird directly into a flight cage which already has inhabitants, without a lengthy period of introduction first.

Hang the new bird high the flight cage within a smaller cage so it can easily see most or all of the area in the flight. After a day or two, when the original occupants seem to have lost most of their curiosity, and the new bird seems relaxed and calm, open the door of the smaller cage and give the new bird access to the flight cage. Don't remove the smaller cage right away, though; leave it in until everybody has settled in comfortably. This will take at least a period of days, and can easily take a few weeks or more. Keep a close eye on the birds during this period to ensure that there are no battles over territory.

All birds should undergo a period of quarantine of at least three to six weeks as well as having a thorough health check by a certified avian veterinarian, before being allowed near an already established flock.

Never keep a sick or ailing bird in a flight cage. It will use far too much of its energy just getting about, which will greatly reduce its chances of survival. Even a bird by itself will not thrive in a flight cage if its health is compromised in any way.

Remember also that a few birds will not (or cannot) use a flight cage. A bird who has become cage-bound will be terrified if placed in a large open flight, in much the same manner a human victim of agoraphobia would react if dragged into the open. Such birds are victims of a psychological disorder, and this should be recognized. It takes time and much care to rehabilitate a bird like this.

It will always take any bird a while to adapt to a new environment, so it is only fair to allow them plenty of time to do this. Perches should be easy to access via short hops as well as longer flights, at first at least, to aid the birds in learning to cope with the extra space. Food and water must always be provided in plenty, in several containers spaced all around the flight cage. They need to be easy to find as well as easy to access, or birds on the lower end of the totem pole will suffer.

There is no reason a flight cage cannot be as, if not more, convenient than a small cage. They don't get dirty as fast as a small cage, and they require much less fussing to clean and service, especially if care is taken in the design and the arrangement of perches, drinkers and feeders.

Flight cages can be visually appealing as well, but some of

by R C McDonald

these designs appear to forget that the *occupants* of the flight should be the visual focus, not the cage itself! Just as with an aquarium, a good flight cage provides an environment in which the birds can be comfortable, as well as showing them off for your own pleasure and delight.

In many cases, lack of money or space does not need to be such a inhibiting factor either. Home-made flight cages, if built with care, can look every bit as good as commercially made ones, but will cost much less, dollar-wise. Even better, there's the advantage of being able to design the cage to fit and complement the space available.

A good flight cage should be as long as possible, while the width needs to be at least several inches more than the outspread wings of the bird or birds which are to inhabit it. While a taller flight cage may not always be possible, it should be as tall as circumstances allow. Remember too that you will need to be able to access all parts of the cage easily, both inside and out, both for cleaning, and in case you ever need to catch an inhabitant.

For canaries, there should be relatively few main perches, to allow as much space as possible to be left for flying. Usually a longer perch on either end near the top, and a lower perch in the middle are adequate, with shorter one-ended perches spaced plentifully about the cage. Swings or toys should be positioned so as to not block the flying space, either hanging quite high, or placed fairly low. The short perches are useful as sleeping perches and for in-between locations where a long perch would take up valuable flying space. Such 'sulky' perches, big enough for only one bird, can be scattered across the cage in plenty, spaced far enough apart that a bird sitting on one can't easily reach the next. These individual perches offer the cage inhabitants a little peace and privacy, as well as assistance in getting around.

Doors should be kept low to discourage escape, as startled birds usually fly upwards. Best is the double-door system, where the first door must be closed before the second can be opened. Food and water dishes are also best kept low, to reduce the mess and to allow ease of access for the caregiver. Problems can develop otherwise, since these dishes need to be changed and washed daily and disinfected regularly, to help prevent illness and disease.

The day draws to a close, and once again I can be found in my seat near the flights. The birds have finished their late afternoon songfest and are busily munching down their dinner. A few are up on the high perches where they will spend the night, and are concentrating on setting their feathers in order.

I chuckle quietly as I relax, thinking of all the people who've told me that they can't see how I manage to handle everything I do and still stay so calm about it all. Those same people will often also be heard to say that a canary is 'just a bird' or that one person's recycling can never make a difference to our planet.

To them there will always be a secret to success. Me? I plan on enjoying my birds forever, if possible. How else would I ever cope?

by R C McDonald

Home Free

Tame canaries can be a lot of fun. But every tame bird requires a fair bit of time and attention, and in the case of a canary, you will need to have the time to tame him in the first place. So what do those of us who have very little free time, but who want our birds to live a quality life, do?

Many people don't realize that it's even possible to handtame a canary, much less know that taking a little extra time to handtame a canary can produce a wonderful pet bird, every bit as sweet and captivating as any parrot. This is especially true when it's possible to get a younger canary, preferably one only recently weaned.

There are actually quite a few people out there who will freely tell you they consider canaries to be untrainable, but that's actually not the case— it's just that taming a canary requires a different approach than is usually used for most other creatures. If you're curious and want to learn more, there's a good article on handtaming canaries posted on our site online; you will find it at *robirda.com/handtame.html*.

But if you won't have a lot of time for building and maintaining a close relationship, you might prefer just to train your canary for limited free flight every day or so. I know several people who don't have room for a larger cage, but who allow their canaries out to fly about in a limited area of their home on a regular basis— in fact, I've done this myself in the past, and it's been my experience that many canaries will thrive on such a routine, even if it's only for a short time every day or so.

Unlike many other species of small birds, most canaries

are quite easy to train for supervised free flight within the home. They tend to be smarter and more adaptable than budgies, finches, or cockatiels, being far less apt to fly off in a blind panic when something surprises them.

Most of us who have trained a canary or a small group of canaries for limited free flight will choose an area that can be fairly easily bird-safed, such as a small room with no furniture to hide under or get trapped behind. Many wash-rooms are excellent candidates for such training— just make sure all plugs are in and windows shut, then lightly mist any mirrors or exposed glass windows, so there is a visual clue that there is something solid there that can't be flown through.

Then just put the cage in the brightest area of the room, prop the cage door open, and place a perch in the middle of the door. This serves as a visual cue that they may come out, and also assists in finding the way back home again.

Sit down nearby (but not too close) perhaps sip at a drink or what-have-you— and watch what your bird does, without staring too closely. Allow him to find his own way out of the cage— *never, ever, take him out yourself!* This is important, because if you want him to be able to return to his cage on his own, he must be allowed to leave on his own first. If he is younger, or is used to flying, this won't take long.

With older or cage-bound birds, it may never happen; but cage-bound birds prefer small cages to flight cages, anyways— they have never learned to fly properly, and most seem to find the whole idea rather threatening. Flying, for birds, is rather like talking is for us. True, it is largely instinctive— but it's also true that if we don't learn how to do it properly when young, we may never get it quite right.

Never, ever remove a such a bird from his cage by hand and then turn him loose. In the case of a cage-bound bird, this is equivalent to tossing a person who can't swim, off a boat while it's in the middle of the ocean. In short, such an action only creates a terrifying, traumatic experience.

by R C McDonald

On the other hand, once he has found his own way out of the cage, he will know exactly how to get home again. All he will have to do is retrace his route. As long as the whole area is bright enough that he can see well, and his cage is obvious, there should be no problem. Even the most cage-bound of elder canaries can often learn to do this, if you are patient and give them lots of time. It may take weeks of allowing him the opportunity before he makes the attempt, but if you are patient and persistent, eventually it will usually happen. Not always, but usually.

Then comes the part most people dread; the reason so few canaries are allowed free flight with-in our homes in the first place. Once he is out of the cage, how do you get him to return to his home willingly?

In actuality, if you use a little creativity along with some insight into basic canary nature, this isn't often a problem. The 'secret' is quite simple.

These are small birds, with a high metabolic rate, and they tend to be quite active. This means that they require food frequently during the day. All that must be done, then, is to see that they do not have access to any edible items when out of their cage.

Be warned if you try this— most canaries will sample *anything* green. In fact, most canaries are unashamed and utter piggies about eating any kind of greenery, so you must be sure before the bird is let out that all house-plants are removed from the room he will be flying in.

Most canaries will generally fly for about a half an hour or so before needing to 'fuel up'. You can help speed this process along, when you need to, using a simple little trick. All you have to do is make a big production of cleaning out his seed cup and then adding a visible treat of some sort, when you want him to return to the cage. Those sharp little eyes miss very little, and seldom will they waste much time before investigating.

A comment here— put the treat entirely inside the cage,

don't just peg it to the bars— because if you do, he will be able to hang off the outside of the cage to eat. Which does *not* produce the effect you want!

The second, most important part of the secret to owning a well-trained, free-flying canary, is getting him to stay inside his cage while you close the cage door. This is easier than it sounds, once you know another simple little trick.

Due to their fast metabolism, canaries see at a faster rate than humans. This is a major factor in why small birds can be so difficult to catch— to them, you seem to be moving rather slowly. This gives them plenty of time to avoid your hand. This can be frustrating for any human, but in fact there is a hidden bonus; if you slow your movements down enough, those same birds will not tend to notice that you are moving at all!

So the trick is quite simple. Once the bird is in the cage and busy eating, all that's necessary is to amble slowly over, looking elsewhere so your gaze does not provoke the bird's attention, and s-l-o-w-l-y ease the door of the cage shut. If you move too quickly he may notice what you are doing, and you may find that he is quite capable of leaping in, grabbing a beakful of his treat, and soaring back out again before you can get anywhere near the cage.

So what do you do if this happens? I've heard various solutions, over the years; some simply make room for a flight cage, and then the question never arises. One of the funnier methods I've heard comes from a pet owner who has five canaries, three hens and two males.

"I think they got tired of performing 'The Great Canary Roundup' every night," she says. "Now I just go out there and wave my arms at them, and they each head straight in to their own cage and wait for me to close the doors! Even my kids aren't always that smart!", she says, and laughs.

Personally, I usually just close the cage door anyways, and wait until they have figured out that they have been (horrors!) locked away from their treat. (This works best if

by R C McDonald

it's a treat they really like, of course.) Once they realize that they need to get into that cage if they want to get some of that tempting treat, (often this takes only 5 to 10 minutes or so), I'll open the cage door again, wait nearby until they are in, then wander slowly over and close the cage door.

This tells the bird clearly that the cage door is going to be shut anyways, regardless of whether he is inside or not. Once he's realized this it never seems to take them very long to figure out that if they want more than a nibble of that treat, they have to be inside the cage when the door shuts.

I have trained dozens of canaries to free-fly within the home this way, yet seldom have I ever had to repeat this sequence more than once, and never yet have I had to repeat it more than twice— it seems our canaries can be quite clever when it comes to accessing a favoured treat!

So if you'd like to provide your canary more room to fly, but can't afford (or don't have the room for) a larger cage, why not give in-home free-flying a try? You and your canary just may wind up having more fun than you ever suspected was possible!

Gardening For Your Birds

You were skeptical at first, but you tried it, and saw positive results from feeding plentiful dark leafy greens to your pet canaries. You've accepted that feeding greens freely is very beneficial to your birds, but you are still left with a quandary; finding a reliable source of good canary greens is not always easy, particularly during certain times of the year. But if you have a small patch of ground, it can be easier than you think to grow your own greens to offer your pet(s) throughout a good portion of the year. All it takes is a little bit of planning to learn how best to set about gardening for your birds.

It really doesn't take much to set up a small area to grow healthy greens for your birds— and you don't even need to have particularly good light or soil— even if you have ground that is often shaded and consists of mostly rocks, or mostly clay, you can still have a fairly decent bird-garden.

Ideally, you want to use a patch of ground that gets sunshine for at least half the day— but in actual fact, a lot of the hardier greens are very undemanding about their location, and many are cool-weather plants that can easily handle a good bit more shade than many other plants would tolerate.

No matter what kind of earth you have, it's a good idea to prepare it a little beforehand, to make sure that all the nutrients the plants need will be available to the growing

by R C McDonald

plants, and in turn, via those greens, to your birds.

Over the years I've started several bird-gardens in ground that 'everybody knew' was worthless for growing healthy veggies. To their surprise and my satisfaction, we all discovered that using organic gardening techniques for building up the soil offered a workable solution, providing effective and productive results.

One of my more memorable gardens was started in only three inches of clay over sandstone and limestone. After a little trial and error, I found that my best solution was to dig 'raised beds' by removing the clay down to the limestone, then make the 'beds' by laying out bales of cheap hay that had gotten wet— usually ranchers will have some bales that got wet, and they will sell them really cheap.

I left the bales unopened, and used them to outline where I wanted the beds to be, then filled in the open holes left on the insides with old grass clippings, loose hay, and compost, layered with screened clay.

An old window frame works well to build a screen— just get one the size you want, then nail ½ inch hardware cloth over one side of it. Lay the wired frame across the bales, then get a small shovelful of dirt and dump it on top of the screen. All you need to do now is to 'scrub' the clay and dirt through the screen, picking out larger rocks as you go.

I'd continue until I had enough screened clay to barely cover the organic material inside, then I'd layer in more organic 'junk'— sometimes even broken-up small branches — alternating with layers of the clay until finally I'd completely filled the gap between the bales. Occasionally I added a sprinkling of bone meal, and every other layer or so I'd sprinkle a few handfuls of wood ash, collected from a fireplace. (If you don't have wood ash, greensand from an organic gardening supply store works well too).

Once the 'hole' outlined by the bales was filled up even with the tops of the bales, I used some potting soil to put a thin layer on top of everything, probably totalling no more than a ¼ inch thick at the most.

The final step was to get some red wriggler worms (mine were from a fishing supply store) and 'seed' a small handful of worms into each 'bale-bed'.

The bales held everything together nicely until it had finished rotting down. It took almost two years before my garden beds had completely finished decomposing, but in the end I had some really nice foot-high or so mounds in the shape of raised beds, filled with wonderfully rich, light, and very fertile loam.

I didn't surround each bed with boards, mostly because that encourages slugs, and in the northwest we get enough of them as it is. True, the bales offered bugs and slugs a certain amount of shelter too— but they also allow enough access to their predators that in reality there turned out to be very little slug problem. Many's the time I've surprised a small flock of wild ducks or quail out in the garden in the earlier hours of the day, 'patrolling' for those yummy slugs. Perhaps they ate a little greenery, too, but if they did, I didn't notice it.

One great thing about this method of garden-building is that just because the beds aren't completely 'cooked' at first doesn't mean you can't use them. I planted my 'bale-beds' the very first year by just digging into them, pushing some of the half-rotted material aside and then putting a fairly plentiful supply of good potting soil into each hole around the roots of my transplants. The rotting compost and hay heated everything up quite nicely, and the whole thing held water beautifully even when it got hot and dry. Meanwhile, the worms I'd 'seeded' kept busy breaking everything down, even while my plants were growing.

The warmth from the rotting bales helped the plants to stave off frost, and that year I was able to plant peppers and tomatoes out a good month before the last frost. They grew incredibly quickly and began to offer ripe fruit a good six weeks earlier than plants grown the ordinary way.

by R C McDonald

Needless to say, we had plenty of greens for everybody that year, the family as well as the birds. It started with small harvests beginning in March and continued all season long. We even had smaller harvests through the winter, as I found I could extend the season by using some protective coverings over the beds, adding more insulation and warmth by surrounding the winter beds with more rotting bales.

As for bugs— try mixing your plants up so that there's no big patches of just one kind of plant, and plant lots of garlic and dill everywhere. This encourages the beneficial insects, brings more small bug-eating birds, and confuses and repels many plant-loving insects. I like to invite garter snakes, ladybugs, chickadees, wrens, and hummingbirds into my garden by putting out the kind of foods they enjoy.

I had no problem inviting garter snakes into my garden, they came on their own— it seems they liked the shelter the hay bales gave them. 'Garter' is an old German term for 'garden', and garter snakes truly are a wonderful 'garden snake'. They are shy, completely non-poisonous and wholly inoffensive. Each one eats bugs like a little bug-eating machine. It wouldn't surprise me to hear that a single garter snake can eat a ton of bugs, over the period of a summer. Well okay, maybe it would surprise me a bit— but only a bit.

The chickadees came originally for the black oil sun flower seeds in the birdfeeder, but stayed to eat bugs off my garden plants, as a kind of appetizer. The wrens came to eat bugs, and stayed for the plentiful nesting spots I provided, while the hummingbirds came for the nectar in the varied array of flowers planted throughout the garden, and stayed to raise their babies on the plentiful bugs.

Even that first year, all my neighbours had cabbage bugs and aphids all over everything they planted— but in my garden, you had to hunt like fury to find a single pest. You might, though, just find your head becoming a perch for a watchful parent hummingbird, and if you weren't careful where you stepped you might find a garter snake shooting out from under your feet. I felt as if I'd been blessed with a miniature Garden of Eden.

We have moved several times over the years, meaning I've had to create a new garden each time. I've used a similar group of 'tricks' several times since to build myself a small garden in an unlikely spot, once on a balcony in the heart of Vancouver, and again in two different community gardens, started while living in an apartment. One such garden was featured in the Vancouver Sun newspaper as an example of intensive gardening. It had 79 different species and breeds of plants all living together nicely, pest-free— with no use of any pesticides whatsoever— in an area 7 feet square.

It had begun in nothing but rock and clay fill that the city had dumped over the swampland that had originally been there, and yet that little garden produced heaps of food and flowers for me and my birds, even in its very first year.

It's a bit of work to set up such a garden, because of the digging and screening that needs to be done— but it is a great way to 'make' good garden soil from next to nothing. When used with interplanting— what is often called 'companion planting'— and including the use of lots of garlic, dill, and various flowers scattered throughout the vegetables— garden pests seem to become really confused. Although I always got a few pests, they hardly ever did much if any damage.

I don't know if you have ever considered trying organic gardening, but if you keep one or more pet birds you might want to seriously consider it. It can be incredibly fulfilling to find your yard full of beneficial bugs and lots of wild birds, as well as heaps of food for your family as well as your pets. I always see lots of wrens in an organic garden; otherwise I seldom see them at all. And they have such a beautiful song! A bonus for me is that they and a few other species, such as the American Goldfinch, and many of the siskins, seem to like to challenge the canaries to singing 'duels', right through the house windows. This produces a show which can be highly entertaining to watch, and is often really quite funny.

As for what to grow for your canaries in your garden, once you have it set up— any kind of greens works well, but I like particularly to grow flowering rape, and the shorter dwarf version of the same plant which the Italians know as 'rapini', and the rest of the world seems to call 'raab' or 'broccoli raab'. You don't even have to buy seed to grow the flowering rape plants, just pick out some of the small round dark seeds from your canary's seed mix, and 'plant' them by tossing a handful over some soil and lightly raking them in.

They are a cool-weather plant, and prefer a similar growing environment to peas, so can be planted at about the same time in the spring. For a really good harvest, plant some every two or three weeks or so throughout the duration of summer, picking cooler and shadier spots for the young plants as the summer progresses.

These are hardy plants, usually quite strong, and resistant to attack by pests. They tend to grow tall and a bit leggy, which is best controlled by continually snipping the growing tips for greens, shaping the plant into a little bush, rather than picking the larger lower leaves. The growing tips can be harvested all season long, right up until hard frost, and if the plants are given a little shelter, they can be quite easily overwintered in many areas of the country.

All of the kales are similarly easy to grow, being hardy and cool-loving, and all are extremely nutritious. In fact, science tells us that kale is the single most nutritious vegetable on the planet!

There is a wide variety of crinkle-leafed and flat-leafed kales of many colours to be grown. I particularly like the tall red-green Russian kale, and the similarly growing peacock kale is lovely too, as well as providing tasty, nutritious greens for both you and your canaries. The dark-green curly kales are perhaps best known, along with the colourful ornamental kales so commonly used to add winter interest to a garden. Yes, these kales are just as edible as the regular kinds, and just as nutritious, too.

Other greens favoured by canaries are leafy endives, chicory greens, nasturtiums (greens, flowers, seed), and of course, their penultimate favourite, the dandelion. Most canaries will cheerfully eat the entire dandelion plant, root, leaf, flowers, and seed, then look for more. I won't tell you what kinds of looks I got from my neighbours when they caught me transplanting dandelions *into* my gardens— I am sure you can imagine. I just wish I'd caught some of those looks on film, they were priceless!

Spray millet is fun to grow, and attractive, too. It is often used in ornamental gardens, and there is known as 'fox-tail millet'. It starts out looking like a little clump of grass, but soon each little clump will put up a 'foxtail' that will eventually become the spray of millet. Each green seed in the spray has a long maroon-red 'hair' attached to it, and the overall effect does look very similar to a fox's maroon-coloured brush sticking out of the earth— if you can imagine how the rest of the fox got underground, that is!

Buckwheat provides plenty of sweetly-scented white flowers, followed by green seeds that are generally adored by canaries, and of course black oil sunflowers look beautiful all summer long. They aren't as large as the giant sunflowers, but they are just as pretty, and the heads are very attractive to a great many species of wild birds. The seeds are greatly appreciated in their green stage by canaries, and are useful when mature and dried as the basis of a good soak seed mix.

I could go on and on, but I think you probably have the idea and can experiment on your own, to find out what grows best in your area, and what foods you and your birds prefer. Just make sure you don't use any pesticides or other such chemicals on your plants, and you will have a plentiful supply of greens for your birds for a large part of the year, and lots of nutritious greens to add to your own soups, stews and salads, too.

I hope you get as much satisfaction, fun, and enjoyment out of your gardens as I do mine— as well as plenty of good hearty food for you, your family, and your birds.

Chickweed, the Bird's Choice

Bird-keepers and gardeners everywhere know it; the former as a wonderful little wild-food that drives their birds into a frenzy of eating, the latter as a pernicious, persistent garden pest that resists being eradicated. Lately research has begun to indicate something our birds have apparently known all along— there's a whole lot of good to be gained from eating chickweed.

Chickweed is a low-growing, cool-loving plant that starts growth as soon as the ground thaws in spring. It loves rich, loamy soil, and is commonly found in gardens— to a great many gardeners' dismay. To these folks, this lowly little green-leafed, sprawling, white-flowered plant is a pest that stubbornly keeps coming back no matter how persistently the gardener tries to discourage it.

Chickweed is closely related to the 'purslane' family of plants, and in one form or another, either it or a close relative can be found over just about the entire planet. Interestingly enough, many plants in this family are a form of succulent; perhaps this is one reason why the greens from this family of delicate little 'weeds' all seem to remain tender and tasty for their entire lifespan. Even when flowering, none of these plants ever become bitter in any way, and they all tend to maintain their crispy, juicy texture and delicate, mild flavour until the day they die.

I've only found one exception to this rule-of-thumb; if the

by R C McDonald

succulent form of purslane is regularly over-picked in a hot dry climate, the resulting regrowth can eventually become toxic, especially to cattle or other ruminants.

Chickweed leaves have a texture similar to lettuce, and are very tasty when eaten in salads, sandwiches, or rolls. Most birds, of whatever species, adore chickweed and will gobble down large quantities, if given the opportunity. My canaries love it so much that if they get to eat it regularly, they will begin to refuse other greens, loudly demanding that I remove 'this horrid stuff' and give them their chickweed, should I have the audacity to present them with anything else!

Unfortunately for them, chickweed does not love the heat, and rarely lasts longer than late spring in the garden, even if deliberately cultivated. So no matter how insulted they feel about it all, sooner or later each year they have to give up their beloved chickweed and go back to eating something else instead.

Even when the yard is knee-deep in chickweed though, the birds never get all of it, because I love it just as much as my birds do— it has a wonderfully mild, nutty taste that resists description, and has to be experienced to be understood. Even the best butter lettuce pales in comparison, once you've eaten the remarkable and tasty little green most usually known as chickweed.

Chickweed has a number of field and woodland relatives, all similar in appearance and growth habits, all with the similarly wonderful flavour, texture, and resistance to bitterness found in 'real' chickweed. Several of these plants are commonly known as chickweed, while other varieties are termed 'miner's lettuce', 'siberian miner's lettuce' or some other such similar name.

These names came about because these greens appear early in the spring, and during the gold rush days were eagerly eaten by miners to stave off scurvy and other such problems. Their efforts were successful, because chickweed and all its relatives are very high in Vitamins A and C.

The latest exciting health discovery about this so-fascinating family of plants is their high content of alpha linolenic acid, one type of the omega-3 fatty acids. This fatty acid may affect human health directly, but the most intriguing possibility is that the body may be able to convert this particular fatty acid into other, related kinds of omega-3 fatty acids, such as those found in fish oils.

Although these fatty acids are so highly beneficial, traditionally there have been very few good dietary sources other than seafood for Omega-3s. More recently some oils, nuts, some grains and other leafy vegetables have been found to also contain some Omega-3s, but so far purslane and its relatives, including chickweed, have been found to have far more of these fatty acids than can be found in any other group of plants.

Researchers have seen evidence that these substances lower blood pressure and cholesterol levels, and make the blood less likely to form clots. Yet for hundreds of years before this scientific finding, many of the various forms of purslane and chickweed have been eaten as foods, and used for treating arthritis, inflammation, heart disease and to promote general good health. The juice has been used as a mild eyewash for sore or tired eyes, and juices and/or compresses were used for treating dry, irritated skin, or rashes. Folk medicine lists many more uses for both purslane and chickweed, and while many 'experts' will remind you that all such 'old wives tales' are suspect, in this case science is beginning to show that these plants have a great deal more to offer than even folk medicine seems to have suspected.

Interestingly enough, many plants in the purslane family are, unlike their relatives in the chickweed group, heat-loving plants that come into their prime in middle to late summer. This means that these little weeds from the purslane family are a good green to offer your birds once chickweed season has passed. Similarly to chickweed, purslanes are also found in fertile soil, and often appear in

by R C McDonald

gardens, where they are most often regarded as just one more unwanted, pestiferous weed. If only those gardeners knew of the nutrition they were throwing away when they uproot these delicate little plants!

One type of purslane has been cultivated for its heat-tolerant and drought-resistant flowers, and is usually known as the 'Dolly Parton flower', for its habit of blooming from 9 am to 5 pm. Meanwhile its smaller 'weedy' cousin has recently begun to receive a great deal of attention as nutritionists and some more creative chefs have begun to discover that this little plant has almost everything; eye appeal, crisp texture, tangy taste, and all the nutrition you could want. If the high content of Omega-3 fatty acids weren't enough, it has been shown that purslane (and chickweed) both contain above average values of Vitamins A and C, yet manage to provide all of this nutrition with only 15 calories in a 100-gram portion, as compared with 76 in a boiled potato.

Purslane has been eaten throughout most of Europe and Asia for centuries, particularly in the Mediterranean. In Russian, it is traditionally dried or canned, to save for winter use, while in Mexico, where it is a favourite comfort food, it is known as 'verdolaga', and is often eaten in eggs or wrapped in a fresh tortilla. It has no bitter taste at all so long as the plants are not picked over regularly, and can be eaten raw in salads or sandwiches, cooked as greens or in omelets, or added to soups and stews, where its gel-like mucilaginous qualities add greatly to the texture and flavour.

Interestingly enough the incidence of heart disease is very low wherever purslane is known to be a traditional component of the diet. I have been enjoying chickweed and purslane as wild edibles for much of my life, but it never occurred to me to wonder just why my birds seemed to like it so well. It seems that in this case, as has happened so many other times, my birds were wa-a-a-ay ahead of me. Maybe they really do know best!

Glorious Greens

One old saying claims that if you scratch somebody who keeps canaries, you'll find a gardener underneath. In my case it's quite true, as it happens, and it seems to be true of a great many of the canary keepers I've met, from all around the world. While not all canary people garden, my experience has been that, by and large, most do. Perhaps there's just something about both pastimes that appeals to us, I don't know. But many of us do know that our canaries certainly do appreciate the garden bounty equally as much as we do, particularly those glorious greens!

Most canaries adore eating greens, and there's a good reason for this; those greens contain more than just moisture, they contain nutrients that canaries (and for that matter, many other bird species) require in fairly hefty quantities, in order to maintain good health.

Vitamin A, for example, is plentiful in a great many dark leafy greens, and most avian species, including canaries, require quite a lot of this essential nutrient, far more, for their size and weight, than we humans do.

Other commonly found ingredients in most greens are a variety of vitamins and minerals, especially the easily-lost water-based nutrients such as vitamin C and many of the B's. Most dark leafy greens also offer plentiful amounts of trace elements or minerals, along with roughage and, yes, added moisture, a particular necessity for birds on an fairly dry seed or pellet-based diet. Even a very busy bird can't always drink as much as it needs, so a little extra moisture with the food helps the body stay vigorous and strong.

One caution you need to be aware of, if you plan to feed greens to your canaries, and that's chemical content. Foods that have been grown with the assistance of fertilizers or pesticides can sometimes turn out to be toxic for canaries, even though the levels used are considered safe for use on food for humans.

The problem is that we humans tend to be much more resistant to negative effects from these substances than our canaries are; and besides, our canaries are simply so much smaller than us. The same quantity of a chemical that won't harm a human child, may very well kill a canary.

Organically grown greens *are* getting easier to find, in many areas of the county, but because they are more labour intensive to grow, they tend to be a little more expensive than commercially grown greens. For me this fact is offset by the fact that they are generally far safer to use, when it comes to feeding greens to your canaries or other small birds.

A lot of people enjoy growing their own foods, when the seasons permit it, and this is an excellent way to produce your own bird greens. After all, if you grow it yourself, you can be that much more certain of just what went into that produce!

The ideal plants for such purposes are hardy, easy-care undemanding plants that are disease and pest resistant, as well as being attractive, tasty, and nutritious. Some plants will self-sow, if given the chance, and will produce plentiful quantities of greens over a period of months or sometimes even years, with minimal care and attention.

Sounds like a pipe dream, you say? There actually is plants out there that fit that description, and we're going to discuss a few of them here.

Broccoli Raba or *Rapini;*

A bit like a leafy broccoli, this relative of the widespread Cole family (that includes cabbages, oak trees and roses, among others) does best in cooler weather. It tastes quite different than broccoli, offering more 'tang' to the bite. It is very easy to grow, being bug and disease resistant, and will do quite well even in fairly poor soil. It is frost-resistant too, and will easily overwinter in many areas of the country, if given a little protection. The spring shoots on an overwintered plant are particularly tasty, and are dense with a rich supply of nutrients. Rapini offers good amounts of omega-3 and omega-6 fatty acids, and a fairly balanced and rich group of proteins and amino acids. It is a rich source of vitamin K, A and beta carotene, and offers a fair bit of vitamin C and simple plant sugars.

Carrots;

Carrots are well known for the nutrition they offer. They are one of the best vegetable sources for vitamin A and beta carotene, and they offer a wide variety of amino acids. What many don't know, is that carrot *leaves* can be every bit as edible as the carrots themselves! The greens from carrots grown commercially, though, are not to be trusted; since most people don't eat the greens, there is often a fair bit of pesticide used on them.

But if you are growing your own, or using organically grown carrots, you can be fairly sure that the greens are as safe as the carrots themselves. As long as they have not been sprayed with pesticides, there's every reason to use these nutritious, peppery-tasting greens. Birds love them, and humans enjoy them added to salads (you don't need much!) or dried and used like parsley in soups, stews, and the like.

If you've never tried these spicy greens, you are in for a real treat. Try leaving a carrot in the ground over the winter, and the next spring it will put up tall stalks with multiple large, white-flowered dill-like heads which attract a great many butterflies. The seeds are spicy and tasty, very much like their close relative, caraway.

by R C McDonald

Chickweed;

Chickweed is a low-growing, cool-loving plant that starts growth as soon as the ground thaws in the spring. It loves rich, loamy soil, and is found commonly in gardens, as an uninvited weed. Gardeners who are better acquainted welcome its presence, because chickweed leaves have a texture similar to lettuce, and even when flowering, it never becomes bitter, maintaining its crispy, juicy texture and delicate, mild flavour until frost.

Chickweed easily self-sows, and is very tasty in sandwiches, salads, or rolls. Most birds, of whatever species, adore chickweed and will gobble down large quantities if given the opportunity.

Chickweed has a number of field and woodland relatives, all similar in appearance and growth habits, and all with the same wonderful flavour, texture, and resistance to bitterness. Chickweed and its relatives are very high in Vitamins A and C. Even better, more recently they have been shown to contain more Omega-3 fatty acids than any other leafy vegetable known.

Chicory (Italian Dandelion);

Chicory is also sometimes called the 'Italian Dandelion', due to a resemblance to its yellow-flowered relative. Like the dandelion, chicory leaves are nutritious but have a bitter edge to the taste, even when young; eating them can be a bit of an acquired habit, but can be very beneficial to your health.

Like the dandelion, chicory is very high in vitamins and minerals, containing essential trace elements that can be difficult to acquire elsewhere in a vegetable-based diet. The greens as well as the blue flowers and the green seed-heads are all greatly appreciated by canaries, and if you dig it up and slice it down the middle before offering it to them, they will even eat the roots.

Chicory is easy to grow; in fact, you could say it grows

like, well, a weed! It self-sows reliably, and will show up early in the spring, even after the hardest winters. Although it prefers cool weather, it is fairly tolerant of heat, though as soon as the days get warm it will insist on flowering and setting seed. But this is no problem if you're feeding canaries, as they enjoy the flowers and seeds as much as the greens.

Besides, those lovely blue flowers are good for bringing more beneficial insects and butterflies into your garden—and who wouldn't want that?

Daylily;

Daylilies are often used in perennial landscaping; they are a grassy-looking plant that puts up lily-like flowers during the summer, dying down in the winter only to return each year. I wasn't able to find out what kind of nutrition daylily buds have; this tasty food is not yet recognized as a food, in most databases. But it wouldn't surprise me to find out that it is every bit as nutritious as, say, chickweed, or some of the other wild foods that have been faithfully eaten traditionally by several cultures for so many generations.

If harvested when newly opened each dawn, each daylily flower can be found to contain a tiny pool of nectar at the base of the blossom. The taste of the flower itself is mild and bland, slightly sweet. In some cultures, the unopened buds are battered and deep-fried, and are considered a delicacy. The roots are also edible, and can be roasted whole, or used to produce a high-grade starch. Canaries adore daylilies in any form, and will readily eat any part of the plant they are presented with, and look for more. Be careful, though; if you try them, you may find you'd rather eat them yourself!

Endive (leafy);

Leafy endive looks a little like a head of loose-leaf lettuce, until you look a little more closely, when you will note that the leaves are long and thin, although they tend to be curly around the edges. The taste is slightly bitter; like chicory, leafy endive (also known as 'endivio') is another relative of the dandelion. Like it's weedy relative, this plant is loaded with nutrition, and is beloved by canaries everywhere. It is more tender than broccoli raab or chicory, and (like a lettuce) will require a bit more tending to grow, (being particular about it's water requirements especially) but the results will be worth it.

Leafy endive offers good amounts of omega-3 and omega-6 fatty acids, compared to most greens, and a fairly balanced and rich group of proteins and amino acids. It is a rich source of vitamin K and A, and offers a fair bit of vitamin C and simple plant sugars.

Kale; Curly, Ornamental, Peacock, Russian;

Kale is, quite simply, the single most nutritious vegetable on the planet. It is very cold-hardy, and in most areas is very resistant to pests and disease, being willing to grow well even in rather poor soil. It will winter over quite easily in most areas with minimal protection, although most kales will then bolt to seed as soon as the weather gets hot. Peacock kale is the exception, and will resist bolting even in the hottest weather until fully adult.

Curly kale and various colours of ornamental kale are the most commonly seen, although peacock kale or the taller russian kale will show up occasionally, or surface in some mesclun seed mixes. All versions of kale are edible, no matter what their colour or shape, and all have similarly high nutrient content. Most kale tends to be fairly bitter in warmer weather, but will become quite sweet and tasty if left in the ground until it has been firmly touched by the first frost.

Peacock kale produces a much larger plant than the more common curly kale. It has larger, flatter leaves, often with some frilling at the edges. It's a beautiful plant, with the dark green leaves blushed with rose tones down their veins, and their distinctive bluish 'bloom' (which can be washed off by rain or sprinkling). Besides its beauty, another benefit is that it's quite mild in flavour even during the summer, lacking the bitterness found in most summer kales. It does well when lightly picked throughout the growing season, making it a perfect home gardener's plant.

Lamb's Quarters or Wild Amaranth;

Lamb's Quarters has beautiful, almost silvery-blue foliage that looks as if it has been lightly dusted, but this lovely plant is often dismissed as a mere weed. It is actually an important source of food and cover to many kinds of insects and birds. Both the foliage and seeds are palatable to humans, while the seeds are an important food source for many of the smaller species of wild songbirds. And yes, our canaries love it too, whether you're talking seeds, flowers, or greens.

The young leaves and stems can be added to salads (the taste is rather bland, and blends well with other greens, wild or domestic), or they can be lightly steamed as a potherb. Similar to its close relative, Amaranth, the seeds are very high in protein. Some tribes of Amerindians reportedly ground the seeds into flour, while others added them whole into a pemmican (or trail food) mixture.

The flowers are tiny, and resemble seedpods rather more than flowers. Canaries enjoy eating the leaves and stems of this plant at all stages of growth, and particularly enjoy this plant during any stage of flowering; whether they are stripping off leaves, chowing down on the tiny flowers or picking out the even tinier seeds, not minding if they're fully ripened or not.

Marigolds;

There are two unrelated plants eaten as marigolds; the first is not actually a marigold at all, but a calendula, sometimes called the 'Pot Marigold'. My canaries love the leaves and flowers of this plant, which has hundreds of years of culinary history. The flower's petals make a wonderful healing wash for dry or damaged skin, and also work well in cooked and fresh dishes, with flavors ranging from spicy to bitter, tangy to peppery. The sharp taste of the flower petals closely resembles saffron, giving rise to its other common name of 'Poor Man's Saffron'.

The pretty petals in hues of golden-orange will help to enhance yellow in canary feathers, while the yellow or orange petals will colour and flavor most foods when chopped and sautéed with them (cooking brings out the colour). Most birds enjoy the greens or flowers equally well, while humans eat the greens in salad mixes, or sprinkle the flower petals on soups, pasta or rice dishes, herb butters, and salads, or use them to add a yellow tint to soups, spreads, and scrambled eggs.

Gem Marigolds (Tagetes tenuifolia): 'Lemon Gem' and 'Tangerine Gem' marigolds are the best-tasting of the edible 'true' marigolds. All marigolds are technically edible, but most are very bitter, and some can carry toxic levels of oxalic acids. Gem Marigolds are also known as 'dwarf marigolds' or 'signet marigolds'. They have a spicy, herbal flavor that ranges from tangy to bitter, depending on the soil and growing conditions. As the common names suggest, they often have a citrus flavor, even though you won't smell a citrus scent. Most of my canaries enjoy these flowers, but I pull off the petals and break off and remove the bitter portion that comes to a right angle, when eating them myself.

If you want to preserve calendula or gem marigolds for the winter, the flower petals can be dried. Add them to nestling foods, or use them yourself in egg dishes such as quiche, scrambled eggs, omelette, or devilled eggs. They're also good in mayonnaise salads such as egg, potato, or chicken, or added to breads and muffins.

Mustard;

'Brassica juncea' or mustard greens are, as the name implies, the leaves of the plant which produces mustard seeds. It's also known as gai choi, Indian or Japanese mustard, or California pepper grass; the leaves can be flat, crumpled or lacy-edged.

One of the most pungent and interesting of all the greens, as well as a very generous source of vitamin A, mustard greens are widely used in French, Chinese and Southern U.S. cuisines. True to style, most canaries enjoy these greens greatly and will eat fairly good sized portions, given the opportunity and free choice.

For human cooking, try mustard greens sautéed with chopped bacon and red potatoes, or simply stir fried in olive oil with a minced garlic clove. Be sure not to over-cook them, and never add water; you'll leach away all the flavour and too many nutrients. Mustard greens are more heat-tolerant than some of the more delicate greens, but do best as a cool season crop. If you're growing them yourself, be sure to rotate them between peas and wheat crops to help prevent root rot.

Nasturtiums;

Colourful, edible, butterfly-like nasturtium blossoms have been considered a vegetable, an herb, a flower, and even a fruit, at different times of their history. Renaissance botanists named it after watercress, ('Nasturtium officinale' in Latin), which tastes similar. The nasturtiums we grow today descend mainly from two species native to Peru. According to Jesuit missionaries, the Incas used nasturtiums as a salad vegetable and as a medicinal herb. Spanish and Dutch herbalists shared seeds willingly, and the pretty, fragrant and easy-to-grow plants quickly became wide-spread throughout Europe.

Leaves were eaten in salads; unripe seeds and flower buds were pickled and used as a substitute for capers. Flowers were common in nosegays, or were planted to adorn trellises or stone walls. The flowers and long-lasting leaves were popular in Victorian bouquets and table arrangements, and nasturtiums were known to help prevent scurvy, since the leaves are rich in Vitamin C.

Keeping the plants well watered helps moderate the spiciness of the leaves and flowers, but how-ever spicy they get, my canaries always seem to enjoy them. They add a refreshing bite to a potato salad, and pair nicely with seafood. A handful of the bright coloured flower petals are delicious chopped into a shrimp or crab salad, and the whole flowers and leaves make a great garnish for a platter of grilled salmon or birthday cakes; press the flowers on just before serving so that they look enticing and fresh. Or, use the petals to decorate any savory open-faced sandwiches.

However you use them, spicy-sweet nasturtium flowers are a wonderful way to introduce edible flowers into any diet, whether for your birds, yourself, or the rest of your family.

Seedpods (green or ripe);

If you're growing your own greens for yourself and your birds, you have another option for use besides simply just harvesting the leaves or flowers— why not allow the plants to go to seed, and feed those to your birds too? Many edible plants set seed that is greatly enjoyed by canaries and other species; besides offering a tasty treat for your birds, the flowers will help to attract a much wider variety of butterflies and beneficial insects to your garden than you would see otherwise.

Many plants will easily self-sow, and save you the effort of collecting, saving, and drying the seeds— as long as you don't mind allowing them to choose their own place to grow, you could end up harvesting food year after year with minimal effort.

Canaries and other members of the finch family enjoy a great many seeds when in the green, or 'milk' stage, as well as ripe. Some useful seed-producing plants for this purpose are lettuce, carrots, dandelions, chicory shepherd's purse, teazel, caraway, canola, millets of all kinds, canary grass, and most of the cabbages and mustards.

Most of these plants are annuals, meaning they will grow from seed and flower in the same year, but carrots are biannual, growing their root in the first year, and flowering the second.

Even if you don't want to bother to over-winter a carrot or two, it's still easy to get carrot-flowers; simply look for a stored carrot that is beginning to grow a bit at the top, trim the root a bit, then replant it in your garden or in a pot on your balcony in the early spring. Keep it well-watered and in a fairly bright location, and it should produce tall stalks of large, multi-flowered heads closely resembling dillweed, except the flowers are white instead of yellow.

Squash Blossoms and Tips;

All squash flowers are edible, not just zucchini. The squash blossom was one of the first edible flowers to become relatively common in the US, thanks to the popularity of Mexican and Italian foods. The young tips of the vines are edible too, and are excellent chopped and quickly stir-fried. Of course, my canaries adore the blooms, pollen and all, as well as the tips!

Mexicans eat the delicately flavoured squash blossoms in quesadillas and in an elegant soup called 'sopa de flor de calabaza', which translates as 'pumpkin blossom soup'. In Italy, the fragile orange-yellow zucchini blossoms (fiori di zucca) are fried in beer batter after being stuffed with soft cheese.

Squash blossoms can be grilled, poached, steamed or eaten raw in salads. Or brush them with a little olive oil, pop them in the toaster oven, and spread a little goat cheese on them when they're wilted and hot. They are extremely perishable and will only last about a day.

→ *See photos of many of these plants online at www.robirda.com/greens/*

by R C McDonald

Why Soak Seed?

I've been asked a lot of questions over the years, but this one (quite commonly heard) never seems to have a simple answer. Finding the right solution for me involved factoring in a great deal of variables— and what works for me, may not work for you.

Nevertheless, as stated in my article 'Soak Seed and Nestling Food' (found online at *robirda.com/soakseed.html*) I have found soaked seeds to be an invaluable addition to my birds' diet, and for a number of years now, using soaked seeds has been a central part of my bird care routines for much of each year. So, for everybody who's ever asked, here's my answer to the question, *"Why soak seed?"*

I first encountered the notion of soaking grain to be fed to livestock years ago. In the midst of a domestic crisis, I faced having to sell my beloved poultry due to lack of money for feed.

"Well, what're ya feedin' them that stuff fer?" one of my neighbours enquired, waving her hand at my last bag of layer pellets.

"Well, I tried feeding them mixed grains, but they weren't doing very well on it, and there was a lot of waste..." my voice trailed off. She was regarding me with the gently patient look she usually reserved for young children or idiots.

"Dry?" she inquired, folding her arms. One foot was beginning to tap, I noticed. I had clearly been missing something and was about to learn what.

"Of course, what other way is there?" I replied, struggling not to squeak.

"—what other way?! *Oooohhh!*" she exclaimed, obviously at a loss for words. Finally, after what seemed closer to an eternity than seconds, she asked, "You mean you've never heard of soaking grain before you feed it to your poultry? I can't believe it! I thought everybody knew to do that. They can't digest it properly, dry, unless it's ground or rolled, and soaking it's so much easier..." her voice trailed off. This time it was my turn to give her 'the look'.

"Why on earth would anybody think 'everybody' would know that?" I demanded firmly, waving my arms in what I fondly believed to be appropriate emphasis, not realizing, of course, that what she was about to tell me would be useful to me (and used by me) for the rest of my life.

It was actually quite simple. You took a mixture of grains selected so their nutrient value would balance as much as possible. This mix was placed in a bucket with twice the amount of water and left overnight. In the morning the water was strained off and dumped on the garden, and the soaked grain was rinsed, strained again, then fed to the chickens.

Her father and grandfather had always done this, she said, and they always had a 'fine fat flock', with little to no problems with unproductive or sick birds. Crushed oyster shells were offered separately, to provide calcium for making egg-shells, and the birds were allowed to roam in a pasture in the afternoons, where they could glean insects and munch on greenery.

At the time, the biggest advantage for me was that this mixture of grains supplemented with the oyster shells, gave my birds a good diet at about half of the cost I'd been paying for layer pellets. Thanks to my neighbour's advice, I was able to keep my flock.

Perhaps due to this background, when I first began keeping canaries it was natural to feed them soaked seed.

The mixture that had served my chickens, doves, geese and ducks would not do for the canaries, however— they did not seem to like the taste of some of the grains in the mixture, and would not eat everything they found in the mix I served them.

I felt that it was important to find a mixture of grains that would be acceptable to them that would still supply adequate amounts of the nutrients needed during breeding and moulting— especially during the critical period when they were raising their babies— and so began a series of experiments.

It wasn't long before I found a mix of soaked grains and seeds that my canaries would eat reliably, but I wasn't entirely happy with the nutrient content, nor was I thrilled with the fact that my birds loved these soaked seeds so much that they would eat them exclusively to all the other foods they were offered, if given the chance.

I could see where this could cause unexpected problems to crop up, particularly during the critical nesting period when they were spending so much energy raising babies. Add in the fact that canary babies require constant supplies of nutrients at a high enough level to support their rapid rate of growth, and I could see the potential for trouble.

Finally, I did not like the fact that the damp, soaked seeds would go sour fairly quickly if offered in amounts greater than the birds could eat in a few minutes.

How could I create a food high in the necessary nutrients that would remain stable at room temperatures for long enough to allow me to reliably offer it in quantities large enough to provide steady nutrition for growing babies?

This was a bit of a quandary, since some days I was away at work for 9 hours or more. Add in the fact that towards the end of breeding season, the weather would be getting consistently quite warm, and you had a recipe with too much potential for disaster, unless I could find a way to help prevent the soaked seeds I offered from going sour.

The problem was less significant when feeding adult birds who required some extra nutrition throughout the rest of the year; say, through the moult, or to help allay stress. I would be feeding only once a day in such cases, and all I had to do was to serve a small enough portion so that it would be eaten quickly.

In the end, I settled for a combination effect. My soak seed mix has varied a little over the years, but nowadays usually consists of something like 50 lbs each of canary grass and black oil sun-flower seed, 40 lbs of canola, 20 lbs each of wheat berries and safflower seed, 10 lbs of buckwheat, and 5 lbs each of mung bean and raw sesame seed. I include the sesame seeds because they are one of the few seeds high in lysine, a necessary protein factor rarely found in other seeds.

These seeds are soaked for 12 to 24 hours or so, and rinsed well, but before being offered to the canaries, the damp, just-beginning-to-sprout seeds are mixed with equal portions of either a good commercially available nestling food mix, or my own homemade nestling food.

My homemade mix is based on ground whole-wheat breadcrumbs, rolled oats, cornmeal, wheat hearts, and (if there are babies to be fed) varying amounts of baby cereal. It also includes balanced amounts of powdered vitamins, minerals, and probiotics.

When served this way, the canaries have to also eat at least some of the dry mixture adhering to the damp seeds, and so they get a more complete diet than if offered soaked seed alone. I was happy to find that, as they got used to the mixture, my canaries began to eat more and more of the mix until soon they were happily eating it all.

The final factor in my multi-pronged approach was to buy cheap paper plates on which to serve the birds my soaked-seed and nestling food mix. These plates help to absorb any excess moisture so the mixture tends to dry out, rather than go sour. This in turn means that parent birds with babies to feed are able to offer edible food to their

by R C McDonald

youngsters for an hour or two longer than if I served their food in the usual dishes, where it would go sour quite quickly on a warm day. As long as I make sure that there is also plenty of dry seed, pellets, and greens available, the parents have more than enough food to offer their growing chicks, even when I have to be gone for most of the day.

Before leaving for work, I serve generous portions, leaving some prepared soak seed ready to mix with fresh nestling food in the fridge. By the time I get home, the birds will have cleaned up everything while feeding their babies, and every-body will be hungry but not overly so. All I need to do is go to the fridge, get out the fresh soak seed, add the dry nestling food, mix it together, and serve it up.

The babies grow rapidly and well with this approach, normally fledging at 17 or 18 days. To my delight when first trying this method with canaries, I realized that they also wean very easily, and are usually eating enough of the mix to support themselves without their parents by the time they are 25 days old, sometimes less.

The same soaked seed and nestling food mix, without the extra proteins of the baby cereal, helps to speed the moult and add a little extra nutrition and interest to my adult birds' diet throughout most of the rest of the year. It may only be served once a week or so during some periods, but the birds stay familiar with it and always seem to regard it as a treat.

I have been using this method of serving soaked seeds with nestling food for over two decades now, and have found that this habit has eased many obstacles encountered by others along the way. So if you are not currently offering soaked seeds to your birds, why not consider giving it a try?

If your birds are anything like mine, they will thank you with increased health, vibrancy, vigour, breedability, and, of course, plenty of cheerful, happy song.

Complete Nutrition?

It can't be emphasized too much, how important good nutrition is to good health. This is even more true when you are raising youngsters, as the nutrition they receive can affect their health for the rest of their life. So many of the commonly seen problems and troubles encountered later in life can be avoided by proper nutrition. This is fact, and applies to our pet birds as well as us. Yet, just what does a good diet for your pet bird consist of?

You will be able to find almost as many theories on what's the best diet for our avian companions, as you will be able to find people who keep and care for them. Some of these theories vary rather widely. So, just who is right? Exactly what does it take, to see that your beloved bird receives the best possible diet for his or her situation?

The answer is not as simple as many seem to think. Very few of the avians commonly kept as companions by humans have been so thoroughly studied by scientists that we can say exactly what their dietary requirements are. Yes, in many cases we understand most of the basics, which general quantities of carbohydrates, fats, and fibres should be present. But what about the trace nutrients so essential to proper operation of the body?

In many species the needed quantities and quality of these nutrients will vary somewhat from the requirements of other species, as will elements considered toxic. Potato leaves, for example, are poisonous to humans, and are usually considered toxic to avian species, too. Yet at every chance, my chickens used to 'gate-crash' my garden and gleefully strip my potato plants of all their leaves in the process of looking for potato flea beetles, to the point where their crops would be bulging with the greens. Yet every single one of these chickens remained extremely healthy, and this occasional 'binge' never produced even the smallest sign of harm in any member of my flock, nor did it affect the quantity or quality of the eggs they laid. I know, because I had the eggs tested for possible toxic content that turned out to simply not be there.

While such an observation is not scientific, and does not provide conclusive evidence as to the actual toxicity of these leaves for that particular avian species, one thing it does certainly indicate, is that more species-specific studies are needed!

Mere observation that chickens have eaten potato leaves and taken no harm does not mean I would be within my rights to turn around and feed potato leaves to my pet canary, either. What if a canary is different from a chicken, and the leaves are poisonous to him? Well, although I don't know for sure whether or not potato leaves actually are poisonous to a canary, I do know that he is indeed very different from chickens, and also that he evolved in an entirely different area of the world.

That is enough evidence of the possibility of essential basic differences right there, to make me refuse to assume that similarities exist, when in fact they may not. But for some reason, often you will find 'scientific facts' produced for 'all avian species', when in fact thorough studies have only been done on a few of the multitude of species in existence.

The production of pelleted foods meant for our avian companions is a good example of some of these kinds of assumptions in play. Various methods of manufacturing pellets exist, and all destroy component nutrients to a certain extent during the manufacturing process. Just exactly to what extent varies with the kind of process used. Differing manufacturing processes use varying amounts of heat, liquid, and pressure to produce the final end product.

Most pelleted feeds produced commercially require that extra nutrients be added after manufacture, in an attempt to replace those lost during processing. The idea is to return the pellets to a state where they may provide something a little closer to 'complete' nutrition. In some cases these additional nutrients are 'soaked' into the pellet, in other instances they are added as an outer 'shell'.

Some manufacturers have studied the effects of a long-term diet consisting of only their pellets on several species, and some research along these lines is on-going. Yet to date, no one has produced conclusive results from intensive long-term studies on the long-term effects of a pelleted diet on the wide variety of avian species found in our homes.

It is true that such a study is both difficult and very expensive to perform; but is this any excuse for assuming that these foods maintain complete health until proven otherwise? Yet in many cases, this is the exact logic behind the sale of these products for our birds' consumption; 'until it is proven inadequate, let's assume that it is as complete as we intend it to be!'

Many people point to the fact that thousands of dogs and cats have been successfully fed for decades now, on kibbles — the equivalent of the pelleted diets manufactured for avian species. Yet how many people remember how many decades into this 'easy-feeding' experiment we were, before it was discovered that the presence or absence of certain elements was causing problems for some animals?

The problems developed by older cats from a long-term diet high in potash is by now well documented, and kibble manufacturers have for many years now been taking steps to correct this problem. This doesn't change the fact that lab development of the kibbles, along with research on the effectiveness of the proposed cat foods before marketing

by R C McDonald

began, failed to show the existence of this problem— it wasn't until multitudes of cats had been eating these foods for years, and began to show up at the local veterinarian's offices with similar symptoms, that the cause and source was pinpointed and means could begin to be developed to combat the problem.

One of the saddest facts in existence is that bird owners, who tend to be so caring, even passionate, about their pets, almost always believe they are feeding their birds well. Yet research has told us, and continues to tell us, that often this is quite simply not true. Over the long term, an inadequate diet can lead to chronic illness, and, if you are trying to breed your canaries, an inadequate diet practically guarantees a poor breeding performance.

One of the more interesting studies conducted on pet birds and their dietary problems was done in New York by researcher Laurie Hess, while working as a vet at the Animal Medical Centre in New York city.

She conducted her study on 135 pet birds, and reported her findings at the first International Symposium on Pet Bird Nutrition held in Hanover. As a guideline for her measurements, Laurie used the recommended nutrient allowances for companion birds as developed by respected avian vets Ritchie, Harrison and Harrison in 1994.

Her findings were utterly appalling. Twenty-seven percent of the birds she tested proved to have less than the recommended levels of vitamin E in their system, while a shocking sixty-seven percent were low in vitamin A. Even worse, ninety-seven percent— almost her entire sample!— were low in vitamin D, and even more, ninety-eight percent, were low in calcium. I find it very interesting that half the birds she surveyed were being fed on 'complete' pelleted diets made specifically for birds.

Equally interesting, to my mind, was the fact that pet bird owners who fed seed-based diets were more liable to be aware that the diet they were providing was incomplete, and so had a tendency to provide extra vitamin and mineral supplements, as is the common practice in much of Europe and Britain. Tests conducted in these countries have shown that, with proper supplementation, a seed-and-vegetable-based diet can work very well, when it comes to supporting and maintaining avian health.

Some say that the birds eating pellets would have tested far differently if they had been receiving enough quantity of the pellets to satisfy their full nutritional requirements. They point at the fact that few pet bird owners feed pellets alone; most 'dilute' the product by feeding fruit, vegetables, and scraps of table foods.

These people want all pet birds to be fed pellets, and nothing but pellets. But I am very reluctant to stop feeding a variety of foods to whatever avian companion I happen to be feeding, from finches to macaws. If they will eat pellets, fine, I will not argue a bit. Usually I will even offer more!

But I also see the pleasure these intelligent, sensitive creatures get from enjoying the variety of foods I provide them, and I see how much energy and time they invest into enjoying these pleasures, and I am reluctant to change that. Maybe they *would* be healthier on a diet of one hundred percent pellets. It's possible.

But I won't be the one to test it, because I know if I did, they would be bored and unhappy with the change, and I couldn't bear it. Besides, I know that a diet consisting of seed, greens, and a few other extras, along with a good, balanced vitamin-and-mineral supplement, can be managed so as to keep my birds both healthy and happy.

Do we really wish to use our beloved pet birds in a similar kind of experiment to that performed on our cats and dogs for so many years? How many years will it be, before we will be able to point with confidence at a particular kind and style of pellets, and say with certainty that this mixture provides a complete and balanced diet for my particular avian companions, and be 100% sure that we are speaking the truth? Until then, I know what my decision is going to be. What about you?

by R C McDonald

Of all the things birds do, moulting is perhaps one of the most confusing to their human owners. Sooner or later (usually sooner) every bird owner will find him or herself asking, "What do I do now that my bird is beginning to...

Enter the Moult

Moulting (or molting) is this really interesting thing all birds do, where every once in awhile they will start to shed feathers everywhere as ageing, hard-used old feathers are replaced by new ones. It's mind-boggling to contemplate the amount of feathers, both large and small, that this process always seems to produce. Cleaning them up can seem endless. Worse, when it comes to canaries, most (if not all) singing will generally stop, and the birds can look rather frowsy until the process is complete.

One canary-keeper described her birds as "looking rather like a lawnmower ran over them backwards," when they were moulting, and often this is a rather accurate description. Many birds are subject to more-than-usual grumpiness during this time, and are apt to become easily stressed, reacting negatively to the smallest change in their environment or routine, even relatively minor ones.

Inevitably, somewhere along the line enquiring minds wondered if canary owners really have to go through all this every year— what would happen if conditions were such that moulting just did not occur?

It was determined that seasonal changes in lighting and heat were the two biggest triggers for the moult in canaries, and an experiment was set up that kept the lighting and temperature the same year round, with no variances. The results were surprising.

True, even after an entire year under these conditions, the birds had not entered a moult. But— and this was totally unexpected— when they continued to be prevented from moulting in the usual manner— eventually every one of the canaries in the experiment died. The conclusion was that moulting, while understandably inconvenient to the owners, was of extreme importance to the birds themselves.

So now we know our birds *need* to moult. With canaries, usually that is roughly once a year, from the middle to late summer. But what else do we need to know about moulting canaries?

First and foremost is that a canary's moult is primarily brought on by the amount of light the bird sees. Lighting is very important to canaries, more so than to any human. Canaries evolved so their bodies respond physically to the amount of light which enters their eyes. This light triggers changes in the bird's endocrine system, and causes the beginnings or endings to some rather extreme physical changes throughout the bird's life. How these changes are carried out can affect each canary's personality, health, appearance, attitude and lifespan.

Every year, male canaries herald the arrival of spring with increased songs and mating displays. Seeing this kind of intensity and frequency of song, their owners become proud that their bird is happy, without realizing what has triggered all the singing— the longer days are telling him it is time to find a mate. In response, he begins to proclaim his ownership of his territory, and his eligibility to mate.

The summer solstice approaches and passes, and suddenly the canary finds its days beginning to get shorter again. The weather after the solstice is commonly the hottest of the year, and to some extent, heat does seem to be a factor in triggering the annual moult. But largely, the canary is sensitive to the lighting that he sees. When the long days of early summer begin to shorten again, each canary's instincts tell him or her that mid-summer is soon to become fall, and *now* is the time to shed all the worn, old feathers, growing in sturdy new ones before cold weather arrives.

Thus the feathers begin to fall, in the age-old ritual of renewal. In the last decade or so, we have learned that more than feathers are renewed during this time, for studies have shown that a canary's brain will grow new brain cells at the same time his body is growing new feathers.

Most of these new brain cells show up in the center of the brain that controls song. Most canaries will stop actively singing much, if at all, while all these physical changes are taking place, but song still plays a very important role in their lives. During the moult they will spend a lot of their attention listening to and absorbing all the audible sounds in their environment, listening for combinations they find attractive. Some may spend time practicing soft disjointed phrases of song as if to themselves, softly under their breath, practicing the feel of producing certain sounds while learning how to reproduce them.

Many of those sounds— the ones each canary finds the most agreeable and interesting, at least— will often end up incorporated into his true song, once the bird resumes singing. But the converse is true as well— if he doesn't hear much of anything that he considers to be of interest while he is moulting, he may not have much of a song to sing by the time his moult is completed.

Stress can cause loss of feathers too— but this is not a true moult. Stress that occurs during the moult can cause what's often known as a 'stuck moult', where the bird's moult simply stops; depending on whether the stress factor continues or not, normal progress of the moult may resume within a week or two, several weeks down the road, or, in some cases, not at all. Such a 'stuck moult' can cause bald spots, most usually a ring of feathers missing around the neck, showing the bare skin.

Bald spots on the back are almost never seen, except in an aviary situation, where they are an indicator of bullying, while bald spots on the front are usually seen in hens wanting to nest; in this case the problem is not due to moulting at all, but to stimulation of the drive to breed.

Some possible causes of stress that can cause moulting problems or even out-of-season feather-fall, are drafts; people (children too) or pets staring fixedly at the bird, causing him to think of them as predators; an inadequate, incomplete, or unbalanced diet; temperatures that vary widely within the same day; or too much silence in the bird's environment. This last is extremely stressful; *no* bird likes things to be quiet! They also don't like sudden loud noises, especially if they are unannounced. A steadily (or rather, predictably) noisy environment, on the other hand, usually makes any bird feel right at home.

How well the moult is completed is controlled largely by the diet. Moulting increases the nutrient requirements, and very often a diet that might normally be considered nicely adequate is not a good diet at all, during the moult.

Available nutrients can make a huge difference in overall health, and especially in the speed at which the moult is completed, because if the necessary nutrients for growing in the new feathers are not available, the moult will not be completed until they are.

For this reason, all birds on seed-based diets need regular vitamin/mineral supplementation. Moulting takes a lot of nutrients, and if they aren't available in the bloodstream, they will come out of the bird's bodily stores— or wait until enough trickles in through the food, if necessary.

A normal moult will usually last for at least four or five weeks, and can stretch to eight, ten, or even twelve weeks, with the normal period being in the neighbourhood of six to eight weeks. If a moult should continue for longer than twelve weeks, other factors are at play, and steps should be taken to resolve them, up to and including, if necessary, a consultation with your local avian veterinarian.

by R C McDonald

One of the most common questions heard from new owners of of a colour-bred canary is, "How can I be sure he keeps his colour?" Many become confused at the variety of conflicting opinions and advice they receive on venturing into owning one or more of the beautiful shades of colour canaries available today. I guess it is inevitable, then, that the next question usually is, "Should my canary be..."

Colour-Fed or Colour-Bred?

Any breeder of these brilliant gems of the Canary Fancy soon grows familiar with this question. Although it arrives in many guises, it usually boils down to the same thing; either the questioner is convinced that colour-feeding is unnatural, useful only to disguise a poorly-bred canary, or they think that the terms colour-bred and colour-fed each refers to a different kind of canary.

In actual fact, the two terms describe two different *aspects* of breeding the group of canaries most often known collectively as 'colour canaries', 'red canaries', or sometimes (although incorrectly) as 'red factor' canaries.

These are the canaries who have the gene that gives them the ability to show red as well as yellow in their feathers. There is a multitude of variations of colour in this group of canaries, but they all share at least two things.

All of these canaries should always be colour-*bred*; that is, each should be the offspring of a similar bird, which was bred to another bird also of similar genetic heritage. But if a breeder wishes to know the true genetic potential for colour that each youngster carries, then he must also colour-*feed* his stock.

Anyone who thinks colour-feeding is unnatural has missed a few basic facts about red canaries. Their background is unique amongst canaries; they are the only breed documented to descend from hybrids of the Canary and the South American finch most often known as 'the Black-Capped Red Siskin', or sometimes as 'the Red Hooded Siskin'.

Achieving a fertile bird capable of throwing young with a cross of this type is very rare; more usually such crosses will be sterile. This is why hybrid crosses between songbird species are often called 'mules'.

History and Science have recorded, however, that unlike most cross-species matings, when a canary is bred to a South American Black-Capped Siskin, approximately twenty-five percent of the resulting young males will generally prove to be fertile. It is from these males, through carefully selective breeding programs, that all of our red-ground canaries of today are descended.

From the Red Siskin these canaries have inherited the ability to concentrate red carotenoids in their feathers, as long as sufficient quantities are present in their blood while their feathers are growing in, while their hardiness and free-breeding style comes from the ever-adaptable canary. Most breeders pay little or no attention to the quality of any red canary's song, but like canaries of all breeds, these birds can and usually do sing, sometimes quite beautifully.

Occasionally you will hear somebody say that a red canary is nothing more than a yellow canary given food dyes while it is moulting, and that the breed of canary has nothing to do with the bird's eventual colour. These people have picked up just enough information to mislead them.

While it is true that many red canaries will wind up looking rather more yellow than red if they are not colour-fed throughout their moult, it is *not* true that a canary with no siskin ancestry can be coloured to look as bright as a true red canary through colour-feeding alone.

by R C McDonald

The first thing to understand is that all canaries derive their colour from the natural pigments in their food. Deprive a normal yellow Canary of all yellow lutein and carotene in its diet while it is moulting, and the end result will be a visually white bird. Deprive a red canary of an adequate supply of dietary carotenoids during its moult, and the resulting feathers will range from pale orange to yellow or even white.

The Red Siskin in its native habitat is able to easily forage for much higher concentrations of carotenoids than is available to a bird from more northern climes, and in fact a Red Siskin fed only on foods easily available in a temperate climate will have much duller plumage than his tropical relatives. This is because most tropical vegetation contains high concentrations of the necessary carotenoids and other such substances he needs to achieve his proper bright colouration; much more than is found in any kind of temperate vegetation.

Since importing tropical vegetation to feed your birds would amount to a great deal of cost, time, and trouble (if indeed possible at all), a compromise was agreed upon amongst canary breeders to use a concentrated compound based on a naturally-occurring tropical carotenoid, which finally offers canary breeders access to the strength and intensity of these tropical vegetable dyes. Using this compound, known as 'canthaxanthin', is no more unnatural, in my opinion, than a human eating bread instead of grain. Canthaxanthin allows red canary breeders, after years of trial and error, to finally see the physical expression of the true genetic potential of their canaries' colours.

A simple experiment is sufficient to prove the difference between various types of canaries and the effects of colour-feeding on their plumage. This experiment is very easy to perform, and I myself recommend it to anybody who thinks red colour-bred canaries should be colour-bred but not colour-fed.

All you need is two regular yellow canaries of any breed,

and two colour-bred red canaries. The experiment starts when the birds begin their annual moult.

Colour-feed one of the red canaries and one of the yellow canaries. Provide the other two canaries with a normal moulting diet, but without any colour-feeding at all. Make sure all the birds receive a diet rich in vegetation, providing items such as broccoli, kale, grated carrot, chopped leafy endives, mustards, crinkle-leafed cabbages (of any colour) and other such foods. At the end of the moult assemble the birds in one cage and compare them.

The colour-bred but not colour-fed red canary should be a good healthy orange, and it should look quite orange indeed when compared to either of the yellow birds. But you may be surprised to notice that it looks rather pale when compared to the rich flaming vermillion of the colour-fed red canary. The colour-fed yellow bird will only look orange (albeit a rather pale orange) if you compare it to the non colour-fed yellow bird— against either of the red canaries it will look distinctly yellow.

I had to perform this experiment and witness the results for myself, in fact, before I was finally able to decide for myself just where I stood on this issue. I had heard so many widely varying and even conflicting opinions on the subject that up until that point I was quite thoroughly confused. But the incontrovertible visual evidence provided by the birds themselves proved impossible for me to deny.

Therefore, although all my canaries are bred first for their song and personality, I frequently allow them to show me their true genetic potential by colour-feeding my red canaries. Their vivid, jewel-like colour combinations are a decidedly distinctive bonus in any aviary or birdroom.

That way, if I'm asked, I can proudly say, "Yes, my canaries are colour-bred *and* colour-fed!"

by R C McDonald

Colourfeeding

In theory, colourfeeding a red canary is simple; get a canary whose genetic inheritance includes the 'red factor'; the gene that allows its body to take red colour from its food during the moult, and put that colour into it's feathers. When the moult is done, you'll have a red canary.

In practice, colourfeeding is rather more complex. What kind of foods and colourfoods you're offering, along with how much you're offering and when, can all affect the end results.

The genetic inheritance of a canary you're considering colourfeeding is *at least* as important as the diet. If the canary being colourfed doesn't have the 'red factor' gene, you can colourfeed all you like, but you will never see the deep, rich red that true red canaries can achieve. The diet the canary is being offered during colourfeeding is equally important, otherwise a 'red' canary can come out of his moult wearing feathers ranging from cream-coloured through yellow, into a range of oranges or even splotchy-looking patches of colour— almost anything other than red.

So what's the *real* story behind colourfeeding? Is it safe, how is it done, and what foods or food supplements are used?

There's a wide range of supplements on the market intended for use when colourfeeding canaries. They vary quite a bit and are usually chosen to fit the method of colour-feeding being used. Most colourfeeding supplements meant for use with canaries include a concentrated form of a naturally occurring tropical carotenoid usually known as *canthaxanthin*. A canary who has inherited the gene for red can use any carotenoid to gain *some* colour, but most of the naturally-occurring carotenoids in the temperate zones of the planet, where most canary keepers live, are not capable of allowing the bird to achieve the depth of colour that can be achieved using canthaxanthin.

This means that if you're planning on showing your red canaries, it's essential that whatever system you use include some form of canthaxanthin. There are several products available on the market meant to be used for this purpose, many including a combination of betacarotenes and canthaxanthin. Betacarotenes help to enhance yellow and orange tones, and are thought to assist in keeping the colour of the feathers bright and rich as well as deep.

Many of these products are meant to be added to the water; this is one of the most effective methods to colour-feed, but it can be expensive and wasteful, because canaries don't drink much water. It's also rather messy, since after drinking canaries tend to flick any water remaining on their beak off. This in turn means you'll be finding little red spots *everywhere*, much further away than you'd think!

Also, because the colouring agent begins to break down and rot once it's in the water, any water including it must be changed *at least* daily or more often, depending on how hot the area gets. Since most canaries moult during the heat of the summer, it's not unknown for colour-feeding canary keepers to have to change the coloured water two, three, or even four times a day in order to keep the mixture fresh and unsoured.

Many canary keepers get around this problem by instead offering colourfood mixed in with a soft food; this is easier and less messy, but can also make it harder to achieve the desired goal of smooth, even colouration over the entire body, because in order for this to happen the feathers must each receive the same amount of colour while growing in. This in turn means that the bird must ingest precisely the same amount of colour daily, or the resulting colour will

by R C McDonald

appear uneven, giving the bird a mottled appearance.

This requires close attention; the amount offered must be adequate to achieve the desired colour, and it must be offered regularly through the moult, without being offered in excessive amounts. The goal is to achieve the maximum levels of colouring agent that can be carried by the blood, allowing the feathers to express the maximum amount of colour the bird is genetically capable of achieving.

This last is best done by closely monitoring the colour of the droppings. This may sound a little odd, but works well. The reason is because once the bloodstream is carrying the maximum amount of colour it is capable of holding, the bird's body will begin to extract any excess colour and shed it through the droppings.

So if you see red in the droppings, you can know you're feeding too much colourfood. Reducing the amount being offered will reduce the amount of excess colouration being removed from the bird's body; again, it will be necessary to monitor the droppings to be sure the right balance has been achieved. The droppings should look normal, with perhaps a slight tinge of pink at the most.

Some canary keepers will claim that their red canaries get red with no special attention to their diet. Generally in such cases it will turn out that the bird's normal diet includes quite a few carotenoids, perhaps in the form of carrots or kale offered daily. Such a diet can offer quite good colour, but the breeder will simply not see the full potential colour being expressed.

Others will be quick to state that they believe colour-feeding using canthaxanthin is 'unnatural'. To them, using carrots or another carotenoid-rich green such as kale isn't colour-feeding. This kind of thing results in occasional tales of a 'canary that remains red without colourfeeding', but generally such a tale is due to a misunderstanding of the process the canary body uses to fix colour into its feathers.

In fact, all canaries get their colour from their food,

according to their genes; withhold items including yellow food colouring from yellow canaries during the moult, and they too will end up with little to no colour in their feathers.

Other birdkeepers refuse to colourfeed at all, having heard that to do so can cause damage to the bird's liver. However, there seems to be little to no scientific evidence behind these fears, *if* the colour-feeding is done correctly. One caveat here; some breeders believe that colour-feeding is not being properly done unless the droppings are bright red. In such a case, liver damage is not only possible but probable, as the canary body is being flooded with colour which can stress the liver and kidneys as they attempt to cleanse the bloodstream of so much excess. In actual fact, a great many substances are benign or even helpful in proper proportions, yet can cause terrible problems if overdone, and canthaxanthin is no different.

I believe it is far more accurate to state the real facts; "Canthaxanthin *can* cause damage to the liver *if misused* through being offered in too great a quantity..."

Remember too, that statement can be made about a great many elements. Our bodies, along with those of our canaries, exist in a delicate state of balance, and if anything upsets that balance drastically, it can have lasting and sometimes damaging results, especially over the longer term.

I've heard many of the old stories about colourfeeding causing liver damage myself, from people who had direct experience with some of the first colourfeeding experiments in the early years of developing red canaries. Their 'data' was based on simple direct observation, rather than being scientifically collected, and there may also have been genetic tendencies involved. But one thing is clear— if colour is showing in the droppings, then that colour is there because the body has absorbed all it is capable of, and the excess is being passed to the feces by the liver.

So yes, it's possible to damage the liver by feeding enough canthaxanthin to produce deep red or even black colour in the droppings (black usually means blood in the droppings, but can also indicate too much canthaxanthin).

Seeing such a colour would mean an excessive amount of canthaxanthin is being used, far more than the bird's body is capable of processing properly. Given that circumstance, I suspect it may be quite easy to damage the liver, especially if the situation continues over a month or longer.

Any liver can be damaged by forcing too much of any number of products through it. This can be achieved through using too much protein, too many fats, or even by forcing the drinking of too much water, along with any number of other ways, too numerous to mention. There will always be some people who take any tale to the extreme; thus, we may hear, "If canthaxanthin can cause liver damage when used incorrectly, we should not use any at all."

To me, that's very like saying, "If breathing too much oxygen can kill, we should try to be as safe as possible and not breath any oxygen at all."

Each is a ridiculous statement; but each conclusion can be 'logically' arrived at, by somebody who's willing to take the idea to the extreme. (Some know this as the "baby and the bathwater" syndrome.)

Much of what we know so far about canary colouration is experiential— there's not yet been enough research done to offer truly scientific evidence. In other words, our ideas about *why* something works is often conjecture based on experience, rather than actual scientific evidence.

Some pet owners (understandably enough) prefer not to go to all the trouble of colourfeeding, but still want their canary to look bright and colourful. Such owners are often heard to enquire as to the possibility of alternative methods of allowing their canaries to show good colour.

Among the few alternative sources for colouring, most breeders' experience will corroborate that the best results are achieved through use of other carotenoids. In the temperate zone, one of the best and most easily accessible natural source for carotenoids is the humble carrot. By offering carrots to your birds daily during their moult, it is often possible to achieve fairly good colouring.

It should be noted that a few colour canaries do exist who will colour up beautifully when fed canthaxanthin, but remain yellow when offered carrots, even though they eat them willingly. Such canaries are not very common; most colourbred canaries in the red ranges can get almost as much colour eating carrots as they can eating canthaxanthin. Their colour will usually be quite intense, but not quite as deep as they are capable of showing if given canthaxanthin during their moult.

Carrots have a higher concentration of carotenoids than most other veggies or greens (although kale comes close), and the birds usually take to them fairly easily. My lot get theirs coarse-grated, but I've known breeders who steamed them and served them in slices or even (if they were tiny) whole.

Keep in mind that a certain amount of yellow colouring is needed to produce a deep, brilliant red; without yellow in the mix you'll get brick red, often considered to be the result of bad genetics and/or overfeeding of canthaxanthin.

But in my own (admittedly small) home experiments, cutting all the yellow from the diet during moult while colourfeeding canthaxanthin, also produced this 'brick-coloured' result.

Another year I deliberately tried to 'thin' the red colour with plentiful use of yellow-containing substances in the diet. This is a practice some breeders say must be avoided, saying that too much yellow in the diet will 'thin' the depth of the red colour, but I found that I simply couldn't do it.

In the end, the only means I could find to reduce the red, was to reduce all the carotenoids— vegetable as well as colourfood sources. But reducing the carotenoids didn't exactly 'thin' the colour, so much as remove it.

Another bit of 'red canary folklore' says to keep red canaries out of direct sunlight, because it will lighten their colour. So one year, I tried to 'bleach' my red canaries by allowing them access to an outdoor, sun-drenched aviary. By the end of the summer I found that all their playing in the sunshine hadn't made a bit of difference to the depth of their colour. It's possible that our Northern rays aren't strong enough. But for southern Canada at least, that tale too seems to be a myth.

Offering carrots during the moult is a great way to learn a bit more about the genetic inheritance of a given bird, because canaries *without* the red factor gene will not get any colour other than yellow, from eating carrots.

If those same birds happen to have the red factor gene that allows them to get colour from carrots, though, it will be very obvious. They will never achieve the depth of colour that is possible for their feathers to show if they were colourfed using a preparation including canthaxanthin—but they will often be only a few shades lighter, a perfectly acceptable and lovely bright colour, as far as a great many pet owners are concerned.

So while colour-feeding using carrots alone really is not appropriate if you want to show your canaries, it can work beautifully for somebody who just wants a bright pet canary without going to a lot of trouble. It must be said, too, that carrots also work well when included with canthaxanthin in a show-canary's diet, to help to keep the overall colour bright and rich.

However you colourfeed, and indeed whether you choose to colourfeed or not, it all comes down to the joy that comes from admiring, keeping, working with, and for some, showing, that unusual group of brilliantly feathered songbirds, our lovely little red canaries.

Building an Indoor Aviary

Most of us love to be able to watch our birds fly and play, but many bird keepers can't afford to buy a larger cage, such as a commercially-built flight cage; they can be *so* expensive! Often it's not too long before the idea occurs, to just build our own. Then all we need to know is the best way to go about building our aviary.

Firstly, let's make sure we're all talking about the same thing. For the purposes of this article at least, I'm defining an aviary as an enclosure big enough for a human to walk in to, while a flight cage, while sometimes known as an indoor aviary, is in reality no more than a big cage *not* big enough to walk in to.

A lot of us think first of building an outdoor aviary. In most areas of the world, this is an extremely expensive proposition; you not only have to provide a good shelter for your canaries, but you also have to prevent access to the inside of your aviary to any number of potential predators and mischief-makers, ranging from the size of a flea or mosquito on up to cats, rats, or mice, owls, snakes, hawks, weasels, racoons, toads etc., depending on just where you live.

Ironically, in many areas it's the lowly mosquito that carries the most potential for problems. Mosquitoes can carry and transmit a wide variety of diseases, ranging from avian malaria to canary pox. These tiny pests can be a

by R C McDonald

problem even indoors, and pose a huge threat to any outdoor aviary. Mosquito netting can help, but it is very vulnerable to claws, little fingers, weather and even normal wear-and-tear; yet all it takes is one tiny hole to allow a mosquito access.

So unless you plan to build the next closest thing to an actual house for your canaries, your easiest and best bet is to spring for the much-simpler-to-build and far-cheaper-to-maintain indoor aviary.

It's a sad fact but true that there are very few books on building any kind of aviary available, especially when it comes to building an aviary for territorial birds such as canaries; most of the good aviary-design books are slanted towards finch or hookbill keepers, who are dealing with species much more sociable than most canaries will ever be.

There is one group of birdkeepers, though, who deal with the same sort of territorial issues that plague so many canary-keepers. They keep and breed some of the many larger and smaller species of grass parakeet or grass parrot native to Australia. Many of these species tend to be highly territorial, so go ahead and take a look at any books from Australia on building aviaries for these kinds of birds that you can find, for inspiration. Of course if you are lucky enough to live in or be able to visit Australia, try to visit some breeders of these kinds of birds, and you might get a chance to share some ideas on design and usability.

It's not often easy to find basic instructions for building your own cages, flight cages, and aviaries. Good clear pictures along with basic instructions are best, but sadly are seldom seen. The problem, I think, may be due to the fact that good wood-and-wire workers may not be good story-tellers or photographers. After all, you need to be enough of an artist to make proper pictures of how the cages go together, as well as enough of a writer to describe the process in a way the rest of us can follow.

There *are* programs that can produce any kind of design

Canary Crazy

for you when given a few basic parameters, but they tend to be rather horrendously expensive. So unless a canary-keeping artist decides one day to produce such designs for us, in the meantime the best I know to do is to write about how we build ours.

Indoor aviaries are basically just really big birdcages. Here's a few basics to keep in mind when building indoor flight cages or aviaries for your canaries.

1. If you are going to use a wood frame, keep it *out*side of the wire! This removes a bunch of little ledges from the inside of the cage. This might not seem like a big deal just reading about it— but it will be when you find you are cleaning droppings from all over the inside of the cage. If you put the wood frame inside the wire, those little ledges will be *heaped* with droppings, faster than you might think.

2. Paint your wood frame *before* putting it together with the wire. Painted wood is *much* easier to keep clean, but painting bare wood under wire is a real nuisance. Use a hard, glossy finish paint for a tougher surface that will stain less and be easier to keep clean.

3. Use welded wire, not braised, for your cage wire, and be sure that it has *not* been hot-dipped. Hot-dipping produces a softer coat of galvanization than welded wire. It can flake or peel quite easily, especially as it ages. If one of your birds eats even the tiniest piece, it will make him seriously ill, if it doesn't kill him. Welded wire is a little more expensive, but is *far* safer.

4. Once you have your wire, roll it out, stake it flat, and leave it in the baking hot sun for a day, then flip it over and leave the other side exposed for another day. Then go over both sides with a wire brush. This will get off most loose zinc or other such material that could cause problems for your birds. As an alternative, you can scrub the wire with wire brush and a cool water/bleach solution of around 10% bleach— but the sunshine method is easier and I've always found it to be more effective, too.

by R C McDonald

5. For finches or canaries, you can paint the wire black once you've scrubbed it. This not only makes the wire much safer and easier to keep clean, the black colour makes it almost seem to disappear to the eye when looking at the cage. This in turn makes it much easier to see the birds inside the cage, especially compared to trying to look through shiny silver wire, which tends to 'pull' the eye away from seeing what's inside the cage. *Budgies, parrots, and all other chewing birds should never be kept in a hand-painted cage; due to their chewing abilities they require a tougher powder-coated finish on their cages if colour is wanted.*

6. Painting wire is easier than it sounds. Start by using a water-based acrylic paint with a glossy finish. Pour a little into your tray, then thin it with an equal amount of water. Using a thick wooly roller, soak it in the paint, then roll it over the wire (I find this process works best if the wire is standing up. If your wire won't stand up on its own, it's too flimsy to be building a birdcage with). Because of the thickness of the roller and the thinness of the paint you should be able to coat both sides quickly this way even working from just one side. Even better, as long as the paint is thinned enough the drips will run right out, unlike if you use the paint at a normal thickness, where you'll end up with half-hardened drips all over your wire. If you're in any doubt, thin it some more; in this case, too thin is better than too thick.

7. You will want to apply at least two or three coats this way. Allow the paint to dry between coats, then let the whole thing stand someplace with good air circulation to cure for a couple of weeks or so. The paint will toughen and harden some more while it cures, and once it's done you'll have a nice, tight, easy-to-clean coating on the wire, with a smooth, almost plastic-like finish that will allow you to just wipe it clean with a damp cloth now and again. It's a fair bit of work producing a finish like this on a homemade cage, but it will save you a lot of time and trouble down the road.

8. As an alternative, especially if you don't have the time

(and assuming you can find a good source) you can use 'shepherd's wire', which already has a plastic coating on it. It isn't quite as easy to clean as painted wire, but the finish is even more durable, and it doesn't take time to prepare.

9. Before you start actually building your aviary, draw up a basic design, so you can get an idea what you'll be working with. Remember, you must either build your cage narrow enough to go through a door, or make it possible to easily disassemble it for moving.

Keep cage doors low, and never design a door that opens up the entire front of the cage, because the birds will tend to fly up and out if something surprises them while the cage door is open. Instead, keep the top half or more of the cage front closed in, and put the access door lower down.

10. Since we are talking about making an indoor aviary for canaries, it's a good idea to think about adapting the basic design somewhat. Most indoor aviaries are basically one large cage. When it comes to canaries, that can cause some rather extreme territorial issues to arise. Instead, consider making a series of smaller cages that line up with each other and have access doors between to link each to the other. Such little inter-cage access doors are often called 'pop-holes', in older bird literature— if you've ever heard any such references, that's what they meant.

In this sort of aviary, rather than one big area, the design incorporates two, three, or more separate areas into one. They abut each other, but each has its own cage doors and trays. Interior access to each of these cages from another is controlled by the use of— you guessed it— popholes. This is essentially a small door between the adjoining flight cages, which you can open or close at will, allowing or not allowing access to each area of the cage; especially useful when cleaning, or you have to catch a particular bird.

11 Be sure to arrange for multiple sources of food and water in each separate area of the aviary, so that if there's any aggression in one area, the picked-on bird can simply go off to another area. This kind of set-up will allow a larger

by R C McDonald

mixed flock of canaries to share a fairly large area much more peaceably than will occur if you try putting a bunch of canaries into one large flight cage, where there's nowhere for a harassed bird to retreat to when dominance issues arise. You'll still have to provide separate breeding cages during the spring, but for most of the rest of the year, your canaries should be able to live in such an shared indoor aviary quite happily.

My favourite design along these lines, is to build one cage long and low; 5 or 6 feet long, 3 feet tall, 2 or 3 feet wide. I put two access doors along one long side, and leave a reinforced slot below them to slide in homemade tin trays (edges carefully folded and hammered flat so they can't hurt little toes). I like to make deep trays, which means I also need to add a flap to the front of the cage, to close the gap left when the tray is removed for cleaning. This is the 'front' of the cage.

Then I build another cage 3 feet by 3 feet by 6 feet tall. It has only one access door, in the middle lower half; most of the interior of the cage cage be easily reached from here or from outside the cage. If I really need to I can just crawl right in. Again, the slot for the trays is on the same side as the door, this makes the front of the cage.

Then I put the two cages back to back in the middle of the room, so I can easily access the doors and trays for both cages— and finally I cut a small 4 - 6 inch 'door' into the wire of the back of each cage, so that the two 'doors' created line up together. When both doors are open I have a 'pop-hole' into the other cage.

Each pop-hole 'door' has another piece of wire slightly larger than it, wired over it on the inside of the cage. This way the cover can be dropped down to shut the pophole, or lifted up to be open, from inside either cage. I usually just use a clothes-pin to peg the flaps up and keep the pop-hole open.

This kind of arrangement gives the birds all sorts of room to fly and play, and makes for far less arguments than you'd normally see among a mixed flock of canaries. I also like to cut other small 'doors' into the two flight cages, and hang other, smaller cages off the sides of the larger cages, lined up door-to-pophole; I'll use different types of show or pet-style cages, and will generally put some treat or another into each cage when I hang it up.

This approach allows the birds to get used to being in all sorts of different styles and kinds of small cages. But even better, they come to associate being in a small cage with getting a treat; this can come in *very* handy, especially when you need to catch a bird. Instead of doing it the hard way, just put up a 'treat cage' or two, then watch closely until the bird you want is in the small cage, and close the pop-hole.

I'm sure you can imagine what a great time-saver this can be, if you ever need to catch a bird in a hurry!

That's just a few of the better ideas I've learned about building indoor aviaries for my birds. If you keep it simple, building for your birds can be instructive, rewarding, and fun, not to mention highly useful.

So jump on in and have some fun with it, and when you're done, do please remember to share what you've learned with the rest of us!

by R C McDonald

Aviary Management Considerations

When they hear the word 'aviary', most people think of a large outdoor cage filled with a variety of birds of several species, all happily living together in a natural setting, similar to how they would live in the wild. Many zoos and nature preserves have displays that do little to dispel this idea. But what most people don't realize, is how much work goes on behind the scenes to maintain this kind of 'natural' display.

Much thought is required when setting up such an aviary. At least some of the birds living in it must be visible to the visiting public at all times, for visual interest to be maintained. This generally entails keeping far more birds in a smaller area than would ever occur naturally.

To counter the stress of crowded conditions and the (for some species) unnerving situation of being stared at by crowds of strangers, most establishments keep a close watch on the inmates of their aviaries, and have 'back-up' facilities away from the main displays. Should an inhabitant begin to show signs of stress or illness, he or she can be removed to these more private facilities and allowed time to recover before being returned to the exhibition area.

Some establishments arrange for each group of birds to have private areas available to them, accessible through 'pop-holes' into a shelter, sometimes decorated to appear as part of the display, sometimes simply placed at the back of the enclosure, perhaps screened by plantings. In such cases, the birds can come and go as they please, and visitors have to take their chances on seeing them.

Other establishments don't have the room or facilities for such a set-up, and rely on having private quarters to which the birds may be removed when necessary. That in turn means that in most cases, few if any birds will remain in these displays year round.

Instead, they are rotated in and out of the main display as conditions and co-inhabitants change, thus allowing their keepers to have a lovely display while at the same time keeping all their stock healthy.

Newcomers to bird-keeping in general and aviaries in particular often have the idea that keeping an aviary offers their birds a more natural lifestyle than would be possible in a smaller cage, and many also believe that having all their birds in one aviary will reduce the amount of care and maintenance needed.

While this is a lovely idea, in most cases it's just that; a pipe dream. In order to provide a setting as naturally close as possible to a bird's own environment, the aviary must offer, not only food, water, and room to exercise, but also adequate territory for each species it holds.

Social though many species of birds are, in a wild environment they will usually flock in groups that include mostly— if not all— members of a single species. Whenever multiple species co-exist closely in the wild, observation will note they are generally quite careful to give each other plenty of elbow room.

This may be achieved in a variety of ways. Different groups will use the same feeding grounds, watering holes, or bathing sites, but at different times during the day. Other species may forage side by side on similar foods, but most members of each flock will keep a careful eye out, ready to fly off at the least indication of aggression.

by R C McDonald

In fact it's not unusual, in the wild, to see a variety of species feeding together, and this fact is often used to justify housing similar species together in an aviary. But if those who note this fact continue to watch the wild birds, they will also note that once feeding is over, these 'flocks' will scatter, each group going their own separate way.

This is just not possible to replicate in most closed-in aviaries. Most aviaries are far too small to be able to offer anything like a truly natural environment for a mixed group of birds, and so their inmates, rather than living the easy and carefree 'natural life' fondly imagined by their human caretakers, instead live a nightmare of stress and constant striving for a better position within the flock, with the goal of gaining a better chance at an equal share of food and drink.

Less dominant members of the aviary may not be able to get a large enough share of resources consistently enough to properly maintain their health, and this, along with the constant stress and competition, can cause a long slow deterioration of their health and wellbeing. Due to the fact that all birds strive to hide any signs of illness, this means that in most cases such deterioration will not be noticed until the bird is near death.

A keeper who has experience keeping birds in an aviary will know to spend plenty of time simply watching the interactions of the birds, and will watch closely for any signs of aggression or lack of energy.

In most cases, a wise birdkeeper uses his or her aviary (or aviaries) as an *accessory to* the birdroom, rather than *instead of* a birdroom. He or she will have made sure that each bird living in the aviary will also have individual quarters available, should the need arise. This way, any birds who appear to be less than optimally healthy may be removed immediately and placed in their own living space.

Once there, they can be more easily observed for signs of illness, or simply given a chance to recover from the stress of aviary life and the constant striving for food and water.

Some General Guidelines to Using Aviaries & Flight Cages

➤ Don't expect to be able to keep all your birds in your aviary all year round.

➤ For small species such as canaries and finches, make sure that you have *at least* 1 to 2 cubic feet of space inside the aviary for each inmate. Note that some species— many waxbills, for example— will require more space than others.

➤ Be sure to have at least 6 to 12 inches of *private* perching space for each bird housed in the aviary. Again, some species may require more. Some species will be happy to crowd together on a single perch, but others will need individual perches well away from each other— and in some cases, out of visual range (use screens consisting of groupings of safe plants, coarse hanging mats or clumps of hanging grasses etc in such cases)

➤ To reduce competition as much as possible, have multiple drinkers available, each placed well away from the others, and placed both high and low in every area of the aviary.

➤ Similarly, have multiple feed cups, likewise placed well apart from each other. You should preferably have at least one food cup for each inhabitant of the aviary, with no less than 1 cup for every 2 inhabitants. Unlike the drinkers, keep all the food cups fairly low, to ease access and reduce mess (and to save cleaning time).

➤ Ensure that none of the food and water sources are underneath any of the perches. This apparently minor detail is of utmost importance to maintaining health and vigour in your flock!

➤ Use your aviary as an *add-on* to your birdroom, not *instead of* your birdroom. Be sure to keep an individual cage available for each bird in your care, whether or not that cage happens to be currently in use.

➤ Be careful when mixing species, and be sure to use

only social species in such mixes. Don't mix larger birds with smaller, or hookbills with passerines, and, of utmost importance, make sure that all the species housed in any one given aviary all eat the same foods. This last is especially important for the long-term health of all the members of your flock.

➢ Prior to allowing any group of species to share the same habitat, be sure to read up on each species and make certain they will be compatible with the other members of the aviary. Some species will be non-aggressive with other species, but extremely aggressive to other members of their own species, while other species will try to boss anything that moves. In direct contrast, there are a few species so mild-natured that any birds not of their own species can push them about terribly.

Paying attention to this kind of detail can seem like a real nuisance sometimes, but will be well worth your while in the long run, for it will allow you to keep your aviaries properly maintained, and your birds happy and healthy.

Moving With Your Birds

The time has come, and you've decided to move. Almost everything has been settled, the packing is almost done, but there's one big worry still niggling at your mind— how are you going to move your canaries without upsetting them too much?

If you have one or more canary hens and happen to be moving in the middle of canary breeding season, as can happen if you are moving during the spring, the dilemma is even worse— how do you see that your hens don't get upset and abandon any babies that happen to still be in the nest? Even if you keep only a single pet hen, being moved while in the middle of laying a clutch of eggs (as even lone hens will) can cause problems up to and including egg-binding, a foremost cause of death for canary hens. You can expect to face these quandaries and more if you plan to move your home and you keep canaries.

There's a lot of details to moving your household at any time of year, and often the problems of how to ease the transition period and actually transport your pet birds will be put on the back burner while more urgent matters are being dealt with. But sooner or later you will have to face facts; no matter how you avoid thinking about it, the fact remains that (unless you sell them all) your birds will have to make the move, too.

If it *is* breeding season, don't despair, chances are good

that you will not lose the entire season. First, check the timing of your planned move. Try to arrange matters so that none of your hens will have any eggs in the nest while the actual move is taking place; if you find any, replace them with fake eggs.

The reason for this is because any chicks still in the egg during the move are almost certain to be killed during the moving process. This is due to being shaken about inside the egg during the drive. The effect is the same as if you picked up the egg and shook it back and forth— this is called 'addling', and in effect it thoroughly scrambles the material inside the shell. Since it is difficult to move a fertile egg without shaking it at least a little, save yourself and your hens the trouble, and let them go ahead and sett on the fake eggs for now.

Remember, once you have the move completed and your hens are comfortably set up in your new home you can let them try for another round— unless you are moving in early summer or later, there should be plenty of time to spare.

Chicks still in the nest or still being weaned are another story. While physically they can handle the move much better than eggs, there's always the chance their parents could get upset about all the changes in their routine, and stop feeding their youngsters.

The answer sounds simpler than you might expect— you need to see that the birds' environment changes as little as possible, and that any unavoidable changes are minimized as much as possible. If you can manage this, it will give you a much greater chance of successfully moving your entire flock, chicks and all.

In order to see that your chicks will continue to be fed by their parents, plan to keep all the birds in the cages they are used to being in; being allowed to remain in their own familiar cage is a large part of the solution, even if it may mean more work for you. If you will be driving during the day, plan to stop regularly to refresh the food and allow some peaceful time to eat and drink.

Once the cages are packed into the vehicle, cover them with a tightly woven light-coloured (preferably white) sheet. This will help keep any drafts out and allow the adult birds in each cage to keep a feeling of privacy, while still allowing enough light through to allow them to be able to see to get around and eat and such.

Of course, that's assuming that the vehicle they are being moved in has windows! If you know that you are going to be driving during the day, try to ensure if at all possible that the birds will have enough light to see by, because it will stress them far less than having to adapt to a pitch-black 'day'.

Even if you've arranged for the birds to be able to see enough to move around, eat, and drink, less of this will happen while the vehicle is actually moving. This is why frequent rest stops are so important. If you can, it's a good idea to try to stop for at least 15 to 20 minutes every hour and a half to two hours or so at the very least— more, if you can manage it.

Take away their water dishes while the vehicle is moving, but be sure to replace them during rest breaks. You can also provide plenty of greens for the birds to eat during the move, to ensure they will all have adequate moisture available when wanted. It won't hurt that most canaries adore greens— if a canary parent will feed anything, it will usually feed greens.

Depending on how far you are planning to move, it may be possible to move the birds at night. This is the most preferable option, if it is available to you, and can reduce the stress of moving tremendously, for your birds and yourself too.

Again, leave them in their own cages. Not long before they go to sleep for the night, pack their cages in your truck, cover them with the aforementioned light-coloured, tightly-woven sheets, then allow them a little time to settle down before full dark; particularly make sure that any hens with featherless chicks in the nest (if any) have returned to their nest and are covering the youngsters.

If the vehicle you're using has windows and you will be driving through territory that tends to have lots of bright lights during the night, you might want to throw a 'black-out' cover over the cages to block all external light, once the birds have settled down nicely.

Then just go ahead and just drive straight through to your new home— once your birds are asleep, it will take a lot of strange noises and rattling about to wake them, so as long as you drive carefully and go easy on the brakes and acceleration, they should be fine. This was how I moved my birds from the coast several hundred miles into central BC a few years back, right in the middle of breeding season. It took most of the night, and I was exhausted the next day, but the birds made the trip beautifully, with all the parents resuming care of their youngsters without a single hiccup as soon as the sun came up in the morning.

Once you've arrived at your new home, leave the birds where they are until daybreak. Then as soon as possible after that you can start bringing them into their new living quarters. Do your best to see that the cages are arranged in as similar a fashion as you can manage to the set-up you used in their old birdroom.

This includes, if you can manage it, orienting the cages in a similar manner as before. For example, if your flock was housed in a room with eastern exposure, if at all possible place them in a room with similar exposure, and try to arrange the cages in a similar manner to the way your old birdroom was arranged. This may sound a little odd, but the fact is, canaries are able to tell which direction their cages face, and may become upset if used to living in a westerly-oriented cage which suddenly becomes easterly-oriented, or some such change.

Your care and attention to these details should help to prevent the adult birds from becoming upset enough to throw them off their food, which in turn could cause them to stop feeding their youngsters. Also, it should help to prevent any just-weaned youngsters from going off their feed from stress due to moving.

Moving is stressful enough for you as it is, without adding the extra stress of worrying about your birds. So plan to take a little extra time to see that this part of your move goes as smoothly as possible, and your care will pay for itself handsomely both during and after the move.

Then you can spend a few minutes in your new birdroom admiring the refuge you've created full of happy, stress-free birds, and don't forget to pat yourself on the back— you've earned it!

by R C McDonald

Translating 'Birdspeak'

Our birds (and their people) all have their own special little ways of communicating with each other, but when it comes right down to it, how much of the time do you know just what your bird is trying to tell you? We all laugh about how our birds seem to 'train' us to provide them with this or that commodity on demand— but how often do any of us wonder if there's actually anything behind this idea?

Okay, it might sound a little off the wall to consider such an idea seriously— but the fact is, research published in February 2005 indicates that birds in general tend to be much more intelligent than anyone, including most avian specialists, had previously believed.

The long-standing scientific belief was that birds tended towards stupidity. Definitions of avian brain structure and function laid out in the late 19th century held that birds had little to no higher brain functions at all, operating almost entirely on instinct with little (or no) conscious thought. Within the last decade or two, great progress has been made towards understanding the intricacies of our world, yet comparatively little progress was made in the field of our scientific understanding of the huge variety of birds we share our world with.

All the same, scientific evidence of what appeared to be logical thought continued to arise, with observations being made among a wide variety of avian species, throwing previous conclusions of avian intelligence regularly into question.

Then came discoveries that our modern birds are likely to be the closest living relatives to extinct dinosaurs. This fact joined the others to prompt ever-increasing numbers of scientists and researchers to query just how firm our actual scientific understanding of birds really is.

As a result, a world-wide consortium of 29 scientists from a half-dozen different countries decided to work together to prove or disprove new and old theories, and at the same time provide firm, statistical evidence as to the reality behind bird brains, their physiological structure, and their function.

Much to a great many peoples' surprise, the resulting evidence indicates that not only are many species of birds capable of much more intelligent thought than had been previously suspected— but in some cases, our birds' brains may come close to rivalling the human capacity for abstract thought!

This is all very interesting, and provides a great deal of gratification to a good many longer-term birdkeepers. The fact is, anybody who has kept birds for any length of time has almost certainly been outsmarted by them regularly.

In the past, this could be a rather humbling experience, but now we can realize that we've actually been outwitted by a creature whose body-mass-to-brain ratio and even brain complexity is not too different from our own, and who possesses a brain that is, in its own way, just as intricate as the human brain— if rather differently constructed.

New credibility has arisen from this reanalysis of avian brains, and lends support to collected evidence of many behaviours that previously seemed rather odd, coming from presumably 'dumb' birds.

New Caledonian crows have been observed to create their own tools, a specialized set of hooks and spears for use during foraging expeditions for grubs and other such

by R C McDonald

difficult-to-catch live food, while Japanese carrion crows have been observed placing walnuts on paved roads. Once the nuts have been cracked by passing cars, the crows wait for the lights to change, apparently knowing that it is only then safe to swoop in for a feast on the nutmeats.

Some species of birds have phenomenal memories; the Clark nutcracker has shown that it can hide up to 30,000 seeds, and find them again as much as six months later. Meanwhile, lab tests on magpies have shown that they become aware at an earlier age than any other creature tested, that an object that disappears behind a curtain has not vanished, but is only hidden. And as anybody who owns or knows an African Gray parrot can verify, these birds not only talk, but many have a rather sharp sense of humour, and can make up new words.

In fact, research on the deservedly famous African Grey Alex, showed that he was capable of distinguishing subtle but important differences in numbers, colours, shapes, sizes, and textures, and understood if they were present or absent. He could talk well enough to converse, and could even sound out the letters of a new word similarly to the way a child would.

Meanwhile, research into birdsong has shown that baby songbirds 'babble' in a manner very like human infants, using the left sides of their brains while learning their eventual adult songs.

This is all very interesting, but it seems to me that it is time to take it a step further. Most of us know that our birds have their own set of calls they use to communicate with each other and us; but apparently nobody has yet tried to find out if each bird has their own unique approach to communicating with their humans, or if entirely different birds come up with similar techniques and sounds to mean similar things.

Most of us know our own birds' individual calls quite well, and can tell you whether we are being scolded, begged from, admired, or reminded of missed 'appointments'. We laugh that we are regularly reminded when it is time to provide food, baths, treats or drinking water, and those of us with tame pets know very well what a demand to be allowed out to play, means!

But it seems there has been very little— if any— actual comparison of these calls from keeper to keeper, and I can't help but wonder just how similar these different demands would sound, coming from different birds. Does a pet conure use the same sort of sounds and motions when asking to be allowed out to play, as a tame finch? Does a pet canary act similarly to a pet cockatiel, when he's upset with his owner's forgetfulness?

I think it's about time we compared notes, and began telling each other how our birds go about communicating with us. If we can get enough information, perhaps it will be possible to compile a kind of 'dictionary' of 'bird-speak' we could all refer to.

by R C McDonald

Pet Bird Communication

We were thrilled to receive so many responses to our last article on how our birds communicate with us. It seems right to share some of these observations and insights with everybody, so we can all continue our own research on pet bird communication.

Apparently birds and how they communicate is on a lot of minds these days; only two days before the first publication of this article in July 2005, an article on avian communication was published in the magazine 'Science', a popular journal of new scientific discoveries and findings.

The study described was undertaken by Christopher N. Templeton and his colleagues at the University of Montana. The researchers recorded local chickadee songs, analyzed them by situation, studied each bird's calls on acoustic instruments, and finally watched the birds react when the songs were played back to them. In a telephone interview, Templeton told an interviewer from the Washington Post, *"These birds are passing on far more information than anyone ever dreamed possible, and only by carefully looking at these calls can we appreciate how sophisticated these animals are. They change a bunch of different features about the call, subtle acoustic features, the spacing between the notes, things we can't hear."*

He went on to say that one variation even a human could spot in the calls were the number of 'dee' notes at the end of the call. *"The more they add, the more dangerous the predator,"* he said.

Most of us know the familiar "chick-a-dee" call, but until now, few of us realized that this call indicates the presence of a stationary predator. Variations in the call specify how dangerous the predator is, whether it is a snake or a mammal such as a ferret or a cat, and apparently even such details as whether it is stationary or moving, flies or stalks, along with exactly where it is.

"We had no idea that any animal was able to distinguish between predators that seem similar," Templeton said. *"It's life or death for them. It's just a fun bird-watching tool for us."*

"Chick-a-dee" can be much more than just an alert, the researchers found— it can also be a call for help, bringing in the whole flock to mob a lurking predator and drive it away.

A second chickadee call, a soft, high-pitched sound like "seet," means there is a predator such as a hawk, owl or falcon flying nearby, Templeton stated. It is a sort of 'duck and cover' warning, he said.

Templeton is now a doctoral student in biology at the University of Washington. He noted that previous studies of the calls have indicated that they can contain information about the location of food and about the flock itself.

Given this information, I found it interesting that several of the readers who sent in observations about their birds' communications made similar comments about their pet birds' calls.

One writer stated, *"minute differences in pitch, duration or spacing give meaning to the sounds."*

Another reader observed of their canary, *"When we travelled with him in the car, it was he who insisted— with loud, persistent vocal inflections he'd learned to use to get our attention, a particular frequency of sound we could not ignore— that any fool should stop driving at sunset and get* some rest!"

Another reader told us, *"My canary will give a single note chirp when he wants his bath water...it sounds like a smoke detector that needs a battery change, a patterned chirp, chirp, chirp, chirp, chirp with a couple of seconds between the chirps. He will keep this up even if I am standing by his cage looking at him and talking to him.*

"I usually try and get his bath ready by 11:00 AM since he prefers bathing about noon. If I put the bath water in early, he ignores it until he is ready... but sometimes he desires early bathing and I get the measured chirp, chirp...

"He will also indicate in the same manner if he wants his food checked. If he runs out of his favorite seed, I get the same measured chirp, chirp, chirp... Guess he has me trained quite well! I get a calmer two-note chirp, chirp when I do as he asks."

Another reader states that she knows when her canary is ready for food, a bath, or play time, because *"I can hear him go, 'beep beep.'"*

Other pet birds were reported too. One reader says, *"I have a yellow-naped amazon who screams in the morning until I fill his food bowl and give him fresh water. At night when I turn out the lights he give me a small quiet laugh and says 'Awww.' I know he is letting me know he is hungry or ready for sleep."*

Another reader wrote of her black-capped lory, *"he raps his beak on things. He likes to rake his beak along the bars for the sound. He also bangs his beak on resonant items (plastic buckets, bowls, cooking pans, his wooden nestbox, etc.) for the sounds they make.*

"You'd think that would hurt a bit, wouldn't you? Yet, he clearly enjoys doing this for attention. He's not exactly a woodpecker, and this is not the behaviour I'd expect from him.

"He also likes hearing his voice inside of containers; many parrot species do this. But, Cato likes to sing into

paper towel rolls, or rattle his head inside a can, and sometimes finishes his performances by looking at me and saying, 'I like it, I like it.'" She adds that while Cato is not a big talker, there is one time when he does talk a fair bit— in his sleep!

One reader wrote in that she shares her quarters with four canaries, three cockatiels, two budgies, four parakeets and an unspecified number of zebra finches. Her 'tiels are her biggest communicators, she says, *"reminding me that it's time to turn their light off at night— they want to go to sleep by nine. They will call to me when I'm in another room (usually when I am trying to take a nap)— they seem to sense that if they keep up the noise long enough, I'll get up."*

She adds, *"They also love it when I'm cleaning up after suppertime, and shriek with delight when I call to them from the kitchen & ask if they "want some 'phagetti'?" (pasta of any kind)."*

Her canaries also talk to her, she says. *"My canaries respond to me when I talk sweetly to them by cheep-cheeping."*

One reader wrote in about her amusing encounter with a friend's African Grey parrot. She says, *"I was a guest in the house of an African Gray, whose person also happens to raise Norwegian elkhounds, several of whom would be in the house at one time.*

"One day things got very quiet, so the bird decided to begin speaking. Just the day before, I had stood at his cage and, in response to his language abilities, said 'That's amazing!' He began his repertoire that day by saying in my voice with the same inflection, 'That's amazing!'

"We had a good laugh over that, the bird enjoying it as well. Later, when he apparently thought we weren't paying him enough attention, suddenly there was a loud knock on the door. The dogs went wild barking. We went to the door but nobody was there. Then we came around to the cage

and looked at the parrot.

"He seemed to be laughing as he gave us another knock on the door. The dogs went wild again. What a jokester."

Given the abundance of stories about our birds, many of which have to do with how clearly they manage to indicate their needs, wants, and wishes to us, tells me that these birds quite likely have a very good idea of what they want to say to us.

Add in the provocative results of the chickadee study and other similar research on avian comprehension, memory retentiveness, and communicability, and I can't help but wonder what other unexpected insights will arise in the future as we continue in our quest to understand these unique and so fascinating little creatures?

Canary Crazy

by R C McDonald

Part 2:
Canary Health Care

Canary Crazy

by R C McDonald

PhotoSensitivity

More than any other factor in the environment of any canary, is one issue. It lies at the heart of each canary's lifestyle, whether breeder or pet. It relates to what they are, why they do what they do, how they do it, and when.

Canaries evolved so that their bodies respond physically to the amount of light which enters their eyes. This will trigger the beginnings or endings to some extreme physical changes, which can affect their personality, their health, their appearance, attitude and lifespan. This trait is known simply as 'photosensitivity'.

It used to be that keeping canaries was a fairly reliable project— a pet canary would sing all year long, except during the summer when he was moulting. Breeders knew just when in the spring they could expect their birds to want their nests, and that there would be time for only two or so nests before it was time for the summer moult.

That was before the advent of artificial light. Nowadays, canaries are only predictable if all they are seeing is natural daylight, or lights which are on only during the daytime. Generally for canaries, the lengthening days of spring signal the start of breeding season. Breeders whose birds produce eggs and/or chicks at other times of the year, have used artificial lighting before or after darkness outdoors, to make the birds react as if the season is different than it really is.

Many breeders deliberately set up their birdrooms to use artificial lighting to get a jump on the season. It is believed that this will allow their birds adequate time to mature before being wanted for shows or sales.

According to my experience though, this may not offer them any real advantages in the long run, as early-season clutches often have a higher percentage of infertile eggs than clutches laid later on. Not only that, but all too often the better birds will turn out to be those that hatched in the middle or later of the breeding season.

One of the biggest problems for many new-comers to keeping canaries is learning to understand that their canaries literally react physically to the length of the days they are experiencing. People are also photosensitive, if to a rather lesser degree. Still, each winter will bring new cases of the disease known as SAD; Seasonal Affective Disorder. This is a kind of depression that has been tied, in humans, to a lack of sufficient natural light.

Most of us don't tend to think much about any of this, though— we are too busy! We think little of hopping up in the middle of the night and flipping on the lights to jot down a note, or finish a task. The fact is, though, that if much of that light is seen by your pet canary, it will stimulate him physically, the same way daylight does.

His system reacts as if it is suddenly dawn. This triggers his internal 'clock' to start producing the physical changes which go with the day and season in which days of that length occur. (For a look at the kind of daylengths canaries evolved with, visit *www.robirda.com/sunset.html* for an online chart.)

Some birds, especially pets in families whose lights swing back and forth unpredictably, are never allowed to complete these annual changes comfortably and in their own time, but are instead physically pushed into suddenly beginning or ending them at the unintended whim of their human family's convenience.

This kind of thing is *very* stressful for a canary, and over the long term, can lead to health problems, and a shorter lifespan than otherwise might be seen. Every year, a great many canaries are tricked into thinking it is spring when the holiday season comes along and suddenly there is more light and longer 'days', due to their human family's increased holiday socialization. Every year I hear of more 'surprise' Christmas hatchlings, and every year, some die, because once the holiday season is over, the house lights go back to more normal timing, and suddenly the canaries find themselves experiencing shorter days again.

In nature, the days becoming shorter means the summer solstice has passed, and winter is on its way— this is a signal to all canaries to get those feathers replaced and renewed, *fast*, before the weather becomes changeable and unreliable. The birds go into a 'winter' moult, thinking it is midsummer. Usually this also means that parent birds will stop feeding any babies still in the nest.

This kind of scenario has made a lot of trouble for newcomers to canary-keeping over the years, and will probably continue to do so for some time yet. The only way out is to try to learn to understand the kind of effect lighting has on a canary. Once you have lived with them for a few years and watched the incredible annual changes they go through, it becomes a little easier to understand how completely this stimulus acts on their physical and mental systems.

When it comes to lighting, creative minds can find ways to get around such limits as when lights need to be on or off, using such handy items as an extra-heavy cage cover, or a separate birdroom where even full houselights won't bother a sleeping canary. The fact remains that, at least for those of us who want to keep canaries, learning how to adapt our lives to accommodate the needs of our canaries has to become a consideration— whether we have a single pet, or a large flock.

One factor often left out of this equation is that of mental stimulation and attitude. Canaries are quite intelligent for their size, and some canary hens in particular can tend to take sudden notions. (Many men will insist this is a trait all females share.) In my experience, some hens adore the idea of babies, and think of them year round. At the slightest sign that it might be getting close to breeding season, they will be busily building nests, and trolling for a response from the males around them. Other hens couldn't give a flit, and breed only when their bodies physically force them to.

My conclusion? They may have similar physical systems, but each and every canary is as much an individual as we humans are. People are all physically similar too— but that has never stopped us from being individuals, each unique in our own special way. My observation suggests that this is equally true of all of the winged, furred or scaled creatures who share the planet with us.

Given that fact, it is my belief that it will serve us well to learn all we can about understanding and relating to this complex little creature known as the 'common canary'. How else will we find out what they still have to teach us?

by R C McDonald

Troubleshooting Problems

Learning how to troubleshoot, understand, and deal with potential problems may be one of the most difficult chores a new bird keeper will ever have to do. Sometimes even the tiniest of changes can be indicators of the start of a problem that can evolve into a serious situation. As a novice bird-keeper, it can be all too easy to miss noticing one of these subtle clues.

Since this is too broad a field to cover in a single article, I will instead use an example to illustrate the process. Apply a similar process to whatever the problem you are trying to cope with may be, in whatever species of bird, and you just may find, as others have, that this is indeed one of the most useful of talents for a birdkeeper to develop. Here, then, are some of the steps involved in troubleshooting what's going on in a canary's care and environment, to discover, in this case, why he has stopped singing.

Sometimes this will simply be because he is undergoing his annual moult, which should happen once a year, usually in the mid to late summer. Growing in feathers takes a lot of energy, and many canaries will not sing much if at all during this time. Once the moult is over he should start singing again fairly soon, usually within two or three weeks of the day when the last feathers fell.

Moulting that occurs at other times of the year indicates a problem, and help should be sought to find and stop the draft or stress causing the unseasonable feather fall.

Available nutrients can make a huge difference in just how long the moult lasts, and lack of nutrients can actually delay the start or end of a moult. This means that adequate vitamin and mineral supplies are especially important before, during and just after the moult. If a moulting canary doesn't have enough of any particular nutrient, it will take him much longer to get back to full health once the moult is over, even if he appears to be acting and eating normally.

Moulting requires a lot of nutrition, and if there isn't an adequate balance of necessary nutrients available in the body's bloodstream, the nutrients needed to grow the new feathers will instead come out of the bird's bodily stores. If that source does not contain enough, his body will wait until enough nutrients trickle in from other sources.

Another little-known fact about moulting canaries, is that what a canary sings after his moult is over can depend quite a lot on just what he hears around him during his moult. Science has discovered that when these little birds are growing in those new feathers, they are also growing in new brain cells. At the same time they are listening intently to everything they can hear in their environment.

Many of those sounds— the ones each individual canary finds the most agreeable and interesting— will end up being incorporated into their songs. But if a moulting canary doesn't hear anything he considers interesting, he may not develop much of a song at all.

On the other hand, if a moulting canary is slow to resume his song even once his moult is over, it *could* mean that disease or illness may be a factor. If you think that might be the case with your canary, be sure to get him or her checked by a veterinarian as soon as you possibly can.

The need will be urgent in any such case, because all birds try their utmost to hide any signs of illness. This instinct evolved in the wild, when any creature showing the slightest signs of weakness was soon to become somebody's lunch. This in turn means that very often the little signs like not singing may be the only clues you will have to go on, until the bird has become too weak to continue to keep up the charade. By then matters are likely to have become very serious indeed.

It's always a good idea, whenever an unexpected change in behaviour happens— especially if there is no obvious cause— to have an experienced avian vet take a look... just in case. It's actually rather amazing how often even a tiny change in habits can be an indicator of a serious problem in development. In fact it's best, if at all possible, to take all your birds in annually for a 'wellness check-up', whether they seem ill or not.

This will help tremendously if any illness should ever develop, and could save you quite a lot of money in case of disease or accident— a vet who knows a bird when healthy, will have a base-line of already-prepared information to compare to and use, when dealing with the same bird ill.

Diet is an important consideration too. Among the questions that need to be considered are these:

What brand of seed or pellets are being fed? How complete is the nutrition offered? If seed, is it 'vitaminized', or not? Is it sold bagged, or out of a bin? How is it stored, and how often is the supply renewed? Is there a lot of dust in the seed?

Fresh seed contains much more nutrition than stale seed. Some indicators of stale seed are a musty, dry smell, and more dust and particulates in the bottom of the container than will be seen in a container of fresh seed. Don't be afraid to taste a few; fresh seed smells and tastes good, while stale seed tastes as dusty as it smells.

Seed stored in a bin ages quite quickly, and will soon be stale. At home, seed or pellets stored in a cupboard will quickly go stale, too— but stored in a freezer they can stay fresh for a year or two, maybe more, as long as you protect them from condensation.

You also need to look at what treat seeds are being offered. What kind are they, how much is being offered, and how often? Over-feeding fatty 'treat' or 'song' seeds is a rather common mistake, especially to newcomers to canary keeping. In practice, *all* treat seeds offered should consist of no more than a teaspoon or so per bird, per week. That's *all treat seeds combined*, NOT a teaspoonful of each kind! Letting a canary have free access to any more than this tiny amount of such highly fatty seeds can lead to some serious health problems.

If there are other birds being kept nearby, you will need to check where he is in relation to them— is he higher than them, or lower? Are they close by, or further away? Does he have his own cage, or are they expected to share?

Canaries do not like sharing cages, and this can limit or even eliminate their song, and can also seriously affect their health, especially if there is any harassment by other birds present.

Even if he lives in his own cage, if there are other birds living nearby, he may find them intimidating, if they are placed so that they are higher than him. Ideally, his top perch should be level with their top perches, so that he knows that he is on an equal footing with them— and to be sure that he knows that he has the right to sing.

If he is kept at a lower height, he is in effect being told that the other birds own the local territory, not him. Since a canary sings to brag about ownership of 'his' territory, he needs to feel that his cage really does belong to him, or even if he's totally healthy, he may not sing a note.

Another factor that needs to be examined is what kinds of fresh foods are being offered. What kind of fruits, if any, are commonly offered, how much, and how often? What kinds of greens are given, how much is offered, and when? What time of day are these foods being supplied, and how much of them does the bird eat, and how fast?

Foods containing a lot of water are better offered earlier

by R C McDonald

in the day rather than later. Canaries do not need a lot of fruit, and soft fruits especially should be offered in limited quantities, if at all; too much can cause problems. Worse, many fruits are treated with some rather strong pesticides during growth; traces of such chemicals can remain on and even in them. Such minute quantities will not be enough to bother humans or even children, but may be strong enough to negatively affect a canary's health.

Many birds are chronically short of vitamin A, and most greens are quite high in it, so it is a good idea to offer plenty of the darker, more nutritious greens, as often as you can— daily, if possible. Some greens are far more nutritious than others, while some can negatively affect the digestion of other elements in the diet. For example, kale has many times the nutrients of any lettuce, but spinach can inhibit proper digestion of calcium.

Try to offer organically grown greens, and avoid those grown with the use of pesticides or fertilizers, if possible; when dealing with the chemically sensitive canary, it takes very little to create a toxic (possibly deadly) reaction.

If you are not feeding pellets, you will need to offer vitamin and mineral supplements designed for use with a seed-based diet. Note that you should not attempt to convert *any* bird from a seed-based diet to a pellet-based diet until you are 100% sure that he is totally healthy. Unless he is a young bird, the conversion process may be difficult, so you need to be sure he is super-healthy before you begin.

A powdered supplement that you can offer on soft food, greens or soak seed is much preferred to the kinds meant to be offered in water, as canaries don't drink often enough or in enough quantity for the latter to be very effective.

Most people provide a mineral block and/or a cuttlebone for their canary to chew on— this not only provides a source for essential minerals 'on demand', but also helps keep the beak in shape. Be careful to tie it on firmly, near enough to the perch that it is easily accessible. Make certain

Canary Crazy

that the softer side is facing the inside of the cage. If the bird seems afraid of it, consider mounting it horizontally rather than vertically; especially at first, some find the latter a bit scarey.

If he is near a window, especially if he gets direct sunshine for even part of the day, you need to be sure that he has shade available when he wants it too. This is *very* important; an over-heated canary can too soon become a dead canary. If need be, clip a smooth facecloth or small hand-towel to shade an area of at least one perch inside the cage, without blocking too much light.

You will also need to be sure that there is no draft, or, if there is one, that there is shelter available when the bird wishes. Often there is quite a lot of heat exchanged through some windows, and in that case any cage within a foot or two of the glass is almost inevitably in a draft.

A lit candle is very useful when checking for drafts— they can be almost impossible to see, but a candle flame will flicker and bend at the slightest stir of the air, allowing you to detect, not only exactly where the draft is coming from, but how strong and how regular it is (or isn't).

Sometimes a computer or other electrical equipment can cause problems, especially if they are near the birds, and are on and active much of the time. Birds are quite sensitive to electromagnetic fields, which computers and similar electrical equipment naturally generate.

Another common mistake is to think that canaries like to live in a quiet environment. This is most definitely not the case! Most birds, including canaries, greatly prefer a loud environment to a quiet one— to any creature who evolved in a forested environment, noise means safety. The only time silence will be heard in a forest, is when a predator is spotted. As far as canaries are concerned, there is no such thing as 'peace and quiet'; silence tells their instincts that they are in a dangerous environment, with a predator nearby who is probably stalking them at the moment. This, as you can imagine, is highly stressful.

by R C McDonald

Remember that canaries sing to claim ownership of their territory. They need to feel they are safe, and that they are 'Lord and master of all they survey' before they will begin to feel much like singing. If you can make your canary feel like 'The Boss', he will be much more liable to want to brag about 'his' home.

Yet another thing to keep in mind, is that many kinds of household products can produce fumes that are harmful to birds. Sometimes, just cooking itself can produce harmful fumes. If you do much if any frying of any sort, you should not keep your canary nearby. Any kind of appliance with a non-stick (except for ceramics) surface is anathema, in a home with birds— some of these products can produce off-gassing that can seriously harm or even kill a bird, and their use in a bird-keeping home should not be allowed.

These can include items such as some oven mitts, baking pans, muffin or bread tins, cookie sheets, irons, ironing board covers, drip trays under stove elements, and more. It used to be thought that these non-stick materials were only dangerous under high heat, but recent research has shown this not to be necessarily true— under certain conditions, normal cooking temperatures can suffice.

So you do want to be extra careful that there is nothing of the sort in your home, if you have a canary living there. (Or for that matter, any other kind of bird.) Be wary of exposing your bird to anything that produces fumes of any sort, including cigarettes, perfumes, scented candles, air and carpet deodorizers or 'fresheners', and many other similar products, especially those made for cleaning. Your birds will thank you by living longer and healthier lives.

Finally, it may seem redundant, but always make certain that you have read over all the reliable information you can find on what is involved in basic care for your bird, before you go looking for more exotic causes. More often than not, the key to finding the answer to any such problem will be to take a good long look at what is included or not included in the bird's daily care and environment, and compare that with known basic needs for that species.

This is only one example of how to trouble-shoot a pet bird's problem— but once you learn to approach all your problems similarly, you may find, as I have, that this kind of trouble-shooting can be worth its weight in gold, when it comes to finding the best and most affordable, workable, and creative solutions for any kind of problem that happens to arise with your birds.

by R C McDonald

The Treatment Quandary

Sooner or later every bird keeper has to deal with the dilemma of how to proceed with the care of a bird that doesn't seem to be quite as healthy and as vibrant as it should be, but which shows no reliable symptoms of illness to act as a guideline for treatment. The decision of what to try next with such a bird can and often does lead to confusion and indecision; just what do you try next?

The following is a single (but common) example of a number of common scenarios. Your canary has a good appetite, but is not as peppy as he used to be, and you're beginning to catch him looking a bit fluffed more often than you like. Along with this, you've found him snoozing more than usual during the day.

You checked for all the usual signs of illness, and found his droppings appear normal, his vent is clean and not swollen, his breast bone is okay, showing that he hasn't lost any weight, and there is no nasal discharge, nor can you hear any wheezing or clicking in his breathing.

Just to be sure, you had a fecal test done, along with a gram stain, and all it came up with was a common bacteria that often show up in finch fecal tests. Your avian vet has recommended trying Baytril (an antibiotic) for 14 days, just to be sure, but you only saw a bit of an improvement.

You provided him with some good probiotics once the course of antibiotics ended, but your bird is still not his usual vigorous self. Your vet is as puzzled as you are, and wants to do some more involved tests on your bird's blood. These tests require a largish sample, and you've been told that this will require drawing blood from the jugular vein, in the neck.

Your bird still 'chats' with you and looks for his food, but you know he is not himself. You want to help, but you are afraid that the measures your vet wishes to take will prove to be the death of your beloved little feathered pal. You want to do the right thing, but you'd prefer to make an educated decision, and you feel as if you don't have the whole story. On top of it all, you are worried that there may be other, perhaps less invasive, approaches that you don't know of.

The first thing you need to check is the time of year. Why? Because if your canary is undergoing his annual moult, which usually occurs in the mid-to-late summer, this could well be the cause of his diminished energy.

As a bird ages, each successive moult can seem to take just a little more 'pep' out of a canary, until the annual feather-fall is over. If you see any feathers scattered about, then it is possible that this could be at the root of the problem.

It's important to check that the moult is a normal one, and it is also important to offer your canary a bit of a dietary boost during the moult. These questions can be fairly involved; for more on moulting canaries, please refer to the articles elsewhere in this book.

But what if his problem is not related to a moult?

Blood *can* be safely taken from a canary in this way, and in fact in some cases it may be the only method possible to allow enough blood to be taken to perform certain tests. But doing it safely can be quite tricky, and losing that much blood can be hard on a canary. It's not like they have much to spare, after all!

I personally would have to be 100% convinced of the need for such a drastic measure before proceeding. On top of that, I'd want written assurance from the vet that in his best estimation the bird would be in no danger. Then, before attempting such a drastic measure, I would first exhaust all other possible approaches.

First among these would be an attempt to boost the immune system. Not all products on the market will work the same way on birds as they will for humans, though, and that's why I prefer to stick to the basics of food, nutrients, and micro-nutrients, or else with avian-tested supplements.

Perhaps the best all-round avian immune-system booster I know of is the product called 'Guardian Angel'. It is manufactured by the Bird Care Co in Britain and sold by a multitude of dealers in the world, both online and off.

I have used this product myself, and liked the results. It works very well when fresh, but has a rather short shelf life, so if you want to try it, be sure it's fresh.

I am admittedly biased towards the naturalistic approach— I have seen it do so much good over the years. But, I also know of cases where if a blood test had not been done, the cause of the problem would never have been found.

In one such case, the problem turned out to be in the house itself— there was a toxic chemical being slowly released in the basement (it's known as 'off-gassing' when buildings do this; apparently it is more common than most of us like to think), and the entire family was exposed.

The chemical being released on this occasion was building up fairly slowly in the bloodstream of those exposed, and did not start to make even their canary sick until it reached a certain level in his liver. By the time the tests were run, it was too late to save their little canary— but there was still enough time to see that the rest of the family survived.

Here's the clincher; had they waited for symptoms to show up in themselves, there would have been irreversible side-effects involved at the very least, and maybe even

Canary Crazy

death. So in the case of that family, those tests— and the presence of their canary— saved their lives.

In another case I know of, the vet was able to determine that the culprit was metal toxicity. After some false attempts to find the source of the toxin, it was determined that the problem had arisen from the coating on the cage! Again, as in the first case, without the tests having been done, the real source of the problem may never have been found.

As you can see, the decision to test or not can be a difficult one; there are pros and cons on both sides, and either way, the decision will still have to be yours, should it ever arise.

While you are thinking, another thing you might want to have a look at is the source of greens and other such fresh foods— if they are commercially raised, your birds might be getting a borderline exposure to some chemical that is toxic to them. A bit too much fertilizer on a greens crop can cause a slight excess of nitrate content, to which canaries are quite sensitive... the same thing goes for several pesticides and such in common use.

I have even heard of cases where people were feeding their birds foods from their own garden, believing that no spray had touched them— not realizing that their neighbours had sprayed heavily with pesticides, and that some had drifted over onto their lot.

In yet another case I know of, all the usual tests were done, but every single one was inconclusive, until the bird owner happened to hear that a neighbour was tearing her hair out trying to figure out why she kept having problems with her youngster getting sick every time he drank the tap water.

Between them, they decided to have tests done on their water supply. It turned out there was contamination in the neighbourhood's water supply— not enough to bother most adults, but more than adequate to bother an extra-sensitive youngster, and easily enough to make a tiny bird quite ill.

Toxicity can build up slowly in a well or watershed, and in that particular case, if it had gone unnoticed for much longer, it could have made the entire neighbourhood sick.

In the last two cases, it was tests on the soil and water that turned up the culprits that were making the canaries ill — so if you have a bird whose problem is due to some such cause, having its blood tested may not be any help.

On the other hand, many chemicals can gradually build up in the bloodstream, and in time, can cause some rather severe illnesses. A blood test could show this, where fecal tests might not. So there's a fairly equal set of chances that having a blood test done could help— or, it might prove useless. And you may not know which, until you try.

As with so many things these days, in some cases there are no guarantees. I don't envy anybody who finds themselves in the position of having to make such a decision.

Hopefully none of you will ever find yourselves, for whatever reason, in any such position. But if a similar problem does ever arise, perhaps you will remember this article. If so, I hope it manages to help you come to the correct decision for both you and your birds.

Air Quality

Air quality is one of those things that we so often forget to consider; after all, air can't be seen with the naked eye, and only relatively strong movement is perceived by human senses, as a breeze or a wind.

Unless there's a strong or unpleasant odour, we don't tend to notice the quality of the air around us, yet clean air is one of the most important ingredients in the recipe that adds up to an optimally functioning living being such as a human, a parrot, or a canary.

We humans are lucky enough to have our own built-in 'air filters'; our noses contain small fine hairs to help to trap small particles out of the air, before the air is drawn into our bodies, and it doesn't stop there; air that is breathed in through the nose or mouth is filtered some more on the way down the windpipe, by tiny hairs known as cilia that move gently to help trap mucus and dirt.

If allowed to enter our lungs, particles could lodge in a warm nook or cranny, where plentiful moisture and warmth could encourage moulds and bacteria to proliferate. By filtering the air we breathe in, our body assists us in staying healthy.

Since we are able to a large extent to deal fairly easily with particulates in the air, we don't easily realize how much more sensitive our birds are to the quality of the air they breathe.

Our birds have no such built-in filtration systems as we do, to help them clean the air they breathe and protect their delicate air passages, so important to their health. Their evolution prepared them to live in an environment where the natural action of the weather would help keep the air they breathe relatively clean. However that is *not* the case in our homes, which means it is up to us to see that the air our pets breathe is as clean as possible.

Unfortunately, many buildings tend to hold quite a lot of particulate matter in the air, and sometimes recirculate it, too. When the weather is cooperative, windows can be opened to allow stale, dust-laden air out and fresh air in, but when it's too hot or too cold out, the dust, dirt, and other particulate content in the inside air can build up to alarming levels more quickly than most of us realize.

This can happen especially easy in homes that rely on venting and ducts to circulate the air (whether heated or cooled) throughout the house, and it can happen even more quickly in a bird room— especially when the phrase 'draft-free' is mistakenly interpreted to mean 'no air circulation'.

Yes, it's true that a constant draft (whether hot or cold) that a bird can't step out of at will can cause illness or out-of-season moulting. But that doesn't mean it's necessary to shut out *all* the air circulation! Good air circulation should *never* be sacrificed in the name of preventing drafts. Instead, what's needed is to provide the bird a means of gaining shelter from any drafts when he wants it. Often the solution is as simple as draping a cloth over one corner of a cage, or moving the cage and stand only a few feet away.

Once cages are properly positioned so as to provide good air circulation along with a little shelter from any drafts in the area, you can turn your attention to keeping the air itself clean.

There's several ways to help you to clean out as much as possible of any dust, dirt, and other particulate matter that's found it's way into the air in your home; in most instances a varying combination of one or more of these solutions will work for you. What kind or combination of systems you choose to use will depend on the heating and cooling system already installed in your home, as well as on the size of your budget.

One of the first options often considered is to add extra or upgraded filters to existing heating or cooling units. When combined with regular thorough cleaning of all vents and ducts, these simple steps can produce surprisingly good results, and remain quite cost-effective too. Vent filters can be added in each room, which, as long as they are changed regularly, will also help increase the effectiveness of the filtration.

Another common approach involves acquiring individual stand-alone air filtration units for each room or series of rooms. Such units can be fairly effective at cleaning the air, especially if used in a limited area.

Most stand-alone individual air filtering units come with their own filters, but look out! Many of these filters cannot be cleaned and reused, but must instead be thrown out when dirty. Leaving dirty filters in place can make your air problem worse, not better, and filter replacement cost can be quite high.

Another drawback is that unless you are willing to pay a fairly hefty sum, most stand-alone models are good for cleaning only a rather limited area, often expressed in cubic feet. Be sure to calculate the actual cubic footage of the area you want to filter to learn if a unit you're considering for purchase will be effective for your home.

You will want to note that a unit used near birds will likely require its filters to be replaced far more often than most sellers' estimates. Those estimates are based on what is considered normal usage in homes without pet birds, and while we all know how wonderful our birds are, it's also true that between the feathers and seed, they can easily produce tremendous amounts of dust.

That brings us to one of the biggest problems with all air filtering and circulating systems, the need for regular system cleaning, and replacement of dirty filters. Whether you use special filters in your home's existing system, or add stand-alone units in each room where you want the air quality improved, it is important to remember that you will also need to clean and maintain the units, and clean or replace the filters as needed.

It can't be emphasized strongly enough, that dirty filters in any air circulation system can be worse than no filters at all. Not only can they pump dust and dirt back into the air, but in some cases the accumulated dirt can begin to breed unwanted bacteria that can also be pumped into the air.

This is particularly true of units that incorporate a humidifier into the design. It can be all too easy to get so busy that we forget to check the air filters and clean out the tank of a humidifier on a regular basis, but to forget these so-essential steps can lead to harm, for yourself as well as for your pets. Whatever system you decide to use, be sure to regularly perform basic maintenance, and check your work often.

Some air cleaning systems don't use filters to clean the air, but instead generate negative ions near collector plates that 'grab' dirt out of the air, while others use ultraviolet light or generate ozone. The latter two systems in particular are supposed to be effective at sterilizing any harmful bacteria that may be present.

Confusion has been known to arise between the systems that produce ozone for cleansing the air, and those that produce negatives ions for the same purpose. In fact, these two systems are very different from each other. Negative ions are beneficial to living beings, unlike ozone, which can be toxic even in fairly tiny amounts. Sadly, this fact is rarely if ever mentioned by most marketers, whose job, after all, is not to be truthful, but simply to sell their product.

Negative ions not only encourage dust and dirt to settle on nearby surfaces instead of floating about in the air, but also lend nearby living beings a feeling of well-being. A bonus is that negative ionizers tend to require very little maintenance, besides being cleaned regularly; unlike most other means of cleaning the air, there is seldom any filters needing to be replaced. In most cases, cleaning simply involves removing the collector plates or generating needles, (following the instructions for your model), washing them off, then reinstalling them once they're dry.

Some air filtration units on the market will incorporate more than one means of cleaning the air into one machine. It's fairly common to see stand-alone units that include negative ionizers and/or an ozonator as well as a filter. A few of these use filters are washable and reusable, but most use filters that will require replacing.

One of the oldest and still most reliable methods for cleaning the air, is the one used by nature; water. Most of us know that rain happens when droplets of water form around particulates in the air, falling to the ground as the droplets grow heavy enough, but how many of us realize that it is this same action that cleanses the air we breathe?

Even when it strikes the ground, water continues to clean the air; dripping or splashing water generates negative ions, and as mentioned above, these negatively-charged ions bind with particulates and make them fall to the nearest surface, rather than continuing to float about in the air.

This's why the air outdoors always seems to smell better than indoor air, and why we all love being near a waterfall or splashing fountain; the air smells fresher, because it *is* fresher, thanks to the action of the water. There is even a few 'bag-less' vacuum cleaners on the market that use water to filter out dirt, and it's no accident that in recent years, the sale of small 'personal fountains' has been proliferating across many markets; they help us to feel better when we're near them, because they help to improve the quality of the air we are breathing.

If you haven't yet taken steps to improve the air quality in your home, try a few of these ideas to find the best solution for you. You just might be surprised at how much easier you and your pets will be able to breathe!

by R C McDonald

Supplemental Lighting

You've decided your canary doesn't get enough natural daylight, and you want to add some lighting to the area where he lives. But what kind of lights should you use? Regular lightbulbs can help to brighten anybody's day— but they aren't anything like natural sunlight, nor do they offer similar benefits.

Our birds evolved under natural sunlight, and their eyes, which see much further into ultraviolet wavelengths than ours do, rely on these wavelengths in order to be able to know each other's gender; to their eyes, a male canary's feathers fluoresce differently under UV lighting than a hen's feathers. We can't see it, but they can.

Moreover, our birds evolved to use sunlight to help them remain healthy; natural, direct sunlight has a wavelength (in the long-wave ultraviolet) that, when sufficiently strong, reacts with the preen oil on the bird's feathers, converting it into the precursor of Vitamin D. This is then ingested while preening and converted by the bird's body into a more useful form of this essential nutrient.

Some owners think that this means our birds will be healthier if they live out of doors. To a certain extent, this is true, but there are numerous dangers also associated with living outdoors; among them are issues such as increased exposure to disease, whether through insect bites or direct or indirect contact with wild birds, as well as exposure to extreme weather, predation, infestation, and more.

What it adds up to in the end is, unless you are willing to put a lot of money into constructing an outdoor aviary that will protect its inhabitants from all those issues and more, our birds are likelier to have a longer lifespan living indoors.

It's tempting to think that keeping indoor birds near enough to a window to be exposed to sunlight for part of the day will help to keep the birds healthy, and it's very true that, as long as there's shade as well as sunlight available, most pet birds will enjoy sunbathing when they have the chance.

Unfortunately, glass windows filter out the wavelength required for the chemical reaction that helps the birds to produce their own Vitamin D, so as an alternative, some bird owners like to offer a more natural lighting for their pets through the use of full-spectrum lighting, made to mimic (as the name indicates) the range and balance (although never the intensity) of natural sunlight.

But it can be very easy to become confused as to the exact quality of a given product— between product names and marketing tactics, sometimes it can be difficult to differentiate between true 'full spectrum' lights, and their lesser-quality cousins with similar names.

For example, some kinds of incandescent bulbs (the ones that screw into a regular light socket) are marketed as 'full spectrum', when they aren't. Full spectrum, that is. They *do* mimic the naturally occurring wavelengths of sunlight to a degree, but they aren't capable of emitting the long-wave UV part of the spectrum that is so useful to our birds.

Another factor that's not always considered (and it should be) is that if you are already offering a good-quality vitamin & mineral supplement, then you don't really need to offer full-spectrum lighting just to keep your bird healthy — reasonably bright lighting of the ordinary kind will do just fine.

Full-spectrum lighting is only an essential for those indoor birds who are not getting vitamin and mineral supplementation as a regular part of their diet— and since even true full-spectrum lighting still wouldn't provide them with everything else they need in the way of vitamins and minerals, and because it is so difficult to supply all the nutrients that a bird needs through the diet alone, the easiest way to ensure your bird is and remains healthy, is to simply supply reasonably bright lighting, and use a good brand of vitamin/mineral supplement.

Full-spectrum lighting *can* help the birds to interact with each other in a much more normal fashion, though, so if you are a breeder and you would like to make use of this kind of lighting to assist your efforts and want true full-spectrum lighting in your bird's area(s), for now at least you will need to go with a fluorescent-type lamp or fixture.

There is a variety of full-spectrum fluorescent bulbs on the market, selling for a rather wide range of prices. Some of these bulbs are better quality than others, and you can't always tell the difference by the price. A good quality full-spectrum bulb should list its ratings and spectrum analysis on the box, for one thing— if you don't see these, you can't be sure that you're getting what you need, no matter what the name is, or the marketing spiel says.

Plus, you need to realize that even if the bulbs are rated for the standard several thousand hours or 5 years, analysis of the light they emit has shown that they are likely to remain truly full-spectrum for only perhaps six months or so. At that point, though still producing light in the visible range of humans, they will cease to emit the long-wave non-burning ultraviolet wavelengths our birds use.

It *is* possible to find bulbs that emit almost all long-wave ultraviolet, with the only visible light emitted being a dark blue. These are most commonly known as 'blacklights'. Blacklights by themselves offer little visible light, and so need to be used in conjunction with regular bulbs, but they can be a useful source of supplemental lighting, when used together with an ordinary 'daylight' style bulb. Since most fluorescent fixtures require at least two bulbs in order to work, setting up such a combination is easy.

One interesting fact I've noticed about blacklights is that my birds love to sunbathe under them— an activity I have never seen occurring under any form of lighting I've offered them, other than natural sunlight.

Learning how to tell the differences between the various types of lights available on the market is an on-going, ever-changing process, as technology advances, discoveries are made, and manufacturing techniques change. It's possible that soon even bulbs that screw into an ordinary light-bulb socket may become able to be true full-spectrum lights— such as the new miniature fluorescent lightbulbs, for example; but for now, we will have to wait, or use other sources.

Graphs of incandescent lights— even those termed 'full spectrum'— show clearly that their intensity of light peaks in the red wavelengths— mostly because an incandescent bulb emits a fair bit of heat. (Actually, that's true of all incandescent bulbs). Sunlight, and fluorescent full-spectrum bulbs, instead peak in the green wavelengths, in the center of the visible spectrum. Plus, a true full-spectrum light will emit a small percentage of ultraviolet light.

One good source of more information on full-spectrum lighting, are the books written by the scientist who did the ground-breaking research full spectrum lights are based on. His name is Dr John N Ott. Among his books are, 'Let There Be Light', 'Health & Light', and 'Color & Light: Their Effects on Plants, Animals & People'. These books should be recommended reading for anybody interested in learning about full-spectrum lighting.

Originally a photographer, Dr. Ott's lighting require-ments for certain shots led him to observe some odd but powerful anomalies in the way we then understood sunlight

by R C McDonald

and its interactions with and effects on plants, animals and people.

It took him years to gather enough funding to conduct proper research, because mainstream science considered research into light to be "a waste of time". Driven finally to soliciting private funding, Dr Ott persisted, and decades later, his labs began producing results.

Some of those results have generated some interesting products— among them, some of the best indoor lights in the world. These are called Ott-lights. They include lamps made specifically to provide birds, fish, reptiles and other such creatures the lighting required for optimal health. These lights are understandably popular with zoos and breeders; they are expensive, but they work. Slowly, as more pet owners try them, they are becoming better known.

Understanding light and how it interacts with living beings— ourselves as well as our pets— is an ongoing process that demands the ability to be willing to adapt our understanding as more information is gained and technology adapts. Light, once thought to be not worth the time to research, is becoming a major modern player in the centerfield of the latest advances.

Recent studies in light technologies have shown that the kinds and quantities of light— or lack of it— can strongly impact our sleep/wake cycles, directly affecting our health and well-being. Other studies indicate phenomenal potential for passing information and storage of data using light. What's next? Keep your eyes peeled, you just never know!

Bird's First Aid Kit

Nobody ever wants to see accidents happen, but all of us should be prepared in case one does. A fully-loaded first aid kit is a very good thing to have, in an emergency! But just what do you need to put in such a kit? Do *you* have the supplies you'll need should an emergency arise?

It can be difficult to think of and prepare for possible future problems, when you have a pet who is lively, bright, colourful, cheerful, and chipper. Yet that is *exactly* the time we should be taking steps to see that our pet or pets remain healthy and vigorous throughout their lives.

It's not always all that easy to know what to include when assembling an emergency care kit for a pet bird. Birds hide illness so well that it is quite common to hear a pet owner state that they once had a lovely bird, and yet one day it simply fell over dead, with no warning.

In most cases, there actually *were* warning signs, but they were so subtle they were not recognized. That kind of thing can happen more easily than many of us like to think, especially for those of us new to birdkeeping. It can take some time to learn to correctly read the tiny clues of body language and change in habits that are often the only outward symptoms of any bird's developing illness.

Unless these symptoms are recognized early enough, too often there will be little if anything that can be done by the time the illness is obvious. Because of this, some avian veterinarians will actually refuse to see or treat small birds. Their reasoning is that too often it is not until the bird is on death's doorstep that the owner realizes that it is sick and brings it into the clinic for examination.

When any creature is so near death, treating them is touch-and-go, and often fails. These vets feel that their lack of ability to successfully treat these birds impairs their chances of developing a good relationship with a customer, and worse, fear that such an experience can lead to mistrust and suspicion of all vets. They hope to build a better relationship with their customers by avoiding these failures. While this may work, it leaves some potential customers out in the cold.

Too few practicing veterinarians have much if any kind of experience working with songbirds these days; they are not a common pet, and while canaries *are* used in some research projects, little to no scientific research has been done on the maintenance of health and longevity for pet songbirds. By default, that information usually comes from longer-term canary caretakers and breeders, who have found by long experience, usually involving a great deal of trial-and-error, what works for them. Their eyes have learned through long practice to spot illnesses or other potential problems while they are still early in development, when dealing with them is so much easier.

One problem exists in this scenario, yet few seem to see it. That problem is the widely differing goals of the breeder versus the pet keeper. Some of the breeder's most useful tools are simply too expensive or too time-consuming for the owner of a single pet to adopt, and a show breeder who is used to thinking in terms of raising and showing his stock may not be able to fully understand or anticipate the needs and wants of a pet owner.

What's needed is a 'translator', a person able to understand both worlds, and mediate between the two whenever necessary. Avian vets are in an admirable position to be able to do this.

In the best possible world, a pet owner will live near an avian vet who has a working relationship with one or more canary breeders. I wish more canary breeders and avian vets would attempt to establish such a relationship, because it can be so very beneficial to all.

Ideally in such a partnership, the breeder has access to a great deal of knowledge, equipment, and resources through his or her contact with the vet, while the vet will have access to a depth of actual hands-on experience in understanding, diagnosing, handling and caring for small songbirds that would otherwise take him or her years to accumulate.

Given that signs of illness in birds are so subtle, no attempt will be made here to establish a method by which you will be able to diagnose an ill bird. That should be left to the experts. But do watch for any changes of behaviour, such as a lively bird becoming lethargic, or a singing bird becoming silent; these are indications that changes are happening.

One symptom especially to watch for, is that of the bird spending a lot of its time fluffed up as if for sleeping, during the day. Generally, with few exceptions, this is a clear sign that something is wrong.

The first thing to do in such a case is to get the bird some heat. The second is to contact a good avian vet, and arrange for a visit. Both should be done quickly.

Since that visit needs must fall within operating hours, it is a good idea for every bird owner to have a basic first aid kit on hand, to know how to use it if needed, and how to provide emergency care for an ill (or suspected ill) bird, until a visit to an avian vet can be arranged.

These are some of the items, large and small, that I like to keep in my own 'Birdie First Aid Kit';

➤ Contact info, location, and hours for a reliable local avian vet. I keep this info with my emergency kit, because during an emergency is the time I will most need it, and have the least time to look it up.

➤ A Hospital cage. My hospital cage is an old, clean 10 gallon aquarium tank, with a plastic grill that fits onto the top. I can throw a towel over the top if needed, or leave it open for air to come in through the grill.

➢ A means of providing supplemental heat to the bird while in the tank. If you have a specially designed hospital cage, it may already have a built-in heating unit, but otherwise you need to choose an arrangement to provide some kind of supplemental heat, so important to a sick bird. All of the following work quite well;

➢ A heating pad, placed under one end of the tank with a firmly towel-wrapped hot water bottle placed above it to hold and moderate the heat. You can use a thick jute or hemp cord to tie the towel firmly onto the hot water bottle, this will look like a 'perch' to the bird, and the familiar look of it will help him be more inclined to sit on top of the hot water bottle. (add no other perches to the cage)

➢ A ceramic heat lamp. These can be useful, but they emit heat from above rather than below, which I prefer.

➢ A lizard 'hot rock' might work for you. These can sometimes have spots hot enough to burn little feet, so it's best to wrap it in a towel before placing it in the tank, if you decide to use one. As with the hot water bottle, tie the towel on. This serves two purposes; it helps to ensure that the towel won't slip off, and, also very important, it helps create a visual impression for the bird that here is the perch.

➢ You will need a thermometer to measure the level of heat in the warm end of the tank. Ideally you want to ensure that the bird is comfortable, and can choose a cooler spot or a warmer spot, as he wishes. If the bird is huddled in the warm area, raise the heat a little— if it tries to get as far away from the heat as it can, lower it. Too hot can be as bad or worse, than too cool!

➢ Clean plain smooth towels or paper towels for lining the bottom of the tank. It's handy to have several, so you can replace them as needed, and wash them later at leisure.

➢ A small pair of sharp scissors. Handy for all sorts of things.

➢ A small jar of unbleached white flour, for assisting in stopping bleeding. Quikstop, often recommended, does work, but stings like fury. Flour is cheaper and just as effective. (Note that corn starch does *not* work to assist in clotting.)

➢ Several small, shallow, undecorated, hard-to-tip-over china soy sauce dishes (or something similar) to hold seed, prepared soft foods or greens, and drinking water. Keep all such items near the cooler end of the tank, so they will not spoil so fast.

➢ Handfeeding formula. Although meant for use when handfeeding young birds, it also works well for birds who are too sick and/or too weak to eat enough food to support themselves on their own. Some use a feeding syringe to offer the food to the bird, but with smaller birds this can be quite difficult. I prefer instead to use a flat-tipped straw, such as is used for eating slushies or ice-cream-and-soda floats, or the broad end of the applicator that comes with the plastic leg bands.

A tiny spoon may do as well; just tap the side of the beak, and when the bird opens it, put the spoon into the mouth and let the bird bite down on it, then pull the spoon out. This is a more natural way for a small bird to eat, and avoids the chance of accidental aspiration which can happen so easily when feeding small birds with a syringe.

➢ A bulb-tipped dropper. This is especially useful for offering the single drops needed for some medication doses.

➢ A good pair of band cutters; this, in my mind, is a must-have. They can come in *very* useful! Before trying to use them on a bird, get some experience by placing bands on soft green-barked twigs such as willow. Practice cutting the bands off the twigs until you can do it leaving the tender bark entirely unscarred. Once you can do that, you can safely remove a band from any canary's leg, should it become necessary. (Or if you have just one pet, you could just ask your avian vet to remove the band for you)

➢ Vet wrap, or some kind of similar bandaging material. Vet-wrap is made to stick only to itself, rather than feathers or skin. It can be very useful in the case of a splayed leg, or a broken wing or leg; ask your vet to let you have some for your kit. You may also find something similar for sale in a medical supply store.

➢ Plastic drinking straws, (or use a piece of the flat-tipped feeding straws mentioned above). A short piece of straw, slit down the side, makes a good splint in the case of a broken leg. Stop any bleeding, then wrap a short piece of straw *lightly* around the leg and tie in place with a small piece of vet wrap. Then make arrangements to see your vet ASAP!

➢ I like to keep a small jug of distilled water along with some alcohol for use in disinfecting if needed, some plain dry cous-cous, and a supply of electrolytes, either fluid (which must be replaced regularly, since they age) in a sealed bag, or the tablets that are meant to be dissolved in distilled water, in my kit.

➢ I usually will also have a small bottle each of Scatt or Ivomec (for treating mites or other pest infestations), Diatomaceous Earth, (to get rid of ants and other such pests in the surrounding or cage environment), a jar of Prime vitamin/mineral supplement with probiotics, a bottle of Calcivet supplement (for treating egg-binding), and some Avi-Culture, a good avian-specific probiotic.

➢ Last but not least, is a small collection of Bach flower remedies, for a variety of uses. For example I have found the Rescue Remedy compound to be useful when treating birds in shock.

This is by no means a complete list of items possible to include in an emergency first-aid kit for your bird/s; but this collection works well for me at the moment. As I learn more, these items may change, but hopefully for now this will be enough to get you started.

All it takes is some research and a bit of imagination to decide what items will best suit your own particular needs. Then you can prepare, clean, and assemble everything you think you may need, so that if or when an emergency *should* happen to arise, you will be as well prepared for it as anybody could manage to be!

by R C McDonald

Encouraging Beneficials

There's more and more discussions in the news these days of the use of bio-friendly products such as probiotics, and how they can be of assistance in establishing good health and disease resistance in living organisms, in both personal and pet health.

It really is rather impressive how beneficial the use of a living probiotic culture can be, if you have access to a good product and use it properly. I've seen problems ranging from simple digestive upset to persistent yeast or fungal infections that resisted all other medical treatment make a sudden turn-around under the influence of a strong, active probiotic culture, in humans as well as in birds.

Probiotics provide assistance to our essential digestive enzymes and encourage and assist the beneficial bacteria required by our bodies in order to properly digest our food. Normally these are cultured within the gut, but stress, poor diet, or the use of antibiotics can deplete the body's natural supplies to the point where these bacteria can no longer reproduce. In order to get the gut functioning normally again, it is necessary to replace them.

Once you've done that, how do you go about encouraging such cultures to thrive on their own, without needing constant renewal from outside sources? 'Scientific facts' are changing every day, as more is learned about how a living body's elements function and interact. This is echoed on a larger scale in the natural world; examples of co-operation between different elements or groups to produce results beneficial to all the living things involved, are found everywhere in nature.

Some of the nastiest diseases in humans or in birds involve problems caused by moulds. I'm personally quite allergic to many common moulds, and my body lets me know in no uncertain fashion when they're around! I've had to learn how to discourage their growth, rather than just battling them; getting rid of moulds entirely is simply not possible. The stronger the chemicals you use, the more you foster the mould's chemical resistance, and the more they will try to grow. Moulds are very adaptable!

Moulds and fungi are interesting elements of the natural world, and although in general I don't much like having them around, I have to admit they do have their place. Their presence is an excellent indicator that something is out of balance in the environment where they're appearing; while their spores tend to be almost anywhere, the mould itself only appears when conditions favour its growth.

This means that those conditions are balanced to foster fungal growths, rather than the beneficial bacteria and enzymes which would normally flourish, and which help the environment— without as well as within our bodies— to achieve its own state of balance.

These beneficial bacteria exist in one form or another throughout the entire environment, wherever life is found. With a little care and attention, we can foster their growth, and when we do, their presence (and the slightly acidified environmental conditions which encourages and supports them) alone will discourage most of the harmful moulds and such from appearing.

Some fungi thrive in slightly acidic conditions; most mushrooms, for example. Some of those are friendly. But that leads into another area of discussion, so we'll go back to moulds for now. Moulds growing on soaking and/or sprouting seed can be very discouraging, particularly to a new birdkeeper. It *is* possible, though, to discourage them from showing up. There's various methods that work fairly well, but one of the best I've found involves adding natural cider vinegar to the water used for soaking and rinsing the seeds, as well as using it for cleansing anything in the surrounding environment. Luckily, cider vinegar is usually quite cheap and easy to get.

If you plan to use cider vinegar, first you'll need to figure out how much acidification your water supply needs, to achieve a roughly 6.0 - 6.5% or so acid balance. Plan on acidifying all the water you use— including the water used to soak the seeds, the water you clean your counters with, the water you rinse the soaking seeds with, etc. Because of this you'll be working with fairly large quantities, so be careful to use enough cider vinegar— a little too much is better than not quite enough.

There's lots of ways to test your water. Some drug stores still sell litmus paper, an older time-tested method, and many pet stores sell water acidity test kits for use with fish tanks. These tests generally work well on ordinary water too. Just add cider vinegar a teaspoon or so at a time to a couple of cups of water, stir until its blended in, and test, until you find the right proportion of cider vinegar to add to your water.

Using raw, natural, non-pasteurized cider vinegar fosters and assists the process of establishing the presence of beneficial bacteria, because it is already alive with existing beneficials; they're concentrated in the 'mother' of the vinegar, which forms near the bottom of the container, but also exist throughout the entire batch. Using this natural source will help establish the process much more quickly than using diluted acetic acid (which is all most white vinegars are).

Another assist to the process is to use wooden chopping blocks and cutting boards, counters, etc, wherever you can; most wood is naturally slightly acidic. This helps to foster beneficial bacteria and discourage the unwanted kinds.

Cure the wood with lemon oil and maybe a little beeswax or linseed oil, and you will have a lovely finish that will itself tend to encourage the presence of beneficials.

The nice thing about all this is that if you persist in adapting this 'acidification process' to the whole home environment, making an effort to sustain a slightly acidified balance throughout, eventually you will get to the point where you won't have to worry about problems with mould anywhere! I regularly mix up a small cup of agar-agar with some water, and leave the mix sitting out on a counter or a shelf for a few days; if there is any mould spores in the area, they will find the agar and begin thriving.

These days, usually all I get is a leaf of dried-up agar, after a week or so. That confirms that the beneficials in that room are doing well, even though I tend to know that already; my allergies begin acting up the moment there's even a few more than normal mould spores around. In the beginning, while I was still dealing with eliminating mould from my living space, the agar cultures offered me a chance to catch and identify the culprit, before it got too well established.

I used to get sick for months on end from moulds and mould allergies, before I learned how to discourage their activities in my household environment. That doesn't tend to happen much anymore. Nowadays I can grow soak seed for my birds trouble-free, and not have to worry about their encountering heaps of mould spores when eating it. That could cause them big trouble.

Some birdkeepers will tell you that soaked seed mixes are dangerous to use because without proper care, a batch might become contaminated with moulds. But avoiding healthy foods because there might be a problem, reminds me of the kind of reasoning that might be used to say, for example, "Breathing pure oxygen is dangerous, so let's get rid of all the oxygen, so we can breathe without danger!"

While such logic can and does sound silly when stated in such a manner, similar logic is used every day by far too many people as an excuse for avoiding substances or foods that could be of great benefit, if used properly.

In the case of soaked seed, all that's needed is to prepare the soaked seeds in a way that will not encourage moulds to form in the first place. There's plenty of reasons to use a good soak seed mix, as many wild birds of a wide variety of species could tell us, if they could talk.

Soaked and sprouting seeds are a naturally-occurring wild food in many areas of the world, particularly during spring and fall. They assist in enhancing overall condition and health, and they are widely used by a great variety of avian species in the wild as an essential ingredient of a natural nestling food. Our birds love eating soaked seeds, and youngsters raised on a good soak seed and nestling food mixture will wean naturally and easily.

In short, a properly used soak seed mix will provide excellent results that are difficult to achieve any other way.

Using soaked and/or sprouted seeds that include mould spores can lead to problems with disease and going light; but this won't happen if the soak seed mix is used and prepared properly. I haven't had a problem with any of my birds going light for going on close to two decades now.

The natural world, with it's multitudinous and interactive systems, has had eons to work out its checks and balances and arrive at efficient, workable results. More often than we know, it also contains solutions to problems commonly encountered in aviculture, just waiting for us to notice them.

All we need to do is learn to understand just what it is we're looking at, then we will be able to solve our problems by simply deciding how we wish to emulate that aspect of nature's solutions in our own birdroom.

Overgrown Beak

As spring approaches and breeding season draws ever nearer, bird keepers everywhere begin to check their birds, trimming nails and examining vents, trying to ensure that every bird in their care is in top condition. Every once in a while a bird will be found whose upper or (more rarely) lower beak is longer than it should be. What causes this, and what's to be done about it?

Our bird's beaks are designed by nature to assist them in eating their food. Many birds, including canaries, have beaks that evolved especially to help assist in the chore of cracking and eating various kinds of seed, which make up a good part of their diet.

Most birds manage to keep their beaks in good shape with no help from their caretakers; frequent 'wiping' on perches, along with regular chewing on a cuttlebone or mineral block, as well as gnawing on other tough items such as the stems and leaves of dark leafy greens, all contribute to this, helping ensure that the top and bottom of the beak stay about the same length, so the bird is able to easily eat their food.

But sometimes things get out of balance, and one part of the beak will become overgrown, resulting in an extension of the upper or lower beak. Whatever the cause, this must be corrected, or the bird will soon find itself unable to eat properly.

Sometimes an overgrown beak can have a simple cause, for example due to the bird, for whatever reason, not chewing on its cuttlebone or mineral block. There is a variety of reasons this might happen; perhaps the cuttlebone is placed so the bird finds it frightening and won't approach it, or perhaps it is fixed so the hard side is facing inwards, rather than the softer, chewable side.

In the first case, simply changing the cuttlebone from upright to horizontal may do the trick; others will break a cuttlebone into pieces, making them seem less threatening, and fasten the smaller pieces into the cage for chewing on. Always make sure that the softer side of the cuttlebone faces inwards, towards the bird; if you can't scratch the surface with your fingernail, the bird won't be able to chew on it either.

Similar problems can arise with mineral blocks; many are made for hookbills, and are too hard for the smaller species such as canaries and most finches. Before you buy a mineral block, make certain that it is made to be useable by the smaller species. Similarly to the cuttlebone, you should be able to easily scratch the surface with your fingernail.

If the cause of the overgrown beak is due to a lack of chewable items, these simple remedies should work nicely. But what about those birds who have and use a cuttlebone and/or a mineral block, but still have an overgrown beak?

In this case, finding the cause may be more problematic. Overproduction of keratinous materials such as beak and toenails can be a sign of liver problems. This could be due to dietary problems, but may also be exacerbated by an inherited genetic tendency. In either case, a long hard look at the diet is necessary. Liver problems need not be deadly, but can and often do take a fair bit of time and patience to remedy.

The first thing to do is to make sure you have the bird in question in it's own secure quarters, rather than in a shared flight or breeding cage. It must be safe from stress and have free access to plenty of fresh water. Look closely at the amount and quality of protein you are offering in the diet. Canaries require less protein than most hookbills, and will do nicely on a regular diet consisting of 12%-14% protein. The *kind* of protein is important, too; most vegetable proteins are incomplete, meaning the bird will not benefit as much from these types of proteins. Worse, a diet based on incomplete proteins leaves the body lacking certain essential nutrients, which can in turn also cause problems.

The proteins from meat tend to be much more complete, but improper processing or handling during preparation of food can cause the spread of disease. Due to this fact, along with the higher cost of materials, most of the protein in many commercial diets (even pellets) is vegetable or seed based.

Careful dietary balancing can blend several types of vegetable proteins to produce complete proteins that will digest fully, but you need to do some research if you want to blend your own foods. A good example of vegetable proteins that complement each other to produce a more complete and digestible protein, is corn and beans. Alone, each adds only a partial protein to the whole. Together, the proteins complement each other and are much more digestible.

What this means is that it's a good idea, when choosing a basic food for your canary, to look a little further than the analysis of percentage of proteins and fats; you want to also take note of the *kind* of proteins and fats. Are they animal based or vegetable or seed based? How likely are they to be complete? If they are seed or vegetable based, you will need to supplement the diet, in order to see that your bird gets the complete nutrition he needs in order to thrive.

Besides kind and quality of protein, dietary fats can cause problems. In fact, too many fats in the diet can stress the heart and kidneys as well as the liver, so it's wise to reduce the overall amount of fats in the diet, when you find a bird with an overgrown beak. Don't eliminate *all* the fat content— just most of it.

At the same time, try to see that the bird gets all the dark leafy greens he can eat— items such as kale, collard greens, dandelions, chickweed or leafy endives. Offer enough so that there is a little left uneaten at the end of the day; that way you can be sure the bird is getting all he likes. The greens will add extra moisture to the overall diet, and will also help to ease the burden on the liver, allowing it to begin to flush out any excess accumulated toxins.

So you've reduced the amount of proteins and fats in the diet, and have seen to it that what's still included is as easy to digest as possible. Now, see that he has access to plenty of easy-to-eat, easily digestible soft foods like cooked rice, rolled oats or cous-cous. The idea is to offer foods that will cause the least amount of stress to an already-over-worked liver.

Make the cous-cous or rice with apple juice instead of water, this will help a little to encourage his liver to slowly begin to detoxify. Don't try to rush the process though; liver detoxification is much the best if it is accomplished slowly and steadily. That's because cleansing out the accumulated toxins entails slowly flushing these toxins out of the liver and into the bloodstream, where they can be processed and removed.

If you encourage his liver to detoxify too quickly, it will in effect dump a bunch of toxins into his bloodstream all at once. This in turn will make him feel quite sick. This can result in his eating or drinking less, which will undo any good achieved through the cleansing.

The trick is to encourage the body to heal itself slowly and steadily, while allowing him to feel good enough to remain interested in eating, allowing him to keep his energy levels up with the high carb content. Slow and steady is key.

Organically grown apples are wonderful for encouraging a slow detoxification of the liver, so you can go ahead and offer a good-sized wedge of apple every day, if you happen to have a good source of them. They will help encourage his liver to start cleansing out toxins, without rushing things too fast.

Milk thistle is often mentioned as a good detoxification agent as well, and yes, it can help— but again, care must be taken to see that the process is not rushed. Strictly limit the amount of milk thistle offered, to be sure the cleansing process proceeds gradually and gently, with as little stress to the bird as possible.

It's a good idea to add a little extra vitamin B to his diet, while all this is going on— this is the 'stress' vitamin, and it will help him to resist becoming ill, and will also assist in encouraging the detoxification process. The easiest way to add some extra vitamin B to the diet is to go into a health or natural foods store and pick up some nutritional yeast.

Try offering him some in a little cup, and see if he will eat it on its own— sometimes they will (many critters, including birds, seem to regard this stuff as being rather like 'cheese', and will eat it greedily). If he won't try it this way, then try sprinkling some onto his soft foods or greens; I love it on my salads, and often, so do canaries. If all else fails, mix a little in with some prepared cous-cous; it's a rare canary who won't eat that.

I have found it helps tremendously to provide plenty of live probiotics in the diet during the cleansing process. If you are unsure whether the probiotics you have on hand actually offer live beneficial bacteria, there's a simple test you can do; just add a bit to some room-temperature milk, and let it stand overnight in a warm— not hot!— location.

If by the morning the milk has thickened a little, then you can be sure you have live beneficial bacteria in your probiotics. If on the other hand, the milk seems to be the same as ever, your probiotics are useless— throw them out and get some fresh.

Whatever else you do, make certain that the bird has access to plenty of good clean water, and make sure that it really is *clean!* If you've been using tap water, boil it and cool it before offering it, and make sure to wash drinkers daily— if you've been letting them go for a day or two, it could be that he's decided that he doesn't like the taste and isn't drinking enough. Plenty of clean water is *essential* to the detoxification process— without lots of water present in the system, the toxins can't be flushed from the liver.

In fact, if there is one element that by itself can tip the scales one way or another, water is it. Access to plenty of clean, safe water is *very* important, in order to keep the body and especially the inner organs properly healthy and functioning well.

Without adequate water, the organs that act as filters for the bloodstream (the liver and kidneys) cannot process all the toxins from the diet, which in turn causes the excess to accumulate in the body, particularly the organs and joints. An ongoing lack of adequate water in the body's system creates an inability to flush these toxins out, and allows them to build up over time to the point where they begin to cause problems such as gout.

Keeping the stress levels as low as possible is another aspect of detoxification, and an important one. The bird must have its own cage, so there is no competition for food or water, and also to make it easier for you to keep an eye on him. This also makes it easier to keep an eye on his droppings; are they large, small, wet, dry? The state of the droppings is a good clue to what is really going on inside your bird.

Of course, after you have done everything you can to see that an overgrown beak won't happen again, you still may need to trim it. It's best, if you can, to have somebody such as an avian vet or an experienced breeder, someone who knows just how the beak should look. This way they can directly examine the bird and tell you if, in their opinion, it requires trimming or not.

Sometimes it's better to leave it alone and let it wear away gradually, while other times the beak will have to be trimmed, or the bird won't be able to eat. It all depends on just how and why the beak became overgrown in the first place.

Mites!

Lately you have been finding what looks at first glance to be iron shavings here and there in your bird's cage, as if somebody had been dropping tiny iron filings around the ends of the perches. But on closer inspection, these little 'shavings' can be seen to be moving, trying to get away from the light.

Like so many others, you may have gone out and bought one of those little 'mite protectors' sold in pet stores and attached it to your bird's cage, only to discover that it made no difference at all. Your treasured pet has been acting lethargic lately, and you're at a loss as to how to proceed to get rid of these pests.

The above description is similar to comments regularly heard from those whose pet or breeding cages have become infested with the pest most usually known as the 'Black Mite', or 'Red Mite'. These mites actually are normally coloured a semi-translucent greyish black, but appear red when full of blood.

They are among the most difficult of all bird pests to get rid of, as they don't live on the bird, but instead live and reproduce elsewhere in the environment, feeding on the bird but not staying on it. They do not like light, and will shelter during the day in any nook and cranny they can find — under the paper lining the bottom of the cage, in the little niches at the ends of the perches, under the cage tray, or in the corners around it.

Sometimes they will leave the cage entirely and take shelter nearby. They have been found hiding in electronic

by R C McDonald

equipment, under rugs, and on occasion, have even been found hiding in or around electrical sockets or in the walls!

These pests are tiny members of a group related to the spider families, which unfortunately means they are quite resistant to anti-mite preparations. Luckily, pyrethrum-based preparations do discourage them. Other products such as Scatt or Ivermectin can't get rid of them for you— but *can* help deter them.

Treating your birds with Scatt or Ivermectin will not end an infestation of these mites, but it *will* kill any mites who actually suck your bird's blood. This is a good place to start, but you will still need to take steps to get rid of the mites living in or near the cage itself and in the surrounding environment.

Depending on where and how you keep your bird(s), this may or may not be all that easy to do— if your birds live outside, it may prove difficult to impossible. Sadly, in many areas these days it is just not safe to keep pet birds living outside, thanks to all the diseases and pests found in the outdoor environments.

Infestation of these mites in pet birds can be due to exposure to wild birds— and it could well be a rather indirect exposure. For example, during the spring breeding season, if you have wild birds nesting on the outside of your house, the mites, who locate their prey with heat sensors, may leave their hosts and discover a way into the house (say, through an open window), where they will hide during the day, then come out at night to feast on your pet's blood.

The first step to take is to administer a tiny drop of Scatt or Ivermectin to your bird. Don't use the dropper that comes with the bottle, it will produce too big a drop, which could be deadly for your canary— these medicines are very powerful. If possible, get a small syringe or dental syringe from your druggist or dentist. If it has a steel needle at the tip, blunt it with a rasp so as to be sure not to hurt anybody by accidentally poking them with it. Then use the smallest drop you can get it to produce.

Get a friend to hold your bird, and use a damp sponge to wipe away the feathers at the back of his neck, until you can see the small patch of bare skin that all canaries have at the base of the neck behind the back of their skull. Get a little liquid into the syringe, then gently squeeze until a small drop forms at the tip.

Touch the drop to the canary's skin, rather than just squeezing until the drop breaks free. This will allow you to be sure you have used a small enough drop so as to not harm your bird.

Neither Scatt not Ivermectin will not get rid of the mites themselves, but it *will* see that they will not stay on your bird, and if any do bite him, they will die. However, if there is enough mites living in the area near his cage, they will continue to bite him, and the loss of blood will not be good for him. Especially if it goes on for too long, loss of blood can be quite dangerous for a canary— being so tiny, they don't exactly have a lot of blood to spare.

So the next chore is to get rid of the mites in and around the bird cage, and anywhere else they might be lurking. Start by giving the cage a thorough cleaning, paying special attention to any nooks and crannies that may have been providing shelter. You don't need to use anything special to do this, just plenty of soap, some warm water, and attention to thoroughness and detail. Make very sure that you clean and scrape and soap every corner, nook, cranny, and niche. If you are in doubt as to how effective your cleaning is, go ahead and throw the item in question out— better safe than sorry, with these little beasts!

This should clean out living mites, but won't affect the eggs, which are incredibly hardy— even exposure to a hard vacuum (no air) won't kill these eggs! So, the next task is to prevent reinfestation, and to kill any mites which happen to hatch from eggs that may still be present.

The best way I've found to do that is to use a preparation used in gardens and fish ponds, known as 'diatomaceous earth'. You don't want to use the stuff made for fish ponds, as it is ground too finely and can cause damage to both you and your birds, if you should happen to inhale it, or if a little gets into your eyes. It is only safe for use in water. There is, however, a grade of diatomaceous earth which is not ground so finely, made for use in gardens. Several brands of pesticides on the market include diatomaceous earth— some include other (toxic) ingredients, while others contain only diatomaceous earth.

Since you definitely don't want the kind that includes other toxic materials which might affect your canaries, you will need to be very careful to read labels and get the right product when buying. You want plain diatomaceous earth, made for use in gardens, and without anything added; be careful, because some mixes include pesticide, something you do *not* want around your canaries. I usually have to get the staff at a gardening center to help me out, in order to make sure that I get the right stuff. They've always been very good about this.

Diatomaceous earth comes from fossilized sea snails, which when ground up consist of thousands of tiny but very sharp particles. In the garden it is used by sprinkling it on the ground, or in a thick ring about plants. It kills bugs when they crawl over it by piercing their chitin and causing them to dehydrate. Because it is not ground too finely, it will settle quite quickly to the ground, and, once it has settled, it is not dangerous to people or pets— including birds.

BUT until it has settled, make absolutely sure that neither you nor your canary breathe any in. This stuff can damage eyes and lungs, thanks to those same tiny sharp particles. So I recommend removing your birds while applying it, and wearing a face mask to be on the safe side. Then give it time to settle before replacing the birds. I find an hour or so works well.

You want to dust the diatomaceous earth anywhere the mites might try to hide. This means all nooks and crannies in the birdcage, including under the tray and between and

Canary Crazy

under any papers used for lining the tray, in all corners and such, and especially including the ends of the perches and any other similar hiding places.

If you use a cage cover, don't forget to clean and treat that as well! Wash it three or four times with lots of soap and bleach, then dust it heavily with diatomaceous earth, let it sit for a week or so, then wash it again. In the meantime, use a different cage cover, or better, no cover at all, to reduce mite hideouts. It's a good idea to remove and wash any seed or treat cups too, as these can also provide shelter for the little monsters.

I had to deal with a huge infestation of mites a few years back, and tried all sorts of ways to get rid of them, before I happened on the combination of using a pyrethrum-based spray, then treating the birds with Scatt or Ivermectin while using diatomaceous earth throughout the birdroom. I found that, while no single product was 100% effective when used alone, in combination they worked very well. Eventually the pests finally stopped reappearing a few days or weeks later.

There is nothing so disheartening as thinking that you have gotten rid of a pest, only to find its come back again some time later. For awhile, I was afraid that I would never be able to get entirely rid of these mites in my birdroom.

But I have used and recommended this combination several times now, in my own and in others' aviaries, and it has always done the trick. The main thing to remember is that in order for this combination to work properly, you need to be extremely thorough.

I then found that these nasty little mites tended to put in a reappearance every year or two, but over five years of trial-and-error happened on a method which works as a preventative against reinfestation. It seems almost too simple, but since implementing it, I have not seen any more mites.

All I did was place all my bird cages on stands— then I got some of the sticky stuff used by farmers to protect their orchards from certain pests. It's called 'tanglefoot', and is painted in a band about the trunk, making it impossible for bugs to climb up the tree from the ground— they get to the sticky part, get stuck, and die.

There's different brands on the market, but if you go to a gardening center and ask if they have anything that works that way, they will probably know just what to give you. Just make sure there's no toxins in it that can harm your canaries.

All I did was 'paint' a wide band of tanglefoot about each leg of each stand. I have to be careful when moving the stands not to grab the sticky part, of course, but for me it's well worth the trouble, as I have not seen a single mite in my birdroom since.

This is what worked for me, to get rid of those nasty mites, and I hope this approach will work as well for you, should these tiny pests ever appear in your home or birdroom.

Resource List

Buhach Pyrethrin Powder
Scatt or Ivermectin
Diatomaceous Earth
Tangle Guard Tree Barrier

Pet Birds & the Avian Flu

'Avian flu' are two words that are showing up more and more in the news these days, and as fear grows and rumors spread, it is becoming difficult to separate fact from fiction. Little to no factual information has so far been presented to pet bird owners by authorities regarding how the avian flu might impact them or their birds, but discussions flourish and rumors grow, seeming sometimes to spread at close to light-speed. Meanwhile, more and more pet bird owners are wondering what the real facts are.

For all the ongoing talk about 'bird flu' or avian influenza in or out of the news, hard data seems to be at a minimum. What *is* known is, while there are dozens if not hundreds of known strains of avian influenza, so far there has been only two causing all the trouble. These strains are termed 'avian influenza H5N1 and H7N9'.

These particular strains of avian influenza are the only ones that have been known to infect some (very few) humans; but the spread of H5N1 from one ill person to another has rarely been reported, and transmission has not been observed to continue beyond one person, while human flu viruses kill thousands (elders and children especially) every year. H7N9 has been seen to spread among ferrets, with only mild clinical signs. Pigs have also proven to be susceptible to this virus, but studies have shown that it cannot be spread either pig-to-pig, or from pigs to other animals. Researchers say that in all cases where humans had died or become extremely ill additional factors were involved.

There are only three 'A' subtypes of known human flu viruses (H1N1, H1N2, and H3N2). Influenza A viruses are found in a great many species of mammals as well as birds and humans, and are constantly changing. Any strain from any source might adapt over time, with enough exposure, to infect and spread among humans.

Dr Leonard G. Horowitz, D.M.D., M.A., M.P.H., specialist on emerging diseases, says, "At this writing (Oct 2005), the H5N1 avian flu virus is said to have killed 'about 65 people' in Southeast Asia during the past two years. Little to no data is available on these individuals who most commonly had immune-compromising medical conditions. Further, all deaths were in Asian countries with questionable health services. Conversely, other forms of flu kill more than 40,000 North Americans annually, generally the immune-compromised elderly."

The US Department of Health and Human Services Centers for Disease Control and Prevention says, "The risk from bird flu is generally low to most people because the viruses occur mainly among birds and do not usually infect humans. However, during an outbreak of bird flu among poultry (domesticated chicken, ducks, turkeys), there is a possible risk to people who have contact with infected birds or surfaces that have been contaminated with excretions from infected birds."

They continued, "The ...outbreak of avian influenza H5N1 among poultry in Asia and Europe is an example of a bird flu outbreak that has caused human infections and deaths. In such situations, people should avoid contact with infected birds or contaminated surfaces, and should be careful when handling and cooking poultry.

"In rare instances, limited human-to-human spread of the H5N1 virus has occurred, but transmission has not been observed to continue beyond one person."

They go on to state that since all flu viruses are known to mutate relatively rapidly compared to other disease organisms, there is a possibility that this virus may one day develop the ability to spread from human to human, but so far most known cases have occurred from contact with infected poultry or contaminated surfaces.

According to the CDC website quoted above, the risk to North Americans from bird flu outbreaks in Asia is very low, but they do state that travellers returning from affected countries in Asia could be infected if they were exposed to the virus. They recommend that anybody travelling to a country with a known outbreak of the H5N1 or H7N9 viruses avoid poultry farms, contact with animals in live food markets, and any surfaces that may be contaminated with feces from poultry or other animals. They do not, however, recommend any travel restrictions be placed on travel to affected countries.

Although it's not said in so many words, these facts indicate that it is likely that good hygiene, cleanliness, and proper care and attention to handling food products, especially raw meats, along with thorough cooking practices, can minimize or even eliminate the risks of direct exposure. It is difficult to imagine that anybody anywhere would work with poultry— especially raw meat products— without careful washing of hands and working surfaces before and afterwards, yet it seems that this is the most common means for the infection to spread.

There has been a fair bit of conjecture that migrating wildfowl could spread the virus over a wider territory, but when examined more closely, this idea seems unlikely. For one thing, while many wild birds are known to carry one or more avian flu viruses in their system— generally these viruses are dormant.

In order to be transmitted, the virus must be active within the bird's system, which will cause the bird to become sick, and in turn will cause the virus to be shed through saliva, nasal secretions, and feces.

by R C McDonald

If you consider the normally occurring stresses and strains on migrating fowl, it seems highly unlikely that such a sick bird would be able to migrate in the first place. Sick birds are rarely if ever seen in migrating flocks— they just don't have the energy to keep up, and instead stay behind until they are well enough to travel.

In Britain, the Royal Society for the Protection of Birds is trying to institute a ban on bird fairs, saying that the trade in birds, especially wild-caught birds, could pose a greater risk of exposure than natural migration patterns.

Meanwhile, Dutch researchers have injected a virus sample taken from a fatal human case into short-haired domestic kittens, and discovered that cats can apparently be infected with, carry, and transmit the H5N1 virus. Their results stated that six kittens became infected, but did not mention the total number of test subjects used in their sample.

One of the biggest threats to bird owners and their flocks is fear. In May of 2004, an outbreak of an H6 avian influenza virus in British Columbia's Fraser Valley led to what officials termed 'depopulation' of 40 commercial chicken farms. But the toll did not stop there; several local bird hobbyists keeping a variety of birds ranging from pigeons to parrots were forced to allow authorities to 'depopulate' their birdrooms and aviaries.

No testing was done, the officials simply took all the birds they could find within a certain range from the commercial farms, whether there was any real risk of exposure or not.

In one case, the birds were very expensive imported Birmingham Roller pigeons. While his birds were being carted off for suffocation, some wild pigeons and ducks landed on or near the owner's barn. He questioned the officials about what they were going to do about all the wild birds that had a much greater chance of having been exposed, only to be told that control of these wild birds was not in their mandate!

Key West Chicken activist Katha Sheehan of The Chicken Store, which among other activities operates a chicken rescue, says, "I hardly know where to begin, defending the Key West chickens against all these allegations of being responsible for a bird flu that isn't even in the USA yet. I always wash my hands when I come home off the streets, after using the bathroom, and before eating. Do you? Do your kids?"

She goes on to say, "If you can't 'do' the flu, don't eat the meat! Factory-farmed chicken eggs and meat products from stores are more likely to bring in foreign bugs, than the Conch rooster standing in the driveway. Germs are everywhere! There are staph germs on that hand railing, tetanus in that potting soil and hantavirus in that deer tick—possibly."

It seems to me that there is an obvious four-step solution for pet birds owners; first, attempt to minimize as much as possible any exposure of your pets (feline as well as avian) to wild birds; secondly, avoid direct contact with the feces of potentially exposed birds; thirdly, be careful to wash and disinfect hands and surfaces thoroughly when preparing food, especially when handling raw meat; and fourth, make certain that meat and eggs from potentially susceptible birds are thoroughly cooked before being eaten.

As Katha Sheehan points out, "What is important is good living to keep a healthy immune system. Most of these germs will never find a foothold with us, and panic can only get in the way of rational decision-making. When you find a pigeon (or waterbird) dead on the ground, remember that they, too, sometimes die of old age! As a civilization, by now we should be far beyond that hysterical and barbaric 'holocaust as a solution'."

I can't agree more.

by R C McDonald

Avian Gastric Yeast
(formerly known as 'Megabacteria')

You think your pet canary may have a problem; although he is acting normally, you've observed that his droppings have suddenly become quite greenish. You blamed it on excessive greens and cut out all fruits and vegetables.

Yet days later, your canary's droppings are still green. He has been active the entire time, although lately he's seemed a bit subdued. His appetite has been normal, but little by little he is eating less each day, and has begun to eat mostly treats and soft foods, rather than seed, even though he is always at one food dish or another. His eyes are still shiny and clear, his wings don't droop, his feathers aren't ruffled, and he preens as usual. What could be happening?

Greenish droppings do show up sometimes, and may on occasion be the result of eating a lot of vegetable matter. But if that is not the case, then green droppings can indicate that there is liver stress present. A good look at all food sources is indicated— were his veggies or fruits treated with pesticides, or grown with chemical fertilizers? Sometimes traces of these will remain in the plant, and can't be washed off— and it doesn't take much to stress a canary's liver. Sometimes seed or pellet sources can be contaminated by the urine of mice or rats, and this too can cause a similar problems; such urine is highly toxic to many avian species.

But there is another possibility too, one notoriously difficult to diagnose; infection by Avian Gastric Yeast. This disease at first was known as 'Megabacteria', which is a complete misnomer, since it is not actually a bacteria at all.

Avian Gastric Yeast destroys the proventriculus and results in two main syndromes; a chronic form that causes a long slow wasting disease, often with whole seeds seen in the droppings, and an acute form that causes extreme gastric ulceration, haemorrhage into the bowel, and malena.

This disease is actually a fungal condition, hence the name change. In and of itself it does not cause greenish droppings, however a bird suffering from it will undergo slow starvation, which in turn will cause liver problems and greenish droppings. The acute form may move so fast that this symptom may never appear, but it is often seen in the chronic form.

Once established, such an infection, more often than not, is unresponsive to more common treatments, but will usually respond to treatment with anti-fungals, available only to practicing veterinarians.

Before things get that far, there *are* steps you can take to discourage this invader from thriving in your bird. Avian Gastric Yeast may be found in many environments, but mysteriously enough, often won't seem to bother many birds— it seems they have somehow developed a resistance to infection, thanks either to their diet or their environment, or both.

AGY thrives in moist conditions, so if you have a bath constantly present, that could offer a place to grow. You can also reduce or even eliminate moist fruit and high-water-content greens, except perhaps an occasional small wedge of apple or a similar hard fruit, and plenty of the denser, more nutrient-rich greens.

Canaries, unlike some other avian species, will do just fine without any fruit at all— and besides, unless they are organically grown, apples, oranges, lettuces and celeries in particular tend to have rather high amounts of pesticides used on them; not enough to bother most humans, but too often easily enough to bother a canary.

It's the darker leafy greens that many birds don't get

enough of; kale, collards, leafy endives, and broccoli raba (rapini) are just a few. Those and similar greens can be offered daily, as much as the bird will eat. I've yet to see any problems caused by too many greens of this kind— in every case I know of where that was thought to be a problem, it has always turned out that the actual cause was something else entirely.

Chemically grown greens, particularly those with higher moisture content, *can* tend to encourage the growth of AGY, more so than in organically grown foods. This is because the salt-based fertilizers and pesticide sprays act to kill off, not just pestiferous bugs, but the benign bacteria that thrive in more naturally grown foods.

If you suspect a potential for AGY infection, offer only the dark, mineral-rich lower-moisture greens such as kale, and try to see that your bird's cage remains dry. Make sure, for example, that bath water isn't getting splashed into a seed cup, because if the seed is getting wet, moisture at the bottom of the cup could be helping to cultivate AGY, known to thrive under such conditions.

Another excellent way to build up resistance to AGY and other such problems, is to add a good probiotic to your bird's diet for a while. These are the body's natural controls for infections— they tend to suppress bacterial and fungal growths, because they foster a slightly acidic system, while AGY and other such less benign pests prefer more alkaline conditions.

For the same reason, you can, if you like, add a little raw apple cider vinegar to the water— up to about a tablespoonful or so to a cup of water. Taste it, to check that you've got it right— it should taste very slightly tart, not unpleasant. It will help encourage the probiotics to thrive, and they in turn will help discourage AGY.

It's really rather impressive how beneficial probiotics and raw (unpasteurized) apple cider vinegar can be, especially when used together. I've seen birds who looked to be practically on death's door make a sudden turn-around and begin looking like a whole new bird in just a few days, once cider-vinegar-water and probiotics were added to their diet.

One of the greatest benefits of both, is the fact that they are beneficial whether the bird is sick or not. No matter what, they won't hurt him, and there's a very good chance that they might help.

Please note that just how much vinegar to use depends on the PH of your water. In the Pacific Northwest, the water is already quite acid, so less is needed in comparison to other areas of North America, many of which have fairly alkaline water.

Having fairly alkaline water means you'd have to add a little more vinegar. That's why it's a good idea to check the taste, because the amount needed to get the water 'a little tart' can actually vary quite a lot.

The probiotics act to replace the essential digestive enzymes and beneficial bacteria that a system requires in order to properly digest food. Normally these are cultured within the gut, but stress, poor diet, or the use of antibiotics can deplete the body's supplies to the point where they can no longer reproduce. In order for the gut to function normally again, it is necessary to replace them.

There is a variety of good avian probiotic formulas available, alone or in combination with other ingredients. Vetafarm in Britain produces several good products that include avian-specific probiotics, while in North America we find 'Prime', by Hagen, and Avi-Sci's 'Avi-Culture'.

'Prime' came about as a result of research conducted at the Hagen Avicultural Research Institute (HARI), and is a probiotic-enhanced vitamin and mineral supplement designed to complement the diet of a seed-eating bird through supplying not only necessary nutrients, but avian-specific probiotics as well. This can be handy when you want to include vitamin and mineral supplements with the probiotics you are offering.

If you do buy some Prime be sure to open the box and check the expiry date on the bottom of the bottle; many stores don't know to check this, and so sometimes you will find an expired bottle still on a shelf. Hagen will replace such bottles with fresh, so don't let the store tell you no, they *can* return them and get you a fresh one instead.

Another good probiotic, relatively new to the market but already noted for its potency, is 'Avi-Culture', available from a growing number of vets, or directly from the website at *www.avi-culture.com*. This is a probiotic without any other additives, other than the basics needed to keep the cultures alive. This kind of probiotic is perfect for when you are quite sure that your canary is getting plenty of nutrition, but you want to ensure that he is digesting it all properly, without risking an accidental overdose due to excess vitamins or minerals.

Many probiotics (including Avi-Culture and Prime) come with instructions to offer them in water, but I myself find this method inefficient when working with canaries; these birds just don't drink enough water for the mix to be very effective before it begins to break down and lose potency.

I prefer to serve such supplements in dry form; I put a little into a salt shaker with a few grains of rice (to prevent clumping), then sprinkle a bit on some apple or greens. 'Salt' things fairly heavily the first few days, then cut back to just a dash for a couple of weeks or so. Once his system is back in balance, you won't need to provide them all the time— in fact, some say it's better to not offer them too regularly— but it's handy to keep some around, as you never know when you might need them.

An alternative method is to mix the probiotics into a nestling food, to be served on soak seed (for more about soak seed and nestling food, check the article online at *www.robirda.com/soakseed.html*)

Again, offer a good sized dose for several days in a row, then cut back until after a week or two you are offering little to none.

It should be mentioned that sometimes a bird who is drastically short on digestive enzymes and bacteria will get looser droppings for a few days, when first given probiotics. This is quite normal. The effect is temporary, caused by the body's habit of 'flushing' accumulated unwanted systemic toxins at the first opportunity.

Such changes almost always cease after a few days— if they don't, you will need to consult an experienced avian vet as soon as possible, to find out for sure what's really going on.

by R C McDonald

This is the story of one bird owner's struggle to find the source of the problem killing her pet birds. All bird owners should pay heed to the lessons she learned the hard way, so as to be sure we and our own pet birds don't pay a similar price someday.

Metal Toxicity

by Sharon Klueber

I've been trying to solve a long and frustrating mystery regarding my canaries over the last five or six years. It involved lots of detective work and much agonizing over what could possibly be the cause of the mysterious deaths of five of my birds as well as many visits to a total of four different avian veterinarians.

While I will never know if I have succeeded in figuring out the reason for the deaths of all of my birds, I believe that at last, with the help of a new vet (number four), I have figured out that in this particular who-done-it, metal toxicity is the killer.

Metal toxicity was not one of my original suspects. I had questioned everything else, from where I bought my birds to fumes from my gas kitchen stove to dirty air vents— all were looked at as being possible reasons my birds kept getting sick and dying. I thought I'd taken all necessary precautions to prevent my birds being exposed to any heavy metals— but I was wrong.

Two and a half years ago, when I finally got it into my hard head that you can't house male canaries together in one cage all year round, no matter how large or well appointed the cage, I set about to find the best cages I could for my birds. Galvanized after weld (GAW) cages (also known as 'hot-dipped') looked to be the perfect solution. They were affordable and easy to clean, and I could get them in a size large enough to allow my canaries lots of flying space. Best of all, they were touted as being safe for birds like canaries and finches that don't chew on their cage wire. They were not recommended for parrots, but as I was looking to house my canaries it sounded like the perfect solution.

So I ordered three nice large GAW cages, specifically made for birds, from a reputable business on the internet.

The cages arrived. Before assembling them I scrubbed them down with cider vinegar and a metal brush; a time-consuming and back-breaking process but it was my understanding this would remove any traces of heavy metal that might be on the wire, help to speed along the oxidation of the zinc coating used in GAW wire and help make the cages totally safe for my canaries.

As it turned out, this widely-held belief is wrong. According to Ritchie, Harrison and Harrison, in their publication 'Avian Medicine: Principles and Application', birds can ingest zinc from cages and clips made of galvanized wire.

Toxicity can be *reduced* (but not eliminated) by scrubbing the wire with a brush and vinegar or a mild acidic solution. This removes any loose pieces and the white rust (zinc oxide) which forms on the wire.

Over time more white rust (which is also poisonous) will form, so enclosures must be re-treated periodically.

In their information pages regarding Proper Avian Care, Mickaboo Cockatiel Rescue says: *"If you have a galvanized cage make sure it is electroplated not dipped. (90% of all galvanized cages are dipped). Birds can get zinc poisoning from living in such a cage even if they don't chew on the bars."*

It seems that a lot of the cages on the market today are

by R C McDonald

not safe. If you are buying a cage, make sure you ask questions like "Can you certify in writing that the cage is lead-free and zinc-safe?" *before* you buy it. If the seller cannot answer this question to your satisfaction, don't waste your money, just go somewhere else to buy your cage. There are several cage companies that will certify, in writing, that their cages are lead-free and zinc-safe.

In the two and a half years since I started housing my canaries in the GAW cages, I have had five birds get sick and die. I consulted three avian veterinarians during my attempts to find help for them, and I currently have one canary, a German Roller, being treated for zinc toxicity— I'll explain a little more about that in a minute.

Alicia McWatters, in her article, "What You Should Know About Zinc," lists the following as common symptoms of zinc intoxication:

- gastrointestinal disturbances
- polyuria or polydipsia
- weight loss
- weakness
- sleepiness
- loss of balance
- seizures
- anemia
- damage to pancreas, liver and kidneys

In retrospect I can now say that four of my five birds exhibited loss of balance and seizures. At least one of them was diagnosed with liver disease which was treated, improved and then regressed— twice— before finally he finally died.

All of them exhibited some weakness and depression, and while I had the feeling something wasn't quite right with them there was nothing definite I could put my finger on. Of the five birds that died, three were necropsied. (the term for an animal autopsy). One necropsy was inconclusive, while another supported a diagnosis of heavy metal poisoning, and the final one indicated liver disease. (This was not the bird who had been diagnosed and treated for liver disease.)

Then when Blitz, my German Roller, started having coordination problems and then seizures, in desperation I contacted a new vet, one who does house calls.

She walked into the room, watched the bird for a couple of minutes, asked some questions about the bird and the cage, caught him and examined him, and told me she thought he was suffering from metal toxicity. Because canaries have such a small volume of blood, she said it was not possible to get enough blood to run the test for metal toxicity without killing the bird.

She suggested treating him with a medication (Calcium EDTA) that would bind to any heavy metals in his system and flush them out. If he was suffering from metal toxicity he would get better and we would see some improvement within seven days. If it was something else causing his coordination problems the treatment wouldn't hurt him. I felt we had nothing to lose by trying the treatments.

Seven days after starting the treatment I have seen some improvement in Blitz's condition. He seems to be regaining a bit of his balance and coordination and was even singing a little bit the other day.

No matter how things work out with him, in the long run I have learned some important lessons. I wish, though, that I had known before what I know now! That is one of the reasons I felt it important to share my trials with you.

I can't help wondering how many undiagnosed (or perhaps misdiagnosed) small pet bird deaths there have been due to similar circumstances, over the years? Many small-bird owners never consult a vet, but instead prefer to try to treat their birds themselves, in the case of illness.

My experience shows that even for those who do consult a vet, a clear diagnosis still may not be reached.

by R C McDonald

One of my new vet's biggest beefs is seeing birds that have been seen and treated by vets trying to cash in on the exotics corner of the market without knowing beans about it. She said frequently it is too late to do much to help because the birds have been treated by someone who tells their owner he knows about treating their pet when really he doesn't!

Blitz has continued to improve but is still not 100%. Next I aim to find out if there is a possibility he may never be 100% (I can live with that) or if he will continue to get better as time goes on. We see him every day so we may not be as aware of changes as someone who hasn't seen him since he was at his worst.

Either way, as the old saying goes, knowledge is power—and the more people are aware that toxic metals are too often and too freely used in the making of our birds' cages, the better.

I hope each one of you will look closely at the homes your avian friends live in, and make certain that such problems as those I have been living with, cannot happen to you! I can assure you, you will rest easier for it, in the end.

The Non-Stick Issue

There's more than one long-time controversy in the world of bird-keeping, and you never have to look far to find one. Of them all, few run the gamut of reactions from mockery to fright the way this issue does.

Non-stick linings can be found all over a great number of homes, these days, and in a wide variety of forms. They have proliferated in an enormous range of household goods, from curlers and curling irons to cookware, ironing-board covers and irons to oven mitts and drip pans, and much more. It's even used on the bulbs in some heat lamps!

There are several manufacturers who produce various analogs of this material, and although the danger of their use near birds is well documented, very few manufacturers have any warning whatsoever on their labelling. This fact has led to the accidental death of many a pet bird over the years, along with a plethora of reactions from bird owners, clubs, and other organizations.

When it comes to the health of my birds and myself, I prefer to err on the side of caution— better safe than sorry, as my grandmother always used to say! But when so much of the available information is hearsay and conjecture, what's a caring bird owner to think?

Well— one issue that's become clear to me, is that there is no question that there *is* some danger to our birds in the use of products coated with many of the more common non-stick linings. To date the sole exception seems to be the new non-stick ceramic type of baked lining. Sadly, far too many companies still opt to go with the older kind of non-stick coatings, similar to that known under the trade-marked name of Teflon. Research has shown that, especially at higher temperatures (and sometimes even at lower ones!) these materials can produce gases that are deadly for birds.

Too often I've heard a bird owner lament, too late, that they knew there was possible danger, but they thought their birds would be okay in another room of the house, well away from the fumes.

Sometimes this is true, but if you live in a house whose heating vents tends to distribute the household air throughout the entire home, seeing that your bird is in another room may not offer him adequate protection. In order for separation to work, there needs to be little to no air exchange between the area where the utensils coated with the non-stick lining are in use, and the area where the bird(s) are being kept.

There are other, lesser-known issues involved in the use of these materials, as well. Studies recently undertaken by the EPA have indicated that there is the potential for nationwide human exposure to low levels of perfluorooctanoic acid (PFOA), used in the manufacture of many non-stick linings, and its salts, predominantly ammonium perfluorooctanoate (APFO). Based on certain animal studies, there could be a potential risk of developmental and other such adverse effects associated with exposure in humans.

But since the same assessment also indicates that there is substantial uncertainty about the interpretation of the risk, the EPA has identified areas where additional information could be helpful in allowing them to develop a more accurate assessment of the potential risks posed by PFOA and other similar compounds, and to identify what voluntary or regulatory mitigation or other actions, if any, would be appropriate.

Because of this, the EPA made the preliminary assessment public to identify the Agency's concerns, to indicate areas where additional information or investigation would be useful, and to request the submission of data addressing these issues.

PFOA and its salts are fully fluorinated organic compounds that can be produced synthetically and formed through the degradation or metabolism of certain other manmade fluorochemical products. PFOA is a synthetic chemical and is not naturally occurring. Consequently, all PFOA found in the environment is attributable to human activity.

PFOA is used primarily to produce its salts, which are used as essential processing aids in the production of fluoropolymers and fluoroelastomers. Although they are made using PFOA, finished fluoropolymer and fluoroelastomer products are not expected to contain PFOA.

The major fluoropolymers manufactured using PFOA salts are polytetrafluoroethylene (PTFE) and polyvinylidine fluoride (PVDF). PTFE has literally hundreds of uses in many industrial or consumer products, including soil, stain, grease, and water resistant coatings on textiles and carpet; uses in the automotive, mechanical, aerospace, chemical, electrical, medical, and building/construction industries; personal care products; and of course, non-stick coatings on cookware.

PVDF, on the other hand, is used primarily in three major industrial sectors: Electrical and/or electronics, building/construction, and chemical processing. Release from manufacturing processes are one source of PFOA in the environment.

The EPA is also soliciting the identification of parties who would be interested in monitoring or participating in negotiations for the development of more enforceable consent agreements (ECAs) on PFOA and on fluorinated telomers ('telomers') which may metabolize or degrade to PFOA. The intent of the ECAs would be to develop additional information, particularly environmental fate and transport information, to enhance understanding of the sources of PFOA in the environment and the pathways by which human exposure to PFOA is occurring.

The EPA's investigation began in 1999, when data indicated that perfluorooctyl sulfonate (PFOS) was persistent, unexpectedly toxic, and bio-accumulative. The data showed that PFOS had been found in very low concentrations in the blood of the general population and in wildlife around the world.

In June 2000, EPA indicated that it was expanding its investigation of PFOS to encompass other fluorochemicals, including PFOA, in order to determine whether these other fluorochemicals might present concerns similar to those found with PFOS. EPA was concerned in part because the studies had also found PFOA in human blood during the studies on PFOS.

In September 2002, the Director of OPPT initiated a priority review on PFOA because of the developmental toxicity data, the carcinogenicity data, and the blood monitoring data presented in an interim revised hazard assessment.

When the priority review commenced, EPA anticipated completing the review within a few months. However, there remain substantial uncertainties associated with the preliminary risk assessment. The EPA believes these uncertainties may be reduced through acquisition of more information, and it is therefore continuing the priority review in order to acquire this information and better inform their decision-making.

This issue could us all, birdkeepers or not. For a full copy of the EPA's report, email *Oppt.Homepage@epamail.epa.gov*

The web address for the Commission is *www.cpsc.gov*

Bald Spots & Tatty Feathers

Your bird began its moult early this year, and it lasted for a long time. His feathers never did finish growing in fully. He has a bald spot around his neck that is gradually moving up to his head, and the rest of his feathers look dull, and are often disarranged.

He used to sing all the time, but has barely sung a note since his moult began. You offer him vegetables and fruit, and you give him vitamins in his water. You've even taken him to a vet for a health check-up, and were told that nothing seems to be wrong. Yet no matter what you try, you still can't seem to get him to feel like his old chipper self, or improve his appearance.

There's a few possibilities that may be affecting a canary seen in this kind of condition. The two most usual causes of bald spots or tatty feathers are;

    1. A condition usually known as a 'stuck moult', and can be caused by stress, drafts, mites, or a fungal infection,

    2. A dietary shortage of some essential nutrients, in particular iodine and/or vitamin A.

Problems like this are often seen to begin with the annual moult, and there's a good reason for this— growing in feathers takes a fairly hefty helping of essential nutrients. If the bird doesn't have enough nutrients in his body and diet to support a full moult, he may not be able to properly grow in his new feathers.

There *are* dietary supplements made especially for birds who are having difficulty completing their moult. The better kinds will provide all the necessary nutrients for a proper moult. One of the best I've used is known as 'Feather Up'; it's formulated to offer the nutrients known to be most needed by moulting birds. Its not usually possible to find it in pet supply stores, but you can buy it online through a variety of venues.

There's another dietary problem that can cause similar symptoms to arise, especially if you live inland, and that is a shortage of adequate dietary iodine. In order to correct this imbalance, you need to find a good source of dietary iodine.

Some folks will remind you that table salt for humans has iodine added to it for just this reason; but too much salt can be deadly for a canary. A little salt is okay, and while it's true that you can regularly sprinkle a little on your bird's soft foods, greens, or fruit, to prevent this kind of problem from arising, you can't add enough to correct an already existing dietary imbalance this way. Note too, that *too much* iodine can be deadly; like many other of the trace elements needed by our bodies, too much can be just as bad (or worse) than not enough.

The easiest method I've found to maintain a healthy iodine balance in canaries is to go to a health food store and buy some powdered kelp. I put the powdered kelp into a salt shaker along with a few grains of instant rice, and every time I am going to offer the bird some food, I shake some kelp over the bird's soft food, using about this same amount I would add if I was salting food to taste. The few grains of instant rice in the shaker will absorb any excess moisture that happens to get into the shaker and prevent the powdered kelp from clumping up, as it otherwise tends to do.

Some vets will recommend switching the bird to a pelleted diet to prevent this sort of feathering problem, but the fact is, few brands of pellets are at all palatable to a

Canary Crazy

canary. An adult canary who's used to eating seed is not all that easy to convert to a pelleted diet, either. Another factor, depending on where you live, is that it can sometimes be difficult to find a steady supply of fresh pellets of the kind your bird will eat. Smaller towns and pet and farm supply stores for more out-of-the-way places may not stock them at all. Worse, they may carry them, but sell so little that their supply is soon stale.

Worse yet, many brands don't yet make a version for canaries, who need softer pellets than most hookbills. In general, the two most acceptable brands of pellets, as far as canaries seem to be concerned, are those made by 'Kaytee' and 'Roudybush'. Even then, some canaries won't eat them reliably enough to stay properly healthy.

If you are finding converting your bird to a pelleted diet is frustrating, then you should know that regardless of what some vets will tell you, it *is* possible to keep a canary healthy on a seed-based diet, as long as you have proper vitamin and mineral supplementation. One of the best all-round supplements I know of, made specifically for birds on a seed-based diet, is 'Prime', made by Hagen. It is sold in pet stores, and most who carry Hagen products can order some in for you if they don't happen to have it in stock.

If you do buy some Prime be sure to open the box and check the expiry date on the bottom of the bottle inside. Many stores don't know to check this, and so sometimes you will find an expired bottle still on a shelf. Hagen will replace such bottles with fresh, so don't let the store folk tell you that they can't replace it; they can easily return out-of-date supplies and have them replaced.

I myself have tried offering pellets to my canaries, and I try to see that they remain familiar enough with them to regard them as food; but in the long run I prefer to use a seed-based diet for my canaries.

You'll find the diet I recommend described in detail in my book *'Brats in Feathers, Keeping Canaries'*, or, in slightly less detail, online in the article you'll find posted at *robirda.com/cansing.html.* The article is actually about how to encourage a pet canary to sing— but the advice on diet and how to make a canary comfortable and happy in his environment applies here too, so if you get the chance you may wish to read it.

One thing to be watch out for when you are offering seed mixes to your canaries— you want to be particularly careful about the amount you feed of any kind of treat seeds such as song food mix, moulting food, honey sticks, egg biscuit, etc. These are all are extremely rich, so much so that one teaspoonful for a canary is roughly the equivalent of a human eating an 8-inch double layer chocolate cake!

This means that when it comes to a canary, you don't need to offer more than a teaspoon or so per week of *all* such treats combined— if you feed them at all, that is— they're nice occasionally, but they are not necessary. In fact they are, just as the name implies, a treat.

One important point about offering vitamin supplements to canaries; I don't recommend using the drinking water, as canaries don't reliably drink enough water for this to be a good method. Even worse, they may tend to avoid drinking water with additives in it, and this in turn can cause them to drink too little fluid. Inadequate intake of water can in turn cause a great deal of trauma to the body, and if continued, can quickly lead to kidney and liver problems.

Instead, I use a powdered supplement such as Hagen's 'Prime', and sprinkle small amounts onto soft foods such as a good soak seed mix, or a little prepared cous-cous. (I use the same salt-shaker-with-a-few-grains-of-rice method that I use for offering kelp.)

In fact, this kind of thing is the closest my birds ever get to seeing something like a 'song food' mix, and they love it! I've had great luck using a good soak seed and nestling food mix as a 'treat'— the birds adore it, and it's a good way to see that they get the nutrition they need. (The basics of using soak seed with nestling food are outlined in the article posted at *robirda.com/soakseed.html* or in more detail in *'Brats in Feathers, Keeping Canaries'*)

At any rate, getting back to our balding bird— another possible cause of ongoing moulting problems is lack of adequate dietary vitamin A. This can simply be due to an indoor bird not being given enough dark leafy greens.

Most people don't realize it, but most canaries can quite literally eat their weight in greens every day! I prefer to offer my canaries a good handful or more daily of chopped dark leafy greens such as kale, leafy endive, or rapini (broccoli raba). These greens are already quite high in carotenoids, which is what the body uses to make its own vitamin A, but you can increase the amount even more by chopping the greens roughly and mixing them with coarse-grated carrot.

Such a mixture is loaded with a wide variety of essential nutrients, and interestingly enough, most canaries appear to enjoy a mix like this and will learn to eat it willingly. This is rather different from what usually happens if you should try to offer a canary a heap of grated carrots on their own. Most often all *that* will get you is a *'what in heck is that?!'* sort of look, with the bird refusing to touch them.

Spinach, chard, sorrel or beet greens should not be included in a canary diet except in small amounts, as they contain far too much oxalic acid, which inhibits proper digestion of calcium.

You want to be careful when offering fruit to canaries. A great deal of pesticides are used during commercial fruit production, and canaries are extremely sensitive to these compounds. Apples and grapes are among the worst culprits. Plus, too much fruit can cause problems with loose sticky stools, which can also cause problems. So use only organically grown fruit if you offer any fruit at all— and be careful to only offer only fairly small amounts.

There's another possibility that can on occasion cause a bald patch to appear on a canary. Once it's been proven to not be caused by an infection, skin problem, or mites, chances are good that either a draft is present, or your canary is feeling *very* stressed by something in his environment. This could be caused by living in too quiet an area, or by being stared at (especially silently) by a human (whether adult or child), or a pet. (For more on this, along with how to check for and prevent drafts, read the chapter on Unseasonal Moulting, found elsewhere in this book.)

Incorrect lighting is another possible source of problems that can cause a bald spot on a canary. Lighting is very important to canaries, who evolved so that their bodies respond physically to the amount of light which enters their eyes. This trait is known as 'photosensitivity', and is covered in the chapter of that name, found in this book.

Hopefully all this will be enough to allow you to figure out just what is going on with your little feathered friend's feathers. Once you've solved his problem, his feathers will quickly begin to regrow, and soon you'll have your happy little songster back!

Feather Lumps

Sooner or later, everybody who keeps canaries of any kind is liable to be plagued by a problem with their canaries' feathers not emerging properly from the skin, during the moult. Theories on causes abound but none seem to be conclusive, and often new owners are left at a loss, wondering just what on earth should be done about their bird's lumpy, bumpy appearance.

A feather lump— sometimes called a 'feather cyst'— on a bird is the equivalent of an ingrown hair on a human. Such lumps are relatively much larger in size, of course, since feathers are larger than hairs, and our birds are so tiny in comparison to us. To date, there has been very little scientific research on the cause of feather lumps. Studies to conclusively prove one cause or another have not been done in numbers great enough to produce proper statistical evidence and until they are, widely varying opinions, many contradictory, help only to confuse the newcomer.

Some theories insist that an improper (or incomplete) diet is the biggest source of this problem, while other theories state emphatically that the tendency a bird shows to develop feather lumps is genetically inherited.

Over the years my experience has indicated to me that while there may be a genetically inherited tendency towards developing feather lumps, the overall diet of the bird in question does seem to be connected to the results seen. I myself have owned birds that in other hands developed feather lumps yearly, during the moult. But while these birds were under my care, I never had any such problem.

by R C McDonald

In particular, a diet including larger amounts of incomplete proteins and rich foods seems to cause feather lumps to happen a little more easily in birds susceptible to them. I should mention here that tradition recommends that birds who develop lumps should not used for breeding, as sooner or later their offspring will usually show the same tendency to develop these lumps.

In fact this problem tends to show up much more frequently in inbred or line-bred show stock. This in turn has caused a great many people to believe that this problem arises from indiscriminate breeding for softer, broader feathers.

Such feathers will help to give a bird that 'chubby' look that is considered so desirable in Glosters, Norwich, and Borders, which are the breeds most often seen with feather lumps. Yet the breed with the softest, broadest feathers of all— the Mosaic, or Dimorphic Canary— is less often seen with feather lumps than you might expect. Feather lumps *do* occur in this breed, but less frequently than would be expected if soft feathering alone was the cause.

Feather lumps can be painful for the bird, depending on their placement. If they are situated where they can put pressure on a nerve or an internal organ as they grow and swell, they can cause long-term damage, and occasionally can even kill a bird!

Feather structure is high in silicon, and new feathers growing in demands a diet with seventeen percent or so of complete proteins. These nutrients *must* be available while a bird is moulting, or the new feathers will not be able to grow in properly (or at all). There's several methods used to achieve this in a bird's diet, with varying results.

My best success has been achieved from using a mix-and-match method to combine vegetable proteins from different foods in order to achieve complete protein when eaten together. Almost all vegetable proteins are incomplete in and of themselves, but can be combined with complementary vegetable proteins to make a complete protein in combination. (For example corn and beans is one such classic combination.)

Quite a lot of research went into designing my home-made nestling food and soak seed mix, so as to allow the ingredients to work together to digest as a complete protein. I've used this method for decades now, and it's always worked well for me; my birds moult quickly and easily, remaining vigorous and active. (For more on this, refer to the F.A.Q. at *robirda.com/faqs.html#nestfood*)

Many people prefer to use animal proteins, which are more often complete in and of themselves. That's why so many birdfood recipes are high in egg. But when working with animal proteins, you need to be wary of the high fatty content that is also often present.

The nice thing about animal proteins is that they are already complete. One school of thought theorizes that animal proteins are harder to digest, though, and that combined veggie proteins are more effective, as well as being healthier because of the lower fat content.

As far as developing or not developing feather lumps goes, the kind and quantity of greens fed also seems to be a factor, although there is very little truly conclusive evidence for this; but it has been my observation that people who feed more of the 'softer' greens (romaine or leaf lettuces, celery leaves, etc...) don't seem to get the good feather results that always seems to accompany the abundant use of kale, collards, savoy cabbages, gai lan, and other such cabbage-family plants.

Perhaps this is because these plants have thicker cell walls, and are higher in silicon? I don't know for sure— but I do know my experience has been that it does seem to make a difference.

I once had several birds who had several lumps each given to me for free— I took them because the previous owner was going to 'throw them out the window'... *(yeesh!!)* After 6 months or so with me, they looked like different

by R C McDonald

birds. Their feathers were smooth and shiny, and every bird was completely lump-free. I never saw another lump on any one of them, during the several years they lived with me.

European breeders, who have the advantage of statistical numbers, suggest that the following amino acids especially, contribute to a successful, lump-free moult; methionine, lysine, threonine, and tryptophan. (These are all separate elements of a complete protein, found in varying amounts in varying foods)

They also suggest that lecithin (an unsaturated fatty acid) also aids in allowing feather growth to occur smoothly. Adequate B vitamins, mineral content (especially zinc), Folic acid and Biotin have also been cited as essential elements required for a trouble-free moult.

Methionine and Lysine especially are thought to be particularly important at preventing the occurrence (or re-occurence) of feather lumps.

Stress may have something to do with the appearance of lumps, too, particularly stress that is experienced by the bird during the time it is moulting. This idea is backed up by the fact that many a canary has gone for two or three years without any sign of feather lumps, only to develop them later in life— and as everyone who's experienced it knows, old age is when the physical results of a stressful life really tend to show up.

I personally have observed that feather lumps can be quite painful for the bird, depending on their placement— if they are situated where they can cause pressure on a nerve or an internal organ, they can cause long-term damage, and occasionally even kill a bird. Such a lump is best removed only by an avian vet.

If your bird gets a feather lump, your first action should be to contact your avian vet and have him or her show you how to best deal with it. Some feather lumps, as noted above, can only be safely removed by a vet. That being said, here's some advice from a long-term breeder who removes her bird's feather lumps herself, re-printed here with her permission and a request to not be named.

"Any time you see a canary with feathers not growing in properly, and most of all if they aren't straight, growing back at an angle or crooked, you can be pretty sure it is feather lumps. They grow on all parts of a canary except the head and feet or legs.

"Many times feather lumps will be found in the tail and preen gland area. It is one of the areas that are prone to them and the area that I hate most of all removing them from. When they are ready to remove they will turn hard, and eventually the skin will split on top of each one. At this stage they are quite easy to remove. Inside there will be a hard, cheesy stuff and bits of feather junk.

"If you see a crooked feather, follow it down the shaft with your fingers. The small ones are easy; just pull it out with your finger nails. As soon as possible, remove those big ones. They stretch the skin and it hurts.

"If you see a bird with a feather sticking out from the wing it is usually a feather lump, unless the bird has been fighting or caught on something. Again, just follow it down and at the end, on the skin, you will find a feather lump.

"I removed my first feather lump via telephone. A fellow club member was on the other end and guided me through it. I had called him about it and he said, "If you are going to raise canaries you must learn to do this yourself." *It wasn't easy the first time. It took me forever and the sweat was dripping down my face until I could hardly see. Now I can do it in five minutes or less depending on the hardness of the lump.*

"First of all get everything together. Peroxide, cotton balls, a sterilized needle (or a small scalpel if you prefer) and some white flour (to help stop bleeding and clot any blood-flow in case you make a mistake).

"Don't try your first time to remove a soft feather lump. It will bleed. Get a good hard one. If it is good and hard the skin will split over it which makes it easy for you. The bird will not feel anything if you just stick the needle in the lump, just far enough to simply lift it out. That's all there is to it if you have a hard lump. You must be careful not to stick the needle into the body of the bird, just into the lump.

"You can lift the lump right out and you will see an empty sac. It won't be bleeding but the mucus lining will look bloody to you. Pretend you make a mistake and you just lift out a part of the lump. You just put the needle back in and lift the other part out; being very careful not to pierce the bird itself. If you are right handed you will be holding the bird in your left hand and be working with your right hand.

"It all dries up very quickly. By the next day you may have trouble finding it. Even the sac shrivels and dries up. If you have done a good job, then just sponge where the lump was with a cotton ball dampened with peroxide. I have never had a bird get any kind of infection from this.

"You can tell if the feather lump is hard and ready to remove by feeling it and by the colour. If it feels soft and is more reddish in colour it is not ready. When they get hard they are a whitish-yellow and sometimes get a split on top. With the split you don't even have to make your opening. Just use the open split, put the needle in the lump and lift it out.

"This sounds worse than it is. However it is not for the squeamish. Most people consider me to be squeamish but I learned to do this because I had to. The bird is in more pain with the lump stretching its skin and maybe pressing against a nerve or organ, than it is with you removing the lump. If you are careful you won't hurt the bird at all.

"Don't try it unless you feel you are ready for it. Just take your time and be sure you have your needle in the ball of feathers and dry stuff, not in the bird. If you get the lump out intact or at least be sure to remove all of it, you will find it won't come back until the next moult. If you leave a piece *behind, even a small bit, it will come back very quickly."*

There you have it; some of the best, most practical advice I have seen anywhere on dealing with feather lumps. I don't think anybody could have put it better, more clearly, or more simply.

It must be noted that there is much still to be learned about the cause and prevention of the phenomenon of feather lumps in our canaries— but in the meantime, this information has proven useful to myself and a great many other bird owners. It is my hope that these thoughts will prove as useful to you as they have to so many others, with the wish that none of us may ever again see a feather lump in any of our birds!

by R C McDonald

Winter, when so many of us spend so much of our time indoors, tends to see more than its fair share of illnesses, including breathing problems that may be exacerbated by the presence of bird dander. Sometimes these problems can develop into serious impediments to the health. This being the case, I have decided that this may be a good time to share my own experience with what is most often known as...

Bird Keeper's Lung

"You should probably get rid of all of your birds," my doctor said, eyeing me seriously. *"There's been many cases of problems like yours amongst birdkeepers, and the best solution is usually to get rid of the birds."*

I gaped at her, speechless. Get rid of my birds? Unthinkable!

But it was clear, too, that something had to be done, as not being able to breathe is unthinkable too. I had recently had a three-month long bout with a serious flu, and had emerged at the other end with multiple allergies and seriously damaged lungs, and my doctor believed my birds were making it worse.

But I couldn't believe it. I had even noticed that my breathing tended to be worse when at work, and improve a little at home— but that could be a time-delayed reaction, she argued, saying that allergies to birds and bird dander were common, and tests were not really needed.

Still, I insisted that tests be done— I was not going to give up my birds until I had solid proof that they were making me worse.

'Bird-Keepers Lung' is the term most commonly used for a respiratory ailment that can afflict, well, bird-keepers, (and their birds). One of the most widely held theories is that it is caused by inhaling too much of the airborne dust from feathers, seeds, chaff, and dried droppings that is so often associated with keeping birds indoors, especially when there is a lot of them and cleanliness is not exactly scrupulously maintained.

It is most often assumed that this problem is due to an infection in the lungs — but the fact is that allergies to inhaled substances can often have very similar symptoms.

I already knew, due to my recent research on my newly developed food allergies, that factors such as allergies to seeds, seed dust, or seed-dust mites could be involved. As I read more, it seemed these factors were seldom considered, yet I had a feeling that such details could be important— maybe even as much as the 'cleanliness' issue.

Testing for the exact allergens my body was reacting to called for multiple visits to the usually-crowded allergist's office, with a long wait often in store, but I found I didn't mind. That office was stocked with magazines filled with the exact same information I was trying to research, and more than once, I stayed longer than I'd planned, because I just *had* to finish reading some article or another.

Among other things, I found that what kinds of seeds go into making up seed dust can make a huge difference in how people might react to it (or not), as can the age of the seed, and the presence (or not), of a tiny, seldom-mentioned critter— the seed-dust mite. These little bugs are relatives of the house-dust mite, but live and thrive in seed dust, just as much as their cousins do in house dust.

It seemed that older, dusty seed, if looked at under a microscope, is often found to be swarming with these little critters, and that many people react very strongly to them. Just as with the house dust mite, they are known to trigger allergic reactions, especially if breathed in.

In fact, just as with house-dust mites, I read that if somebody without any allergies was exposed to heavy concentrations of these tiny bugs for long enough, their chances of developing an allergy to them would grow increasingly high. I also noted that they tend to be very few or non-existent in fresh seed, and that freezing would kill any adults (although not their eggs).

But one article I found, tucked away in a magazine dedicated to allergists world-wide, fascinated me no end.

This article did not mention birds, but discussed research on reactions produced in people through the inclusion of a certain seed in the diet, both ground as a component in prepared foods, where it is common, and as an extract (as in oils), where it is also common. That same seed is common as a component in seed-based pet bird foods, too— they were talking about canola.

It seemed that studies in hospitals in Britain had shown that canola, especially when inhaled in particulate form, can be what they termed an 'allergen trigger'. This meant that they had found that regular exposure to the dust of this seed could trigger a body to produce allergic responses to multiple substances in the diet or environment, not just to the seed itself. They found that the longer the exposure, the higher the odds were of general allergic reactions to all sorts of common substances beginning to develop.

This information fascinated me, and thinking back, I realized that I had begun to show mild allergic reactions within a year or two of beginning to live with birds in the house, although I did not at the time recognize them.

There doesn't seem to have been much attention paid to this research yet amongst the allergy-oriented community at large— but I believe it could be a factor in understanding why allergies sometimes so suddenly arise, in some people at least— and I especially believe it could make a huge difference in many bird-people's lives.

My test results, when they finally came in, reinforced the ideas that were slowly developing as I read further. I was relived to find that I was not allergic to my canaries, my finches, my waxbills or my softbills— but I did react very strongly to parrot dander, chicken and chicken eggs, and dust mites. And yes, I was allergic to canola.

I had to face the fact that I could no longer keep my hookbills, and began with a heavy heart to look for good homes for them, while at the same time taking some basic steps to remove as many house-and-seed dust mites from my environment as possible. Seed was bought in smaller lots and kept in the freezer, and I bought a vacuum that used water for a filter— I could vacuum to my heart's content, and no dust would ever escape that filter!

At the same time I removed all canola from my house and diet. I began to scan labels when shopping, and stopped buying any foods including canola or canola oil. I even designed special seed mixes for the birds I was keeping, containing *no* canola seed. This generated some surprise from my dealers, as canola or rapeseed is a common ingredient in most small-bird seed mixes.

Finally, I bought and set up air filters. After some research on initial cost, filter-replacement costs, and overall effectiveness, I settled on small units that used easily-available and relatively inexpensive Hepa filters, and included a built-in ionizer to increase their effectiveness. I found that these worked quite well, although it was true that I had to replace the filters up to twice as often as the manufacturer recommended.

To my great relief, once these steps were accomplished, I immediately noticed a dramatic improvement in breathing. I also find it very interesting that over the longer term, I have noticed a gradual decreasing of the number and severity of my allergies— if this keeps up, within a few years, I will be back to having few if any allergies at all. My birds have continued to do well without any canola in their diet. I was careful to see that my new seed mix presented a similar balance of nutrients as the mixes that include canola, and my birds don't seem to miss it.

It's certain that there's a lot more to learn, when it comes to this kind of issue— but I find what's come to light so far to be v-e-r-y interesting indeed. My breathing continues to slowly but steadily improve, and more than ten years after I was told I had to get rid of my birds, I still have them. A minor success, perhaps; but *highly* satisfying.

Air Sac Mites

Of all the pests that can infect canaries, these tiny mites are among the most misunderstood. It's true most canary owners know of their existence, but it's also true that many believe that every time they see a bird having difficulty in breathing, the problem is due to the presence of air sac mites. So what's the real story behind these tiny pests, and how can you learn to tell whether or not your bird *really* has air sac mites?

Air sac mites are tiny insects distantly related to spiders, that prefer to live inside a bird's lungs, particularly in the air sacs and windpipe. Here they can cling to the air sac walls, where they find plentiful warmth, moisture, and easy opportunities to feed and lay their eggs.

Canaries and Lady Gouldian Finches tend to be more susceptible than many other passerines to this tiny pest, so difficult to diagnose, and are more often found infected with air sac mites than most other avian species commonly kept as pets.

Even birds of these two species won't be much bothered by a few air sac mites, but over time the infestation can grow to be quite serious, as the mites become more plentiful. When that happens, their constant feeding begins to gradually weaken the bird. This is exacerbated by the fact that their presence in the bird's lungs and air sacs inhibits the ability to breath fully, reducing the amount of oxygen available to the blood supply.

At this point, a dry, almost rasping clicking sound may be heard as the bird breathes in and out, if it is held next to the ear. It's most often a rather quiet sound, not loud at all, in fact not loud enough to be easily heard unless the bird's beak is very near the ear. This small clicking sound is often considered to be symptomatic of air sac mite infestation, and it is common to hear of canary and finch keepers medicating their birds for air sac mites on this symptom alone.

However, it should be noted that other lung and air sac problems can cause similar, sometimes louder sounds, so in fact, a bird whose breathing produces these clicking noises could actually have a lung infection of some kind, whether bacterial, viral, or fungal in nature. Or, lack of adequate vitamin A in the diet can cause the lungs and air sacs to produce excess mucous, and this too may cause the bird to produce a clicking sound as it breathes.

This means that a clearer diagnosis should be sought before medicating *any* bird for the presence of air sac mites. Any infestation of these mites in a bird's body has to be fairly substantial before these small clicks can be heard in the breathing. That in turn means that it should be possible to verify the air sac mite infestation by shining a small, bright, very focused light over the windpipe or just behind and below the eye.

If the light is bright enough, it should be possible to spot small, pepper-sized grains of darkness within the windpipe, or just under the skin behind and below the eyes. If you watch long enough, you may see these small black 'grains' moving about. A careful examination in either or both of these locations should produce definitive verification of air sac mite presence, as long as the light is very bright, with a small, focused beam.

When asked about dealing with and treating air sac mites and their symptoms, long-time canary breeder Julio Valella, a member of the Lone Star State Canary Club, says,

"Observation by microscope of actual mites in saliva samples or the observation of tiny dark spots in the airsac tracks just under the skin below and behind the eyes under

a careful exam with a strong light are generally acknowledged as the more accurate diagnosis. It takes two trained people to do this. Simply listening to 'clicking sounds' is not enough.

"There are other causes of 'clicking sounds', and all indicate respiratory system problems. Clicking can also be chronic, caused by scar tissue remaining from prior airsac mites or other infections; viral, bacterial, or fungal. Most infections of the canary air passages cause lesions in the soft moist internal tissues that when they heal create scar tissues. When the bird is stressed and breathing heavily and rapidly, or is sleeping and breathing cooler air that constricts the air passages, the scar tissue restricted passage can produce 'clicking sounds'.

"When the 'clicking sound' is caused by this old, established and stable scar tissue there is simply no treatment that will eliminate or 'cure' the 'clicking sound'. Many breeders have experienced owning such a bird, that for years while a 'clicker' was healthy, fertile, productive, and otherwise normal.

"Other causes of 'clicking' can occur, such as a bacterial infection that causes air passages to fill and drip a clear liquid, that often dries up around the nostrils and leaves a chalky residue upon drying. Some stressful digestive infections can lead to depressed immune system and air passage congestion caused by improper hydration, mainly a partially dehydrated bird will suffer from lack of enough natural and normal moisture in the air passages that in turn triggers an over production of mucous fluid in the frontal passage directly behind the nostrils, and that can cause 'clicking'.

"So, a thorough overall exam and diagnosis of the bird is needed first. If any signs of digestive or respiratory infection are observed, sample cultures and/or immediate micro-scope slide observations of the feces, the saliva and any nostril discharge should be done.

"NOT all offending pathogens will be observed but mites

by R C McDonald

will, and also any other parasites. The cultures should be observed and also tested for gram positive & gram negative susceptibility to determine an indicated effective antibiotic, IF ANY.

"Based on the observed conditions, and diagnosis (if any), a treatment regimen can then be defined.

"Of course this is well beyond what most can afford or will do. So, typically the few things that can be done and may help are:

1. Isolate the bird, another room altogether is best. Prevent spreading the problem.

2. Provide warmth and draft free, sheltered, stress free rest. Increase sleep (rest) hours slightly.

3. CLEAN the cage daily, if there is any liquid droppings clean out paper at least twice daily!

4. ENSURE bird is fully hydrated, observe amount of water taken up daily to verify. IF compatible with treatment add juicy, high calorie fruit treats. Watermelon, sweet orange... These help hydrate, add calories, improve appetite, and acidify the gut, all benefits.

5. Feed a high calorie, easy to digest and very nourishing supplement. The favorite is couscous laced with royal honey jelly or powdered bee pollen. Provide ample, varied, fresh food and monitor the bird IS eating well. The goal is to get the bird to INCREASE caloric intake and if possible gain strength & weight.

6. When there is evidence of digestive problems, somewhat similar to 'going light', add treatment with a bird specific supplement (acidic, with minimal 4 live active cultures, and enzymes).

"This regimen, cleaning, and observation followed for about a week often yields full recovery. The bird should remain segregated for another 21 days to verify there is full recovery and no relapse.

"Remember, when the bird has old scar tissue and is a

chronic 'clicker', it will be found to be in very robust fit shape upon examination, often looking ready for the show bench, yet it may still 'click at night'."

How birds manage to contract these mites is another often-discussed subject amongst bird keepers, as is what to do about a possible infestation; once the presence of air sac mites has been verified, recommended treatments can vary quite a lot, depending on who you're talking to.

So we went looking for the definitive answers to these two questions from the professionals; avian veterinarians. We were referred first to the article on air sac mites at exoticpetvet.net, which states, *"Transmission is thought to occur from the bird coughing the mites up into the mouth, or by the mites crawling into the mouth, where they are wiped from the beak by a bird during feeding or rubbing the beak along perches, where they may be transferred to another bird. A parent bird may pass mites to its offspring through feeding.*

The article adds, *"Treatment by an avian veterinarian may be attempted using invermectin, dosed precisely. However, if a large number of mites all die at one time, this may cause a fatal reaction in the infested bird.*

"All birds in a room with a bird diagnosed with air sac mites and treated with Ivermectin should be treated at 10 day intervals for at least three doses. A cage containing infested birds should be thoroughly disinfected."

Another method of treatment, claimed by many to be as effective as Ivermectin without the need for retreatment, entails the use of the product 'Scatt'. This product is based on moxidectin, a close relative of ivermectin. Birds treated with 'Scatt' are often thought to need only one treatment, as unlike Ivermectin, Scatt will stay in the bloodstream for two or three weeks or more.

However, the idea that only one treatment is needed could be misleading in some cases, as Julio Valella notes, *"...airsac mites can 'come back' even after a proper and effective treatment. That's simply because it's very difficult to achieve 100% kill. If any adults are not killed by treatment, or if any eggs and/or larvae survive to hatch out later, a reinfestation can emerge. That is why often retreatment is recommended within 4 weeks of a diagnosed infestation."*

Many avian veterinarians believe this feared and pernicious pest to be less common, even in canaries and Lady Gouldian Finches, than is believed by many bird-keepers. As discussed, the symptom of clicking may be interpreted as indicative of an infestation of air sac mites, when the actual cause is something else. But in cases where the problem has been verified to actually be caused by these pests, understanding the situation, how to diagnose it, and what can and should be done about it, can be invaluable.

My preference would be that no bird should ever have to suffer from these difficult-to-see pests, nor should any bird keeper ever have to agonize over what to do about them. But if you should ever come to suspect that *your* bird has contracted air sac mites, it is our hope that you will find this article helpful in resolving your questions.

Quarantine

Bird-owners have a saying to the effect that owning birds is like eating potato chips— one is never enough. It's meant as a joke but interestingly enough is actually an accurate observation when it comes to a good many birdkeepers— we just can't seem to stop at one!

As soon as you start thinking of making the move from owning one bird to owning two or more, another factor enters the equation. Too often though, nobody remembers to consider it, yet it can often literally mean the difference between life and death for all the family's birds.

Webster's dictionary tells us that the word 'quarantine' is a modification of the Italian word 'quarantena', referring to the quarantine of a ship, from the word 'quaranta', meaning 'forty', and the Latin term 'quadraginta', from 'quadra', or four, plus 'ginta', meaning 'twenty'. Webster goes on to give four definitions of the word quarantine;

1. : *a period of 40 days.*

2. a : *a term during which a ship arriving in port and suspected of carrying contagious disease is held in isolation from the shore* **b** : *a regulation placing a ship in quarantine* **c** : *a place where a ship is detained during quarantine.*

3. a : *a restraint upon the activities or communication of persons or the transport of goods designed to prevent the spread of disease or pests* **b** : *a place in which those under quarantine are kept.*

4. : *a state of enforced isolation.*

by R C McDonald

Although these definitions originally applied to ships and shipping practices, the word quarantine has come to be used to refer to the isolation of any being or group of beings where health concerns or potential pest problems may exist.

In the case of birds, in most cases international laws demand that birds being shipped from one country to another enter a government-monitored period of quarantine before being released to their purchaser. The aim is to determine and/or verify the bird's state of health, and to ensure that it will not carry any communicable pests or diseases upon being released to the purchaser.

Depending on the source of the birds being quarantined and the country the purchaser resides in, often medication is required to be administered during the quarantine period, with the goal of eliminating any pests or diseases the bird may be carrying, whether actually detected or not.

Unfortunately, many birdkeepers regard the quarantining of birds as being a procedure followed only by the bigger breeders, or those who for whatever reason wish to import or export birds. While it is true that quarantine is an important part of these procedures, by no means is the usefulness of quarantine limited to only those situations.

These days, with more and more avian diseases showing up in the headlines of the news all over the world, basic quarantine procedures are becoming the rule in the homes of more pet bird keepers, as well as in the homes of most who keep, breed, and show birds. Full quarantine procedures are not only followed when acquiring new stock, but are also applied when bringing home birds that have been in a show, or for that matter anywhere else where they may have been exposed to other birds.

Ideally, the birds being quarantined will be kept in complete isolation from existing stock or pets. If this is not possible, they should be placed as far away as possible from any other birds. If the house has forced-air heating, consider shutting off the air circulation to and from the quarantine room, and arranging to draw air into the room from outside the house. This will assist in preventing any possible air-borne contamination or diseases from getting into the vents and eventually spreading to the rest of the house.

Achieving an ideal quarantine set-up is not always possible for all of us, but even if you live in a fairly small apartment, you can establish a limited quarantine by placing any new birds as far away as possible from your existing pet or breeder birds. If possible, they should be in another room, to prevent airborne contamination.

The next step to consider, is the length of the quarantine period. If you randomly ask any group of birdkeepers for their recommendations on quarantine length, you will find the responses will vary quite a lot, depending on who you're talking to. Some feel that two weeks is perfectly adequate, while others recommend three or four weeks or more. Many avian veterinarians have been heard to recommend a minimum of four weeks, with others recommending a extended six week quarantine as preferable.

The whole idea is to keep any new birds in quarantine long enough that any diseases they may be carrying will finish their incubation period and become active and visible in the bird before the quarantine period is over. Given the rather long incubation period of some of the diseases our avian friends could be carrying if exposed, I myself consider the longer quarantine periods of six or so weeks to be the safest.

One of the most difficult parts of observing a quarantine, is to keep possible exposure between the quarantined birds and your own stock to a minimum. This is easiest to do if, whatever the situation, the quarantined birds are dealt with last. Always feed, clean, and maintain your own birds, before approaching a quarantined bird for care, interaction, and maintenance.

If possible, keep a clean smock or some other article of clothing at the entrance to the room the quarantined bird is

by R C McDonald

being kept in, along with a pair of slip-on shoes and some clean, empty garbage bags. Change out of your everyday clothes into these before approaching the quarantined bird for day to day maintenance or any other chores. This makes it easier to be sure you won't accidentally pick up anything and carry it out of the quarantine room on your clothes or shoes.

Speaking of shoes, it's a good idea to keep a filled 'footbath' containing a disinfectant solution safe for your shoes, to walk through on your way into and out of the quarantine room. Once you're finished with the daily chores of maintaining the quarantined bird, walk out through the footbath, remove your slip-on shoes, and throw the smock into one of your clean garbage bags, for transport to the laundry. Then take a shower before carrying on with your day.

This kind of routine can complicate your day of course, but depending on the circumstances, it can save lives, along with a sometimes fairly hefty investment of time, effort, or money. Depending on the situation, a less strenuous routine may fit your needs better, but it's a very good idea to know all the options (along with the risks and benefits) well enough to be able to adapt the routine to fit to the situation, rather than expecting the situation to adapt to your needs. Besides, the latter will almost never happen anyway!

Depending on where the quarantined bird came from, you may also wish to administer medication during the quarantine period. For example, if your new bird had access to an outdoor aviary, and that exposure included access to soil, you may wish to treat for possible soil or water-borne pathogens such as intestinal worms, giardia, or coccidosis. Some avian suppliers sell a handy 'quarantine kit' that can help you to see that your new birds don't expose your existing birds to any such problems once the quarantine period is finished.

That brings us to the next step. Once the quarantine is over, what's the best way to introduce your new bird to your existing bird or birds?

Perhaps the most common approach is simply to bring the new bird into the same room as your existing birds. If you only have one or two pets, this is fine, but if you have several (or more) birds, you might want to take a different approach. Once the quarantine is up, rather than putting the new bird into the birdroom, instead bring one or two of your regular birdroom inhabitants out to live near your new bird or birds for awhile. Say, a couple of weeks or so.

This is safer than the reverse, because it allows you the chance to learn if your new bird is carrying something to which it is immune, but that your other birds could catch. This way, if your already established birds should happen to become sick when exposed to the new bird, you would lose only a few, instead of the whole flock.

This kind of situation is admittedly not too common, but it *can* happen. Given that it is far easier (and cheaper!) to replace one or two birds than a roomful, this extra step is really not all that unreasonable, at least for those of us who have a birdroom with more than a few inhabitants.

The USDA Veterinary Services Organization has published an excellent and definitive website on backyard bio-security, with clear guidelines for preventing the spread of disease in your home and flock. To read about their recommendations and to learn more about why and how such procedures should be implemented and when, see the webpage at *www.aphis.usda.gov/animal_health/birdbiosecurity/*

Careful quarantine and monitored introduction of new birds into an existing flock or birdroom can seem like a lot of trouble to some of us, and others might pooh-pooh the whole idea as being overly cautious. But when you consider the potential disasters that instituting the use of quarantine procedures can help you avoid, it seems only common sense to make use of them in *your* home, when you find yourself wanting to add another bird to your life.

by R C McDonald

Unseasonal Moult

One of the most puzzling problems that can arise for a new pet canary owner, is learning to understand the causes of (and learning how to prevent), an out-of-season moult.

Winter or summer, feather-loss problems are easily caused by drafts from a heating or cooling system, either directly, as in a draft from a vent— or indirectly, say, from a current of air bouncing off a wall into a corner, or blowing down from a duct, or something similar. Sometimes heat rising from a heating vent can get trapped under a cage cover, and when that happens, it is highly stressful to the bird, almost always causing feather loss and cessation of song, due to the widely-ranging temperatures it can cause.

So particularly if you find fallen feathers in the morning when you uncover your bird, be sure to check that there is no hot air rising from a nearby register into his cage at night. Generally all you need to do to solve such a problem, is either to block the draft so it no longer reaches him, or sometimes just provide a sheltered area where he can step out of the draft.

Most canaries will stop singing when they begin to drop their feathers, whether that feather-fall is due to an unseasonal moult, stress, or illness. Only an exceptionally well-nourished canary will sing while he is growing in feathers, because doing so takes quite a lot of energy and nutrition. And if there is feathers missing, his body will be trying to grow in more, even if you can't tell any are missing by looking at him. If you can manage to find and stop the problem that is making him drop his feathers in the first place, you will probably find that he will resume singing within a couple of weeks or so of the time when he finally has all his feathers back.

Missing feathers around a canary's neck is a sign of what the old-timers used to call a 'stuck moult'. The most usual causes are a draft that he can't get out of (the most common cause for this symptom), or lack of adequate nutrition for growing in new feathers (another fairly common cause), or stress.

Stress can be caused by many things, including being harassed by another bird sharing the cage or living nearby (especially if the cage and perches in the nearby cage are higher than those for the canary's cage)— or it could be generalized stress where multiple factors combine.

That leads us to another important cause of stress, his regular diet. (All of it, including treats, greens etc.) It is almost always necessary to take a good overall look at diet as well as environment when trying to solve problems, as even small items missing or given in too large quantities can make a huge difference in a canary's health.

One of the biggest problems that can be caused by the diet is fatty heart, kidney, or liver problems, from feeding of too much fatty foods. Most often, this is due to offering too much treat seed. These mixes are usually *very* fatty; one teaspoonful of one of these mixes for a canary, is the equivalent of you or I eating an 8-inch, fully iced, double-layer chocolate cake, all by ourselves. As I am sure you realize— to do so might make him very happy, but it certainly won't do much for his health!

So try to make sure that your canary doesn't get more than a teaspoonful or so per week of any song of the food mixes or other such treat seeds, *combined*. A diet that includes daily doses of such foods can easily cause a bird to become too fat and/or too sick to sing, from stress caused on his body by a fatty liver, kidneys, or heart. Moulting food, song treat, eggs and egg food or egg biscuits, honey treats, millet, and all such treats tend to be very high in fats

— often 60% or more. Even a heavily moulting bird should receive no more than a tablespoonful per week or so of all such treats combined. Outside of the moult, he should see no more than a teaspoonful or so per week, again, not of each, but of everything combined.

Another (quite common) cause of loss of feathers is skin problems. This can occasionally be caused by mites or even a fungus growing on the skin, but the most common culprit is long term lack of vitamin A. The fact is, vitamin supplements are *always* necessary for a seed-eating bird.

Especially over the longer term (for a canary at least) not being given enough dark leafy greens can lead to problems. Most people don't realize it, but most canaries can literally eat their weight in greens every day. Even if you think your canary has been getting adequate amounts of vitamin A in his diet, there should be no harm in increasing the amount of foods in his diet known to aid the body in producing its own vitamin A, to see if it makes a difference or not. Much of the time, it can make a rather astonishing difference in quite short order, in actual fact.

I prefer to offer a good handful or more per canary, daily, of chopped dark leafy greens like kale, leafy endive, rapini (broccoli raba), and other similar greens. I often mix these greens with coarse-grated carrot, which increases the overall nutrient content even more. Most canaries will take to eating a mix like this fairly easily.

As mentioned above, regular vitamin/mineral supplementation is an absolute necessity if your bird is eating a seed-based diet— it is utterly impossible to supply an indoor bird with all the nutrients needed through a seed-based diet alone. I prefer a good basic supplement such as the Vetafarm products, but perhaps the best on the market is 'Prime', made by Hagen. It is sold in many pet stores, and most who carry their products can order it in for you, if you ask.

If you do buy some Prime be very sure to open the box and check the expiry date on the bottom of the bottle—

many stores don't know to check this, and so sometimes you will find an expired bottle still on a shelf— but Hagen will replace such bottles, so don't let them fool you and tell you that they can't replace it— they *can* return them and get you a fresh one instead.

I like to serve these vitamins dry, on a soaked seed mix — this is the closest my birds ever get to a 'song food mix', and they love it.

If the seed mix your canary eats has lots of dark seeds in it, then it is too fatty— the darker seeds are all quite high in oil. If you do see a lot of dark seeds in his mix, you might consider changing to a plainer brand of seed mix.

As for drafts— I can't tell you how many times I have spoken with people who have been totally certain there was no draft anywhere around their bird— but when they tested using the following method, they found one.

Drafts tend to frequent the vicinity of windows, and heating and air conditioning vents can cause problems too. The fact is, that while many people worry about exposing their birds to drafts, most don't realize that there is a very simple and effective way to check *any* area for drafts— simply use a lit candle.

As long as you are careful with the flame, this is a very easy and effective way to check for the presence of an unsuspected draft. Simply remove the bird's cage from where it usually sits, then put the lit candle in the same place the cage usually occupies.

Wait for a few minutes for the candle flame to steady down, then observe it from a little distance. Is it flickering? Then it is certain there is a draft. If it is *not* flickering, there is still some checks to perform— open and close nearby doors or windows, turn the furnace on and off, turn air conditioners or fans on and off again, watching the flame all the while.

Whenever it flickers, a draft has gone by; make note of its source and direction (from the way the flame leans) and

by R C McDonald

remember to provide your bird with shelter from it which he can use if he so desires— a draft is no problem, as long as the bird can step out of it if he wishes! Often this can be as simple as a smooth cloth draped over one corner of the cage, sheltering part of a perch.

Another thing to keep in mind, is that many kinds of cookware can produce fumes that are harmful to birds. Even a tiny trace of some of these fumes can cause some quite serious problems, even if they were not strong enough to cause death or noticeable damage. Because of this, your canary should be anywhere but nearby if you do any frying, and of course, any kind of appliance with a non-stick surface is anathema in any home with birds, with the sole exception of the newer ceramic non-stick bakeware.

Bird-toxic non-stick surfaces can be found on oven mitts, baking pans, muffin or bread tins, cookie sheets, irons, ironing board covers, drip trays under stove elements, and other similar items. It used to be thought that these non-stick materials were only dangerous under high heat, but recent research has shown this not to be true — under certain conditions, normal cooking temperatures can suffice. So you will want to be extra careful that there is nothing of the sort in your kitchen, if you have a canary living in your home. (Or for that matter, any other kind of bird...)

Finally, remember that canaries sing to claim ownership of their territory. They need to feel that they are "Lord and master of all they survey" in order to feel like singing about it. Once his feathers have grown back in again, you will want to see if you can make him feel like "The Boss" so that he will be more liable to want to brag about 'his' home.

Take a good close look at your canary's diet and environment, and I am sure it won't be long before you'll discover the cause— and solution— to your pet canary's feather loss and lack of song.

Canary Crazy

Hot weather arrives each year with a vengeance, in most of the Northern Hemisphere, and when it does bird-owners are suddenly faced with an urgent question. How will their bird (or birds) handle the heat, should it get extreme? It's time to learn what can be done to help our avian friends to...

Beat the Heat

"Oh, I don't worry too much about them, they'll adapt," he told me, smiling his charming smile. I wasn't fully convinced, but didn't feel I had the right to comment— I was just another relative newcomer to keeping canaries, visiting a widely respected canary breeder who had been keeping and breeding canaries for more than 70 years.

"But we're supposed to be starting a much worse heat wave than is usual for around here," I protested, feeling sorry for the birds in his outdoor aviary— they had no shade at all that I could see available to them, unless they went inside a mostly closed-in wooden shed. The roof was a combination of tin and corrugated plastic, and it seemed hotter in that shed, than outside in the sun. I knew, because we'd just been inside it.

He mopped his sweating face with a handkerchief, and admitted that it was indeed hotter than usual, but told me that he had never had any problems with his canaries from the heat, and he was sure they would adapt, even to this extreme.

I looked at his canaries again, and while they all looked okay, experience gained in my farming-country youth told me that some of these birds were going to be in serious

by R C McDonald

trouble, and soon, if they weren't provided with some way to help them cool off.

But I didn't feel I had enough canary-related experience to justify further protest. He had decades of experience behind him, so why not wait and see? Perhaps canaries were hardier than I thought.

I have one of those transparent faces that clearly shows all of my thoughts, and this one must have been as easily read as a book. He looked at me and chuckled.

"Not convinced, eh?" he chortled. "I don't blame you, I wouldn't be either, just going on what you can see here. There's a bit more to my aviary than this though!" His grin spread as he saw my puzzlement.

"Come on," he threw over his shoulder, as he turned and began walking away, his long legs devouring the ground at a deceptively easy looking pace.

I scuttled to keep up, and noticed with interest that I'd completely missed seeing the small path we were on. It led past the back corner of the aviary around the shed and under a group of alder, birch, and aspen, to a sheltered area that had been completely hidden from what I'd originally been able to see.

Here, in a small clearing behind the shed and almost completely shaded by the surrounding trees, was another simple extension to the aviary. A corrugated-plastic roof covered a large extension to the main flights, connected by a narrow wire-mesh alley only nine inches wide and perhaps a foot tall, running along the side of the shed under the eaves. Birds were flying merrily back and forth through it, ducking each other in flight.

In the center of the sheltered area this 'flyway' led to was a large multi-level fountain, easily four feet across at the base. It had four large pools stacked in tiers, each smaller around than the one below it, none more than a couple inches deep. They were all fed by a low spout in the center of the top pool, bubbling up musically from the middle. As

Canary Crazy

each pool filled, excess water flowed over the rim, falling in a gentle shower to the pool below.

Canaries were everywhere, showering under the falling droplets, splashing in the pools, or simply perched nearby, preening. I was awed and fascinated, but couldn't help but wonder how on earth he managed to keep the water so clean, given the steady use it obviously got— especially in such heat!

He showed me with pride how the overflow from the lowest level fell into an artificial stream-bed which led to a small area he called 'the swamp', filled almost to the brim with sand, moss, and cat-tails, where the water sank out of sight. He called the whole thing his 'cleansing stream', and pointed out the heart of the whole affair, almost a hundred feet away from the aviary, and perhaps eight feet lower, where the water ended up— a smallish natural pond, with a simple spout in the center.

Large, colourful fish could be seen here and there in the depths, and dragonflies hovered over the bunches of water-lilies and cat-tails that decorated the surface. A grace-note was added by a small flock of tiny Ornamental Ducks paddling serenely past. He told me how a pump in the middle of the lower pool continuously circulated the water, while another pump at one end drew water from near the bottom and sent it up to the aviary fountain, where the birds could bathe and refresh themselves, after which it was returned to the pond through the natural filter created by the sand in the cleansing stream and the bio-activity in his miniature 'swamp'.

The whole affair was remarkably beautiful, and provided his birds and his family a great deal of pleasure, helping keep everybody cool and happy through the hottest of weather. Most of us can't afford such an elaborate set-up, but that doesn't mean our birds have to suffer through the summer heat! There's some simple but effective steps that can be taken to help them weather the hottest days of the year with ease.

by R C McDonald

First though, it's a good idea to know how to recognize signs of heat stress in a bird. These are fairly simple, but if you see them, you need to act immediately, as they are a sign of urgent need. If that need is not met, death could occur.

Like stress from fear, in birds heat stress involves slicked-down feathers, held as tightly to the body as the bird can manage. When a bird is afraid, this serves the purpose of making it look as small as possible. In the case of heat stress, the goal is to reduce the heat retention of the feathers as much as possible.

Usually a bird suffering from heat stress will be gaping, again similarly to a fearful bird— however in this case, the open beak allows the body a little bit of cooling through the process of evaporation. The wings will be held out from the body, assisting in the circulation of air around the body.

The real problem is that birds don't have the built-in physical means of dealing with heat that we do. Birds have *no* sweat glands or other such option to help their body get rid of excess heat, but instead rely on air for cooling. Keeping the air circulating around them can help them to shed a little heat, and combined with their ability to find shelter from the sun, this is usually enough.

But when we cage our birds, we remove their ability to find shelter, unless we think to provide some shelter within the cage. If a cage should happen to be left sitting in the sun with no shade available, heat stress can occur in short order at any time of year. If this should happen in the heat of summer, it can initiate an all-too-rapid progress towards death, more quickly than most of us would think possible.

If you see signs of heat stress, you must act immediately! Remove the bird from the sun right away, and make sure clean drinking water is easily available. Then, (and make it quick) mist it lightly with some room-temperature water. Don't spray the bird from close quarters. Most birds find this a bit too much, and don't like it. Instead, stand back and aim over the bird's head, allowing the water to fall gently, as in a light rain-fall. This is almost always enjoyed by most birds.

But what can be done to prevent heat problems from arising in the first place?

First off, consider the cage itself, along with the layout. It's a good idea to ensure that there is plenty of room to move about. Remember, birds are creatures of the air! Floor space means very little to them. Just as we enjoy living in rooms that allow us to walk freely without having to worry about bumping into something, so do our birds prefer to be able to fly, at least a little, without having to navigate a maze. Flight also increases the amount of air flowing through the bird's system, and so can assist the body in its effort to divest itself of excess heat.

Birds like to be where they can see everything that's going on, and so their cages are often placed in front of a window. But if the sun is going to be coming through that window for even part of the day, you need to ensure that, no matter what the time of day, there is at least one perch always available in an area where the sun can't reach. It's no good having the cage partly shaded if there's no perch available in that patch of shade!

Always remember to include one of the most important elements to coping with heat— water. Clean, plentiful, and if possible, cool, water. Almost all living beings on this planet require an adequate supply of water in order to thrive, and during the heat of summer, this element is even more important, especially to our birds.

If possible, provide plenty of easy-access drinking water in a container that does not encourage bathing (to slow bacterial build-up) and provide a separate bird-bath. The enclosed ones that hang from the side of the cage work well — not the huge dark ones, but the smaller, lighter ones such as are pictured near the bottom of the Basic Canary Care article at *www.robirda.com/cancare.html*.

A few ice cubes in the bathing water will be gratefully

accepted by most birds, and, just as with children, the splashing and playing is not only fun, but helps to keep these small but high-activity creatures cool and happy.

When the weather gets *really* hot, many of us resort to fans, air conditioners or other such cooling systems. These can help birds to keep cool as much as they do us, but care must be taken to ensure that the bird is not living in a draft that he can't get away from. Remember, there's no problem with a breeze being present, as long as he can get out of it if he wishes. So long as there's even one draft-free perch, a breeze from a fan or air-conditioner should not cause a problem.

Often setting up a draft-free area of the cage is as simple as clipping a small piece of heavy paper, or perhaps a piece of cardboard or even tightly-woven cloth, to part of one or two sides of the cage. It's not necessary to cover much area, usually, and care must be taken to not block too much light.

In general, if it's too hot for you— chances are pretty good that your bird feels similarly. It's our hope that these tips will help you and your birds to weather any summer heat waves with ease and flair!

Canary Crazy

by R C McDonald

Part 3:
Breeding Canaries

Canary Crazy

by R C McDonald

The Breeding Quandary

Pet canaries are territorial little birds, and are really not very social at all. Yet time and again I've read, in books written for pet stores to sell, and online in websites aimed at selling birds or birdcages and cage accessories, that canaries need company in their cages.

This is, quite simply, just not true. In fact, pet owners trying, with the best of intentions, to follow this advice probably cause the majority of premature deaths in pet canaries. No explanation has been found for why any reputable author, (many with multiple books to their name) would make such a mistake, yet such statements are fairly easy to find. In my opinion errors like this throw the reliability of *any* information from such a source into question.

Even if you have a really large cage, (big enough to walk into) it is still quite difficult to keep canaries successfully caged together year round. While the hens in general are a little more socially inclined, even they like to have their own space to claim, while breeding— and it is not always easy for a new pet owner to understand just what 'coming into breeding condition' means, or how it affects their canaries.

Canaries can often be kept together through the moult and for some months afterwards (that is, from late summer through the fall and winter) but as late winter passes and early spring draws near, the males need to be separated out, to prevent undue aggression.

The primary mechanism that triggers their response to

the changing seasons is the lighting. The light a canary sees is very important, because canaries have a trait common to many species of songbird, but rather rare in most other pet bird species, known as 'photosensitivity'. This means that a layer of cells in their eyes responds to the lengthening days of spring, and tells their bodies to begin to prepare for their spring breeding season.

This involves actual physical changes. Examination of the birds' vents at this time will reveal that an adult canary in full breeding condition will have a more swollen abdomen than at other times of the year. This is also the *only* time when such an examination can reveal the bird's true gender.

The rest of the year (in other words, when the birds are *not* in breeding condition) there will be no obvious difference to the human eye between the genders, but when in breeding condition, the male's vent will protrude more than the hen's, while the hen's, being somewhat wider, will also protrude a little, but not as much. The difference is subtle and best learned by directly comparing two birds of known gender when in full breeding condition.

Canaries who try to breed earlier or later in the year have been kept under lights that (whether deliberately or by accident) mimic the lengthening days of spring. If such stimulation happens accidentally, the lighting can come in sporadic bursts. This may cause the subsequent death of any chicks that manage to hatch, as nights of irregular length can mean that the hen will not be able to feed the chicks just before dark. Since canaries can't see at night to feed their youngsters, the tiny chicks rely on getting an evening feeding in order to be able to survive the long hours of the night.

Sometimes a non-feeding hen may not have access to what she considers appropriate food to feed her chicks, and that can result in chick death too. Other times she may think she is guarding her chicks from a too-aggressive male. The solution is not always obvious, and there may not

by R C McDonald

be much time for experimentation. In fact, raising canary chicks successfully is a lot of work, for both birdie parents *and* birdie owners!

Until you have actually seen it, it is hard to believe the quantity of food a growing young chick can eat. It is quite astonishing! A canary youngster can (and normally should) literally double in size every day for the first 10 or 12 days of its life. This rate of growth takes a *lot* of fuelling!

People who are truly determined not to be a breeder generally won't buy a hen— but accidents can and do happen. Many a 'male' canary has suddenly and without warning (as far as the owner knew) laid an egg. This does not mean that the bird changed gender, as is sometimes claimed, but rather that its gender had not been correctly identified when sold as a male.

Other new canary owners, thinking that their canaries need company to keep them entertained and amused, will purchase a second male canary, believing that will be less trouble than buying a hen. But expecting two male canaries to share a cage at *any* time of the year can lead to trouble.

Imagine two very macho men, strangers to each other. Then imagine them being forced to share a bachelor apartment all day every day. It would be surprising if they didn't fight, yes? That's similar to what happens when we expect two male canaries to peacefully share a pet-sized cage. It *could* work out— but it almost always does not.

It's a little different when you are dealing with a male and a hen. In a flock of canaries, hens tend to rule the roost, and outside of breeding season the males generally will let them. Their humans will think that they are getting along just fine, but wonder why their male has stopped singing. You see— most males sing very little if at all, when they share their cage with a hen.

Other pairs may argue from the first, then suddenly decide to get along, while yet others may be fine for awhile, then suddenly begin trying to kill each other. Especially during the spring, one or the other may come into breeding condition first, and this can cause any number of problems, most to do with fighting and aggression.

They don't often do this kind of thing while you are watching, either. Generally there is lots more going on in our birds' lives than we realize. Cluing in takes effort on our part, to learn to understand their basic nature and ways of expression. These are quite different than ours— but quite understandable, too, once you get the hang of it.

Canaries are rather complex little creatures. Many an experienced hookbill breeder has scratched their heads in puzzlement over their canaries, who are so different in so many ways from other common species of companion birds. Most of the species we tend to keep as pets are originally from tropical regions where there is, not the four seasons found in temperate climes, but two; the Wet, and the Dry. Species who evolved under such conditions tend to be what is usually known as 'opportunistic' breeders, meaning that they breed only when conditions are right.

Many of these species have little to no photosensitivity, which means they will usually do quite well even under the variable lighting commonly found in our homes. But when it comes to our canaries, such variable lighting will affect their behaviour drastically.

Most of us find it easiest to follow a lighting schedule for our canaries. These can stick fairly close to nature, or we may, for convenience or other reasons, want to shift the seasons a little, one way or another. You can easily adapt such a schedule to your needs, just remember that canaries need a steady lighting routine to allow their bodies to maintain a natural balance with the seasons as they perceive them.

For an example of a schedule based on the annual days and nights found in the Canary Islands (that part of our planet where canaries evolved, which they are physically most naturally adapted for), see the chart found online at *www.robirda.com/sunset.html*

by R C McDonald

There's another reason to house canaries separately; besides preventing fights, that is. The dominant canary housed in any community cage will come into breeding condition first, and may (and often will) harass the other inhabitants of the cage during the process, slowing their progress into breeding condition.

The process of assisting canaries to come into full breeding condition occurs much more reliably and steadily if the birds are housed separately, and the pairs introduced to each other only *after* both parties have come into full readiness to breed.

Once this occurs, the eggs will begin to arrive. Each egg laid amounts to as much as 25% of the hen's mass. This means that a great deal of a hen's bodily resources goes into making each egg, which in turn means that laying too many eggs can make her seriously ill. When you own a canary hen, it is not a bad idea to get a liquid calcium supplement to keep on hand, in case of emergency. This can save an egg-bound hen's life.

Incubating her eggs after she has laid them is a natural process, and whether or not you want chicks, she should be allowed to go through it. If instead you remove the eggs, she will simply lay more eggs, and yet more, trying to get a clutch to incubate. This is far harder on her than allowing her to incubate a clutch of empty eggs! Even if you don't want chicks, you will still need to allow her to spend some time sitting on her eggs, as her body will tell her she needs to do. This will allow her body time to replace the nutrients that went into making those eggs.

Fake eggs don't hatch, and also have the advantage of not drying out and losing weight over time, as infertile eggs will, so replacing the real eggs with the right kind of fake eggs (usually sold only by those who specialize in canary breeding supplies) can help give her a longer time between laying clutches, since she will not abandon the fake eggs as fast as she would infertile eggs. This means less over-all egg-laying through the spring season, which is generally healthier for a pet hen.

Egg-binding, that is, difficulty in laying the eggs, has a variety of contributing factors. Most involve a diet lacking in adequate nutrient intake levels, particularly calcium and the vitamins and other minerals needed to properly digest it. Another factor, often disregarded, is the general physical condition the bird is in. This last is directly related to the amount of flying she is allowed throughout the rest of the year.

I have always found that allowing the hen adequate exercise *before* breeding season comes along to be a very important part of preparing for breeding season. The time to allow flying is not when a hen is setting on her eggs, but during the winter, while the days are shorter. Given the chance, most hens will fly almost ceaselessly during the latter part of the winter, trying with every second of daylight to see that their bodies are properly prepared for the rigors of breeding and laying eggs soon to come.

This is why canary hens, even those kept strictly as pets, should have large cages, or else be allowed to fly about in a bird-safed area on a fairly regular basis. This can be easier to do than you might think; see the chapter 'Home Free' elsewhere in this book for more information on safely 'free-flying' a pet canary inside your home.

It is well known that we canary people are regarded by many other bird owners as being quite unreasonably attached to our birds. Many of us have numerous other people in our lives who just can't understand why anybody could possibly care so much about 'just some silly birds'.

But you see, we know what they don't. We have the disease known as 'Canaryitis'... and, it's completely untweetable! ;-)

by R C McDonald

Predictability or Adaptability?
(the Controversy of Diversity)

Linebreeding, a form of in-breeding where carefully selected related birds are chosen to breed to each other, has been practiced for centuries, with varying results. The last century has brought much new information to add to the accumulated years of experience, but that has done little to settle the heated discussions on the controversial topic of canary line-breeding, and whether predictability or adaptability should be the preferred goal of canary breeders.

Go to any bird show and listen, and it will probably not be long before you begin to overhear varied snippets of conversation centering around breeding winning showbirds. This is a favourite topic at most shows, and you will find that there are as many different proponents and systems as there are birds at the show. Yes, I said birds, not people. It's been my observation that many of the people at these events may hold several systems dear. A newcomer to the Canary Fancy can become incredibly confused in very short order listening to all these (many conflicting) ideas and methods, particularly if they are looking for advice on buying a breeding pair.

I try to tell anybody who asks, to listen to everybody, at least to start with; sort through all the advice and categorize it, then apply that good old yardstick, common sense. Any one approach or technique that everybody agrees on is quite likely to have a lot of validity, for example. On the other hand, you still have to watch out for that old bogey, the 'old wives tale.'

Line-breeding is a fairly commonly approach to breeding show-quality canaries. There are a variety of methods for producing the desired goal, but they all have the same aim; to produce a strain of related birds who look and act as much alike as possible. Ideally, you would choose anywhere from two to six or eight top-quality birds to begin with. These birds should all display the physique, colour, and temperament you wish to propagate. They are paired up to produce offspring who will in turn be paired together.

Each generation of offspring is heavily culled of any birds which do not display all of the desired characteristics before again being bred to each other. Some sell such culled birds as pet stock, others put them down. Many systems also advise crossing back to one of the 'founder birds' on a regular basis.

Why this produces more predictable offspring is because this approach will directly reduce the diversity of the gene pool. The birds grow to be more and more reliably similar over the generations because they each carry more and more identical genetic coding.

What many proponents of such a system often forget to mention, or perhaps they do not know, are the problems which can accompany such an approach. Genes are made of a large number of chromosomes which govern the traits of the living thing which contains them. When the chromosomes are fully diverse, each is different than its neighbour, and the genes are able to carry the codes for a vast number of traits and abilities, some expressed, some not.

It is well known to food-crop husbandrymen that if you reduce the amount of genetic diversity the species carries too far, you will also lose an unpredictable and unforeseeable amount of adaptability and, often, quite a lot of disease

by R C McDonald

resistance and hardiness.

Canary breeders can easily be found who stress the idea that since show stock is so expensive, you will want to see that you get the greatest possible production out of any birds you might buy. Often line-breeding is quoted as proof that the pair will reliably reproduce themselves; the babies will be as similar as possible in size, colour, and type to their parents.

Well, that is true, as far as it goes.

It is at times like this that a basic understanding of genetics and how it works comes in handy. Many's the person whom I've overheard saying, 'Oh, genetics is too complicated for me, I don't understand it.' Okay, genetics is a subject with an incredible range of possible complexity, that I will grant you. But if you look at it awhile, it will soon become clear that the basic premises are actually quite simple.

I like to compare genetics with chess. In chess, there is a finite number of defined moves, possible in limited and qualified ways. It is in combination and in interaction that the moves acquire their complexity. It is the same with genetics.

Birds who carry many similar chromosomes, as is true of most line-bred stock, will hatch out similar to each other as well as the parents. It is also usually true that this group of birds will all tend to be susceptible in the same degree to the same diseases, and that they will all have similar levels of resistance to any other problems which come along— average levels often markedly lower than that of more genetically diverse stock.

Diversity of the gene pool gives rise to higher levels of diversity in the chicks, resulting in more variation in colour, body shape, and expression of personality. Babies from the same nest may look and act quite different from their sibs and their parents when adulthood is reached. Many could turn out to not be considered fit for the show-bench.

Canary Crazy

The one fact I find many people forget to include in their calculations, though, is that most of these birds will tend to be hardy specimens and very good breeders, and will be perfectly acceptable as pets or breeding stock, if carefully mated. Those (admittedly fewer) babies produced which are good enough to show will be every bit as strong and healthy as their less showy siblings, and will often stand up to the rigours of stress and adversity far better than their 'hot-house flower' cousins.

It has been my observation that if careful notation is kept of the ancestry and outstanding characteristics of each chick and its parents, it is possible to get at least fifty percent or more predictability of the youngsters a bird will throw when adult, when their lineage is considered in combination with that of their mates.

Let's take a simple example having to do with physical markings. A dark hen bred to an evenly-marked male might throw 2 dark chicks, 3 mottled variegated chicks, an almost evenly-marked variegate, and a clear over two nests. The mates for these babies will come from a clear bird mated to an evenly-marked variegate; the babies were mostly variegate, with one being 3/4ths dark, and two clear.

Pair one takes a clear bird from each nest. (We are pretending for now that they have complementary feather types.) You can reasonably expect to get about 50% clear or lightly ticked babies from this pairing. The rest will be mostly variegates, ranging from lightly ticked to almost fully dark. You may even see a self, or all dark bird, particularly since there is one within two generations of the chicks' lineage.

Nest two pairs one of the dark birds from pair one with the 3/4 dark from pair two. Here the babies should be about 50% dark, with about 25% of the rest being fairly heavily variegated. Here again, you will see the odd lightly-marked or even a clear bird, but most of the offspring will be dark.

Nest three pairs two of the variegates, and once again the

results are fairly predictable. About 50% of the babies will be variegated, and the other 50% will be split fairly evenly between birds that tend to be either heavily dark, or most or even all light.

Nest four pairs a all-dark bird to a all-light bird, a match most breeders will tell you should not be done. If you are speaking of interbreeding two birds from two completely different lines, this is usually true, but in this case both these birds have both all-dark and all-light birds in their direct ancestry, on both sides. This is a fun pairing, for me, as I have often found nests of this sort to produce both fully dark and totally light babies in even amounts. I love to show people a nest with two dark babies and two clear babies, and see their faces when they realize that all four babies are full blood siblings.

You can probably imagine enough by now to continue the theoretical matchings by yourself. Besides colour, you can affect song, breeding traits, conformation, and even many personality traits. One delightful result of promoting genetic diversity in your stock is the increased chance of seeing a truly new mutation, remote though it still is. But with a fully diverse gene-pool, almost anything can (and often does) happen.

Remember that percentages are based on averages out of a hundred. Since you will rarely if ever get a hundred babies from a pair, the odds can give you two 'long-shot' babies in the first nest. It may be years, however, before you see that particular mutation again if you are not careful to preserve its presence. Take the time to study your birds and their traits; that way you will be better able to spot a potential mutation.

The possibilities grow more complex and varied as diversity of the gene pool is expanded; the sky is literally the limit! So enjoy your birds, and practice whichever methods seem best to you, keeping in mind one of the first laws of nature; 'infinite diversity in infinite combination'.

A Hen's Gotta Lay
What a Hen's Gotta Lay

It can be difficult to always be sure what gender the canary you are buying actually is. Every year I hear from people who end up owning a canary hen, when they thought they were buying a male. Others may buy a pet canary hen rather than a male because of her appearance, personality, or even price.

Many pet owners, especially those new to canaries, don't realize that keeping and nurturing a canary hen as a pet can be rather different than keeping a male canary. The fact is, whether you have a male canary with her or not, and whether you plan to breed her or not, as long as she is healthy, sooner or later your canary hen will prove to you that a hen's gotta lay, what a hen's gotta lay.

I can't tell you how many people I've talked to who were shocked to find that their happy little pet hen canary, living all on her own with no male in sight, has suddenly turned around and laid an egg. It's a fairly common misconception that as long as there is no male, there will be no eggs.

"You mean they're like a chicken?" is often the next question— frequently delivered in tones of shock, understandably enough.

Well, no. Not exactly. But the fact is, a canary hen *will* lay eggs at the appropriate time of year, if she is old enough and healthy enough. Some hens will try to lay eggs even if they are *not* really healthy enough. Whether these eggs have been fertilized for her or not actually has nothing to do with

by R C McDonald

whether they will be laid, but only with whether they have the potential to hatch.

Generally egg-laying will happen sometime during the spring. If eggs appear before or after that, it is usually due to her having been exposed to artificial lighting before dawn or after sunset. This leads her system to react as if it were spring, by pushing her into breeding condition.

Many pet owners don't really want to raise babies, but don't want to give up their hen, either. Others assume that whether they want to or not, eggs will mean that they have to raise babies. Neither is necessarily true. So what's a puzzled pet owner to do?

Well, if you just take the egg away, chances are good that she will just keep laying, another, and another, and another, until her body's resources are too low to lay more. By then she will be a very sick little bird.

Each egg a canary hen lays amounts to the equivalent of as much as 25% of her total physical resources. Yet her body, in breeding season, will try to make her lay an egg a day until she has an entire clutch (ranging normally from three to five eggs) to incubate. This is pure instinct for canary hens, a powerful impulse that will not be denied.

So if you simply remove the eggs, you will in effect be forcing her to lay more eggs than she otherwise would. This in turn will use more nutrients, which will be pulled from her muscles and bones in favour of producing the eggs, unless her diet is sufficiently rich in the necessary minerals and vitamins needed for producing eggs.

Proper muscle function also requires a mineral supply. These nutrients ensure smooth operation of the muscles throughout the body. So when a hen's body is so lacking in dietary minerals and the vitamins needed to digest them that it is forced to use its own supplies in order to make an egg, the bird's muscles lose much of their smoothness and power. This can lead to eggbinding, where the hen is unable to pass her egg. If left untreated, this condition can kill within 24 hours; in effect, she must lay the egg or die.

If ever you should happen to find a hen in such a condition, liquid calcium given orally, along with heat, may help her to pass the egg. Far better, though, is to take steps to prevent such an occurrence in the first place.

The best thing I have found to do begins well ahead of time, by obtaining a batch of fake canary eggs. Every owner of a canary hen should have at least a few of these relatively inexpensive and indispensable little items on hand for when they are needed. They are cheap and readily available from various suppliers such as Redbird Products, found online at *www.redbirdproducts.com,* or Just For Birds, located at *www.justforbirds.com.*

Then, when she shows signs of wanting to nest, you can go ahead and give her the nestpan, and let her lay her eggs. After each egg is laid, once she is off the nest, remove the real egg and replace it with a fake, until after a few days the clutch is complete and she begins to sett.

Handle the eggs gently, from end-to-end, and there should be no problem with breakage. If breakage does occur and it seems as if the shell is too weak to be handled this way, then you will know that the egg-shell is too thin, and the hen needs to have her nutrient content increased, especially calcium.

Once the clutch has been completed the hen will begin to incubate them. The old term for this is 'sett'. Real eggs, if infertile, will begin to slowly lose their water content after a week or so of incubation, which will make them lighter in weight. This in turn will be noticed by the hen when she is turning them, and her instincts will tell her to throw them out and lay more 'good' eggs.

Wise canary keepers know this, and keep plenty of fake eggs on hand to offer a broody hen. These fake eggs cannot lose weight, and in turn, the hen's instincts will tell her that she is incubating fertile eggs. This usually means that most hens will be quite content to sett and wait for their eggs to hatch, rather than tossing them out and laying yet more eggs, as they might if allowed to sett on their own real, though infertile, eggs.

Let her incubate her fake eggs for at least a couple of weeks or more before you even begin to consider removing her nest. Some hens will want to repeat this nesting cycle right through the spring, until she begins her summer moult, and her body tells her that breeding season is over. She may even abandon the nest willingly herself, at that point.

Many canary hens will try to breed for up to half the year if their environment encourages it. That's why I feel it is quite important to not trigger the start of breeding season too early, as it can be difficult if not downright impossible to get a pet canary hen to stop, once nesting is underway.

The best way I have found to control breeding is to monitor the amount of light she is getting, and be sure she does not see too much artificial light before sunrise or after sunset, particularly during the winter.

You will often hear that reducing the amount of light a hen is seeing can stop her from wanting to breed, and as far as it goes, this is true. What is too often left unsaid, though, is that the reason this works is because a reduction in the amount of light will usually trigger a moult, and that this is what will bring about the bodily changes that will put a stop, for awhile at least, to her wanting to breed.

You want to be careful using lighting as a means to stop a hen from breeding, though, as if you should happen to increase the lights once her moult is over, she is quite likely to once again try to begin breeding— because as far as she is concerned, lengthening days is a signal that it is spring, and time to begin breeding.

Personally, I prefer to not mess with what nature has worked out, and try to follow the pattern established by the birds' own heritage. This means using a lighting system based on the hours of daylight canaries evolved with.

Canary Crazy

As the chart posted at *robirda.com/sunset.html* shows, the shortest day of the year in the Canary Islands, where the ancestors to our canaries evolved, is ten and a half hours long. In midsummer, the longest day is fourteen hours. I use these extremes as my guidelines, and follow the pattern of the rest of the year's days as best I can.

After the midwinter solstice, I begin to increase the amount of time the birds lights are on by about 15 minutes every couple of weeks, until they are at the maximum of fourteen hours. There they will stay until the summer solstice, when I begin decreasing slowly, until I hit ten and a half hours. At this point the lights stop and hold steady again, waiting for midwinter, when the whole cycle begins all over again.

Once you have this routine established, you will be able to keep your pet canary hen's urge to breed satisfied without sacrificing her health. Granted, she won't have much if any interested in interacting with you while she is on her nest, but never mind that, it won't last forever.

Once her nesting instinct has been satisfied and breeding season is over, she should return to being her normal, active, happy little self, and you will have a wonderful, healthy pet canary hen for the rest of the year, and hopefully for many more years to come.

by R C McDonald

An Ethical Breeder

Breeding canaries or any other species of bird is a wonderful activity. The babies are endlessly endearing, and it's an experience that can't be described, watching the pairs mate, produce eggs, and hatch, feed, fledge and wean their babies.

In all the excitement, it is very easy for new breeders to get so involved in helping their birds to produce babies, that they forget to consider how they are going to house, feed, and train these babies, or exactly what will be involved in finding them good homes. Yet these thoughts are perhaps the most integral part of becoming an Ethical Breeder.

Difficult though it can be to rein in the excitement of your first breeding season, it can't be emphasized how important it is, before allowing your treasured canaries to begin breeding, to sit down and carefully consider all the factors that will be involved in your operation. Careful preparation can help tremendously in dealing with any of the problems that arise, but first you need to have a basic understanding— *before* getting started— of everything you will soon be confronted with.

Here's some of the questions I believe every breeder should ask themselves beforehand;

"*Do I understand how my birds are going to want to breed?*"

A successful breeder *must* have a thorough understanding of the wants and needs of his birds. Many species have fairly strict breeding requirements, and will not produce any healthy chicks for you, if these needs are not met.

Look for books, articles and websites on your chosen species, and read everything you can find on them. Talk to people who keep and breed them, if you can find some. Try to get a feel of what kind of conditions the species evolved under, so as to be able to better understand their breeding triggers and the dietary requirements of their breeding diet. Then try to mimic those conditions as much as possible, in the environment you set up for them to live and breed in.

"Do I have enough cages to house all of my breeding birds individually if necessary, as well as enough extra cages to adequately house any babies once they are weaned?"

This is one of the most important questions any new breeder can ask himself, and it is perhaps the one most often forgotten, ignored, or skimped on. Yet it can have a tremendous impact on, not just your lifestyle, but the health, longevity, and, yes, the personality of the birds you raise.

I couldn't tell you how many times I have heard people agonize over throwing out fertile eggs, when they finally manage to get their birds to breed and suddenly discover they don't know how to get them to stop! Too often the cages fill up much faster than expected, and suddenly the breeder is faced with a quandary— if he or she allows those extra eggs to hatch, there will be too many birds.

It can seem like sacrilege, after struggling so hard to get your birds into condition to produce fertile eggs at all, to find yourself throwing them away in quantities later on in the season— I've even heard it referred to as a 'crime'.

But if it *is* a crime, then the results of allowing such eggs to hatch is an even worse crime— because it is nothing more or less than cruel to put just-weaned youngsters into a crowded cage where competition rules. Such youngsters will almost certainly have trouble getting enough food, water, and perching space, and will undergo a *lot* of stress.

Crowding is much more stressful for birds than it is for humans, even for the more social avian species, and that is even more true of youngsters, who have higher nutritional requirements than adults, while their bodies are maturing.

For the territorial species such as most songbirds, overcrowding can be a death sentence to birds lower down in the 'pecking order' of the flock. These birds will have great difficulty getting adequate amounts of food or water, and will never be allowed to eat peacefully; each mouthful will be gotten grab-and-run style.

In short, in a contained space like a cage where no escape is possible, such birds live in a state of constant fear. This severely impacts a youngster's ability to mature properly, and often winds up negatively affecting their state of health life-long.

"Are my flight cages large enough to allow my babies to fully develop both physically and emotionally?"

Crowded conditions are sometimes excused on the notion that the crowding is only temporary, until some birds are sold. But that approach does not take into account the fact that youngsters continue developing for quite some time once they are out of the nest— their bodies are still growing and developing for several months afterwards, and at the same time, they are also learning the physical and social skills they will use the rest of their lives.

Housing for young birds should provide plenty of room for exercise, a wide variety of nutritious foods for their maturing bodies, and plentiful safe and entertaining toys and perches to stimulate their minds and bodies and help encourage positive interactions, between each other as well as with humans.

All this, while still leaving enough room for the birds to practice flying. Most young birds can fly as soon as or shortly after they leave the nest, but will still need plenty of practice in order to learn to manage themselves properly in the air. In particular, they need to learn how to take off and land. Birds who do not learn basic flight skills when young, are likely to never learn them properly at all.

This makes it very important that all young birds learn how to fly properly, while they are still quite young. This also helps strengthen their growing body and encourages proper musculature and skeletal development, as well as assisting in producing a confident, outgoing personality.

"Will I need to sell any or even all youngsters produced? If so, can I keep them housed well until they are finished their baby moult, and mature enough to sell?"

Some species, and canaries are one of them, undergo a nestling moult shortly after weaning. Care should be taken to never sell any bird until their moult is finished, except in rare special circumstances where they will go to somebody prepared to deal with the special needs of a younger, still-maturing baby.

Most birds are highly susceptible to problems during the moult, particularly if they also have to deal with a changing diet and environment, so be careful to keep track of this timing before committing to any sales.

"If you are planning to sell your youngsters, do you know an ethical wholesaler or retailer you can sell your stock to, or are you planning to sell your birds individually to private homes?"

This is another highly important question so often missed by beginning breeders, but which can make a world of difference. While you may be paid more per bird, it can be a lot more work to retail the birds directly to their eventual owners. They need to be able to find you, so you will need to figure out what, when, where, and how to advertise, and just what your sales and return policies will be. Then, you will need to decide what you'll do when your customers want to come and visit, to choose their new bird.

It's not a good idea to let just anybody into your birdroom; let them look in the door if you like, but don't let them in to just wander around— not only could they scare your birds, but there's a possibility of insect or disease transmission, especially if they have been around other birds.

You will also need to be sure that they know how to care for their birds— this was why I designed my Basic Canary Care Sheet. Everybody I sell a canary to receives a freshly-printed copy. On it is space to enter a brief description of the bird, its band number, and my phone number and email address, as well as basic care instructions. (You can use the same care sheet yourself; to learn more about it go to *www.robirda.com/care.html*)

Selling your youngsters to a wholesaler or a pet store is far easier— but rarely will such dealers take very good care of the birds temporarily in their care. It is up to you to research such buyers and decide for yourself what will be best for you and your birds.

Nobody will know better than you how to make sure that your youngsters will be treated with the same care with which you raised them— and that should not change whether you are selling them to a wholesaler or directly to the family who will keep them.

Maintaining an ethical approach to breeding may seem like a lot of work, but I can personally vouch for the fact that not only are the rewards well worth it— so is the peace of mind you achieve, knowing that the youngsters you raised so lovingly and carefully will be cared for as well as you would yourself.

That's the kind of peace that no amount of money can ever buy— and it will stay with you and your birds for the rest of your lives. What better reward could anybody ask?

Gender-Specific Behaviour

Canaries are among those interesting creatures whose gender is difficult for humans to determine, especially when they are young. They are able to easily tell the difference between themselves, but for us it's another story!

Since with very few exceptions there's nothing obvious to go on unless the birds are in full breeding condition, many canary owners will be tempted to look for a set of actions or habits that they can use as gender indicators.

The problem with most such observations, is that they can't take individual personality into account; yet that single, so-often-ignored factor can make a tremendous difference. I can't tell you how many times I've seen a mellow, non-aggressive male mistaken as a hen, or how many aggressive hens I've seen judged to be a male.

For example, it's tempting to think that two canaries who consistently fight with each other whenever they have access to the same area are both male, based on their aggressive behaviour with each other.

But in actual fact, many canary hens are just as liable to be every bit as aggressive as a male, particularly in regard to defending herself or an area she considers to be her own personal territory. This means that using aggression (or lack of it) as a gender indicator can lead to mistaken identities as often as not. These kinds of traits and actions can vary not only from individual to individual, depending

by R C McDonald

on personality, but also from flock to flock, depending on conditions and genetic inheritance.

In some flocks, all males are aggressive, while all the hens are mellow and easy-going. In other flocks, the exact opposite conditions may prevail. Unless you happen to know the history of the flock your canary came from, using such actions to indicate gender may not be too reliable.

There are, of course, some actions that *are* specific to each gender, especially during breeding season — but even many of these can fool you, particularly if you're relatively new to keeping canaries.

A good example of this is nest-building. It seems to be quite true that only a canary hen can build a proper nest. It can be tempting to take this to mean that only a canary hen will collect nesting material, and that only a canary hen will attempt to build a nest— but in actuality, usually this is not the case at all.

Especially during the earlier days of spring, many canary males can be seen eagerly ripping paper, and picking up shreds of paper or other materials, trotting about with it in their beaks while twittering excitedly. Female behaviour? Not necessarily! Many male canaries will do this just as eagerly as any hen will.

Others will tell you that only a canary hen will sit in a nest and incubate eggs, however this too is sometimes wrong. I have known many male canaries who would sit in the nest, and I have even heard of one case where a proven male successfully finished incubating, hatching, and rearing a clutch of eggs that the hen had abandoned half-way through incubation.

I myself have seen many a male canary try to encourage his hen to begin nesting by sitting in the nest himself, occasionally lifting up a little to look down into the nest, twittering softly as if 'talking' to imaginary chicks. When the hen gets curious and comes over to see what's going on, these males would begin feeding her— and more often than not, in fairly short order they would have their hen first sitting in her nest, then building it, while they eagerly fed and bred her.

What all this means is that these kinds of behaviours can be beneficial to the male, in that it shows the hen that he will make a good father, one who is eager to assist her, and has shown her his skill in feeding and caring. This makes her feel more comfortable with him, allowing her to be more willing to rely on him to feed her and, once the chicks have hatched, increases her tendency to trust him to protect her babies while she is away from the nest.

Some male canaries will even go so far as to put nesting material they've collected into the nest, and attempt to pack it down; but if you watch carefully, here is where you will see a distinct difference between the genders. Although it's rare for a male canary to want to build a nest, it *can* happen, so an attempt to build a nest is not necessarily an indicator of gender. Such a male will collect nesting material and drop it into a nestpan or other likely-looking receptacle— and he may even have a pretty good idea how to go about actually building a nest, too. But he will be quite hopeless when it comes to knowing how to tamp all these bits of material together into a tidy nest. That knowledge seems to rest with the hens alone.

So if a singing canary builds a loose, sloppy-looking nest, he probably is a male, irregardless of 'his' nest-building attempts. On the other hand, some hens build fairly sloppy nests, too, and although in general the males sing much better than the hens, occasionally a hen will hatch who can and does sing very much like a male. So, song is not always a reliable gender indicator either.

Some people say that a hen will only sing when she has too many male hormones in her system, usually pointing at a dietary or seasonal cause. It is true that this can happen, and when it does, such singing hens will usually be heard mostly after the moult and through the winter. As the winter turns to spring and they begin to come into breeding

by R C McDonald

condition, these hens will gradually stop singing, ceasing entirely once each has achieved full breeding condition.

Not all singing hens fit this description, however. While they are not common, some hens will sing right through breeding season, even when incubating eggs, which quite neatly obliterates the hormonal theory of hen's song, as a breeding hen's hormones *can't* be out of balance— if they were, she would not be able to breed successfully, lay her eggs and incubate and rear her babies.

What all this means is that a singing canary who builds a neat, tidy nest is almost certain to be a hen, regardless of how well it sings.

Of course, once breeding season is well under way, there *is* one time-tested and thoroughly reliable method of telling the difference between genders. This particular method is indisputable; if a bird lays an egg, it's unquestionably a hen.

Every once in a while I'll hear somebody claim that their bird suddenly changed gender, that it used to be a male and suddenly became a hen; while that actually can happen with some of the more primitive species, it has never been known to occur in canaries.

A more probable scenario in such cases, is that any bird who has laid an egg was actually a hen all along— regardless of how well s/he sang, or what gender her owners were originally told she was.

Indisputable proof of gender in a male canary only occurs when it is seen that he has produced fertile eggs with a hen. While it is true that only a hen can lay eggs, it is also true that only a male canary can fill those eggs so that they will produce live young.

Some people believe that it is possible to tell any canary's gender at any time of the year, through an examination of the bird's vent. Many pet store people rely on this kind of 'gender identification' to sort any youngsters new to the store, and it's quite common at bird marts to see people casually flipping a bird over to check the vent area.

Canary Crazy

While the state of the vent *can* be a good and even reliable indicator of a canary's general condition and state of health, it is *not* a reliable method for separating youngsters by gender. As long as it is clean, not swollen, and has no traces of old droppings adhered nearby, the state of a canary's vent can verify that the bird is in general good health, but that is about *all* the vent area will tell you, unless the bird you're looking at happens to be in full breeding condition.

The problem is that until a canary is ready to breed, his or her vent will look exactly like any other canary's vent. When a canary is *not* in breeding condition, there simply is *no* obvious visual differences in appearance between a male and a female canary, with the exception of a few gender-linked canary colours or feather types.

People who tell you otherwise, are, quite simply, either sadly mistaken, or lying through their teeth— or they may have mistaken a different condition as an indicator of gender, when in reality there was another cause altogether.

The fact is, being in breeding condition is not the only time a canary can have a swollen vent; some diseases can cause exactly this symptom as well. For example, a problem with an enlarged heart, liver, or kidneys can cause a bird's vent to swell in a fashion that can look remarkably like a bird in breeding condition, as can other medical conditions — but if you watch such a bird's actions, you will soon realize what is actually going on.

Any canary with such a problem will not act at all like a bird preparing for breeding season, but will instead be much more lethargic, spending little to no time flying, or ripping paper and tearing at string toys. In such a case, observation of the bird's actions can give you the clues to its true state of health, if not its gender.

Observation will always play an essential role for a caring canary owner; it lends invaluable assistance in learning to understand just what these small gems are all about. Just remember to use such observations as indicators, rather than definitive facts. That way you will continue to learn more about just what you're seeing and hearing when you watch, look, and listen to your canaries.

In my experience, the lessons these wonderful little songsters have to share with us will never end— the more time you spend around them and the more you learn about them, the more you will realize there is left to learn.

It *can* be quite a challenge— but after all, isn't learning to deal with challenges what life's really all about? And maybe, in the end, that's why some of us seem to find canaries so endlessly fascinating.

Wintering Canaries

When you're new to keeping canaries, it can be difficult to realize the tremendous difference the changes of season can bring to these small birds. The kinds of physical changes brought on when their bodies experience the changing length of days throughout the year can affect their actions, their health, their state of mind, and their overall quality and length of life.

Just how important these seasonal changes can be to our canaries is not easy to imagine; they literally can mean the difference between life and death. This was recently brought home to me yet again, when I received a letter.

He wrote, *"I put my two canaries on a natural light schedule for the last year, and for the first time I have had my canaries moult at the correct time of year. I hope to keep these guys for a long time. Unfortunately my first canary died in Feb after only 2 years. When I got him I thought it was great to have him sing late at night. I didn't realize canaries are so light sensitive. When I found out otherwise I put him on a natural light schedule, but he just never 'got right'. I guess an ounce of prevention is worth a lot more than a pound of cure. I would never knowingly have harmed my bird."*

No caring owner would *ever* knowingly harm any bird in their family, but many birds, canaries not the least among them, can have ways so alien to our own human nature that

by R C McDonald

it can be difficult to learn to really understand just what they need. The matter is not helped by the fact that there is so much misinformation in the few industry-published books available on keeping canaries. It can be very difficult to sort through all the conflicting ideas, trying to figure out what is right and what isn't.

In the end, too many new canary owners find out the hard way what not to do, by losing their pets to one or another problem that could have been easily prevented, with the right information at hand.

How a canary spends his winter will have a tremendous impact on his health, state of mind, and yes, his song, throughout the following year. It can seem to be counter-intuitive to spend the winter preparing your birds for a healthy and active spring breeding season and the eventual summer moult— particularly if you're a pet owner and not planning to breed— but this species' seasonal approach to life means this is exactly what we need to be thinking of in the fall and winter, in order to keep our canaries' health at optimal levels through the entire year and into the future.

In the Canary Islands, the wild relatives of our birds' ancestors experience daylengths varying by less than four hours over the year; the longest day receives a little less than 14 hours of daylight (not counting about twenty minutes each of dawn and dusk), while on the shortest day of the year, the time between sunrise and sunset will be just under 10 1/2 hours.

Not exactly a huge difference! Yet canaries evolved to use these changing lengths of day to cue changes that control how they live, eat, act, and sing, as well as having a strong impact on their overall health and physical condition.

While it is true that our pets and show-birds are often as much as hundreds of generations away from their ancestral wild canaries, their bodies still rely on the age-old triggers of light and dark to tell them what the season is, how to act, and when. These instincts are set so deeply into canary physiology that it seems impossible to separate them; a study done on the annual moult showed that canaries who were kept completely away from any seasonal stimuli did not moult or attempt to breed, and, in a period of slightly less than two years, all eventually died.

The study concluded that an annual moult was essential to maintaining canary health, but did not emphasize the fact that it was the lack of exposure to seasonal change that was the root cause behind both the failure to moult and all the birds' eventual deaths.

All the experienced canary keepers and breeders I have met use the annual cycles of daylight and darkness to help prepare their canaries for seasonal changes. Some simply use direct daily exposure to natural sunlight, while others use artificial lighting, changing their bird's days to suit their own needs. But if you ask any to explain their solution, it's not all that unusual to get a different explanation from almost every person you speak with.

Some breeders supplement the natural daylight their canaries see with artificial lights, while others arrange to keep their canaries completely away from exposure to the outdoors, preferring instead to provide artificial lighting at their own chosen hours, 'time-shifting' the seasonal changes forward by as much as two or three months by controlling the lengths of their birds' days with lighting.

This is thought to allow the young birds more time to mature before they will be shown, which can perhaps be an advantage at the earlier shows— but as some experienced showmen are quick to point out, these shifted seasons also mean that the birds are expecting the approach of breeding season during the later shows towards the end of the year or early in the next. This in turn means that such birds may not show at all well so late in the season, being far more interested in courting hens than in displaying their traits to the judge.

Another popular approach involves a more drastic cycle of seasonal change than that found in the canaries' native islands; this approach also requires that the birds be kept

by R C McDonald

where they cannot see any indications of the season outdoors. The lights are taken up to 14 hours or so a day for breeding, but then are suddenly dropped in late May or early June to only 8 or 9 hours of daylight. The lights are kept at this level right through the summer.

Then, in early September, the length of the days is again increased by a half hour or so, the same being done again in October. The lights are slowly increased at a gradual rate in this manner until breeding has begun and 14 hour days are reached, then the lights are maintained at that level until mid-May, when once again the lighting is suddenly dropped to 9 hours a day, and breeding arbitrarily ends.

For this kind of approach to work correctly, it is essential that the birds not be allowed any way of being able to tell what the weather outside of their birdroom is like. If this fact is not emphasized strongly enough when this approach is outlined to canary-keeping novices, results can sometimes be close to disastrous.

If the birds are allowed to garner any clues as to the real season outdoor, novices to the hobby may instead find their birds (and themselves!) undergoing a *very* long breeding season, with the birds refusing to stop attempting to breed until well after midsummer or even into early fall, when the days outside have finally become short enough to have an impact on the birds' perceptions.

By then they will have expended so much energy in their attempts to breed over so many months, that they will have problems completing their annual moult, having spent the physical reserves that would normally support them and assist them through this physically difficult time (growing feathers takes a *lot* of energy even if the diet is top-notch).

In turn, difficulty moulting can lead to such physical exhaustion that the winter will not be long enough for the bird to recuperate properly, meaning in turn that he or she will not be able to come into proper breeding condition at the right time during the following spring.

So, whichever kind of schedule you decide to use, whether you plan to follow the normal days outdoors, or artificially shift the seasons with your schedule of lighting, be sure you understand all the aspects of the schedule you will be using before you start. If your birds' days aren't similar to what's happening outdoors, take steps to ensure that they will not be able to see and be stimulated by exposure to any amount of daylight, no matter how little.

There's another aspect to wintering canaries that is often missed too. Winter is when all canaries, males too but especially canary hens, need to fly as much as possible. Flying strengthens not just the wings, but the long muscles that run the entire length of the body, from keel-bone to sternum. It is these muscles that support the wings; the male will need them to be strong enough to allow him to fertilize his hen's eggs, while those same muscles will help the hen to lay her eggs.

When it comes time for egg-laying, the stronger and more well-exercised her wings and flying muscles are, the better it will be for the hen. Pet canary hens who won't be allowed to breed are also likely to lay eggs during the spring, so even if you are not planning to allow her to do any breeding, preparation to assist her ability to lay her eggs is a *very* good idea.

While less crucial to their life and health, winter-time exercise is important to male canaries too, especially if they are going to be used for breeding. During mating, the male must hover over the hen for a crucial second or two in order for proper fertilization to be achieved. He must be a skilled and strong flier to be able to do this, so the more flight time he's had, the more skill he is liable to be able to achieve during mating. This, in turn, will impact fertility.

It's always possible to find breeders who never allow their birds much room to fly, but whose birds go ahead and breed at the proper time anyways— but it's been my own experience that while yes, it is possible to breed canaries without having allowed them much if any time to fly— you'll get much better results, higher fertility and overall less problems in general, if the birds have had plenty of practice flying throughout their winter.

Luckily, most canaries tend to squabble less during the winter months, so many canary keepers will provide one or two large flight cages for their birds during this season. As long as there is plenty of individual perching spaces, near the top of the flight in particular, and there are plenty of food cups and drinkers scattered about the flight cage, spaced well apart to minimize squabbling, many canaries are willing to relatively peacefully co-exist with each other for a time— at least until the days again begin to lengthen, telling them it will soon be time to begin to claim territory in preparation for breeding.

Whether you plan to breed and show, or are interested in keeping one or more pet canaries, how each canary spends their winter can drastically affect a great many aspects of their lives. Understanding this can lead you to a much richer and far more rewarding experience with each of your canaries.

Conditioning Canaries

Just what is *conditioning* when it comes to canaries, and just how is it done? In canary fancier circles, this is one of those simple-sounding yet mysterious operations that can seem to arbitrarily change definition, sometimes rather drastically, depending on who you're talking to.

Trying to sort out just what procedures are involved in conditioning a canary can be very confusing to a newcomer, who is still trying to assimilate all the ins and outs of keeping this sometimes rather complex species, and who usually prefers to pin down each definition with terms as exact as possible.

It doesn't help matters that this word is used for entirely different actions, too. Canaries are *conditioned* for show; or they are *conditioned* for breeding. The procedure in each case is quite different, and methods can vary quite widely. Each fancier has his or her own procedures, often arrived at over years of trial and error, that work best for him or her; often each is firmly convinced that his or her method is the best for everybody, since it's the best for him or her.

In fact, what works best for who, really depends on a wide variety of factors, chief among them what breed you're working with. And let's not forget elements such as the personality, inheritance, and gender of the bird.

Then there's environmental considerations; what's the local climate like, is it warm and humid, hot and dry, cool and dry, or something else entirely? Does the bird live in a birdroom with a controlled environment surrounded by other birds, or is he a pet, sharing a household with a variety of humans and other pets? All of these and more, can and will affect the results achieved when conditioning a canary.

Conditioning a bird for showing is best learned from an expert in showing the type of canary you want to work with, as techniques and needs will vary widely, depending on whether you're working with a type, colour, or song breed.

Conditioning for breeding, however, is something almost every bird breeder has an opinion on— or, in the case of a new canary breeder, *wants* to have an opinion on.

Many older canary-keeping books refer to conditioning a canary for breeding season through the use of foods; some certain items, when added to the diet, are supposed to help get canaries 'in the mood' for breeding; or if you like really bad puns, 'egg them on'.

While it's true that some foods can help push a canary into breeding condition, successfully doing so can be tricky, as too much of these same foods can actually prevent breeding from happening properly, instead of enhancing it as intended.

For example; feeding extra amounts of oily seeds is often advised to encourage canaries to come into condition for breeding. But feed too much, and you will have a fat canary, and a fat canary can't breed. Oh sure, they'll try— but any eggs will almost certainly be infertile.

Another example is wheat germ, high in vitamin E, which is often cited as a useful supplement to encourage canaries to come into full breeding condition. While it's true that vitamin E *can* help to encourage breeding and egg-laying behaviour, it's equally true— and seldom mentioned— that *too much* vitamin E can cause the birds to become so hyperactive that they will be unable to properly settle down to brooding and raising the babies.

Too much dietary E can cause over-aggression and restlessness. Males will become prone to disturbing the hen, and hens become less inclined to incubate their eggs or feed their youngsters, instead abandoning existing nests — even those containing fertile eggs, or live chicks— in favour of more mating and more egg-laying.

I find it easier to understand the process of conditioning, by looking at the root idea behind it all. To learn how best to encourage a canary to come into breeding condition, let's take a look at the natural system canaries and similar species have used for millennia.

For these creatures, breeding season is during the spring. In nature, the approach of spring is signalled in many ways; the lengthening days bring warmer weather, and with it comes new growth to provide plenty of the plants and bugs the wild birds rely on for feeding their young. Spring also tends to bring plenty of water; besides rain, there is water everywhere from the melting snows of winter.

As a result, spring brings wild canaries far more than just longer days. Along with those lengthening days comes warm weather along with plenty of rainfall. This offers, not just water to bathe in, but ensures an abundance of small, soft-bodied high-protein insects to eat, and all the water-rich greens a canary can devour.

So if we want to to encourage a canary to want to breed, why not mimic these conditions?

The first and most important part of the recipe is the lighting. This has been covered in more detail in other articles, which you can find elsewhere in this book. For now, suffice it to say that if you want to breed canaries, you will have adopted a lighting schedule that, among other things, has your canaries seeing shorter days during their 'winter', then lengthening days to bring in 'spring'.

As long as your canaries can't see outside, the lights can be timed so as to create the seasons at whichever point of the year is more convenient to the breeder, so in fact

by R C McDonald

midwinter might be closer to early summer in some birdrooms. But for now, suffice it to say that introducing 'spring' entails lengthening the days.

The idea of feeding vitamin E to stimulate the desire to breed, comes directly from the 'spring-time' scenario, too, although you might not realize it at first glance. It's true, though— because spring brings sprouting seeds galore, particularly amongst the grasses that wild canaries favour. What many people don't realize is that most sprouting seeds, particularly grass seeds, are naturally quite high in fresh, potent vitamin E.

Many old-timers will tell you they increase the amount of protein in the birds' diet while conditioning their canaries for breeding. This too derives from the same scenario of attempting to mimic the spring-time conditions that wild birds rely on. In the wild, dietary protein is most likely to consist of small, soft-bodied insects, which are much more plentiful during the spring than at any other time of the year.

Such soft, high-protein foods *must* be readily available to any birds wishing to raise chicks, and rarely will you find any species attempting to raise their young when there is no such foods to offer them. Our canaries have learned to eat protein-rich nestling or egg foods instead of the insects their wild cousins rely on, but the basic needs are still the same.

Another element of conditioning for breeding, one that is often overlooked, is water. Plentiful fresh clean water, preferably as cold as possible, should be available for both drinking and bathing, if you want to be sure to put your canaries reliably 'in the mood' for breeding.

There's still another element to consider, and it too is one that is often missed. In order to breed successfully, it's necessary for a canary to be in tip-top shape, physically.

For this reason, many canary breeders will keep their breeding stock in large flights through the winter months, encouraging their birds to fly as much as possible. Frequent flying strengthens the entire system, enhancing blood circulation and increasing oxygen conversion rates, as well as increasing general strength in bone and muscle, along with good muscle tone and stamina.

For the hens, this exercise helps to ensure they will be strong enough to be able to mate properly. In order to acquire fertilized eggs, a hen needs to be able to firmly grip the perch and maintain her stance during the mating process. This is much easier to do if she has developed some physical strength.

Good muscle tone will also assist her greatly when it comes time to lay her eggs, and afterwards, will help to see that she has enough stamina to get through the hard work of raising a nest of young after remaining almost entirely immobile during the two weeks she spends incubating her eggs.

Strength and flying agility is important for the males, too. During mating, the male needs to hover over his hen for a critical moment, in order to be able to ensure fertilization. It takes great strength and flying skill to be able to accomplish this task properly, otherwise the results are infertile eggs.

Even if they are not entirely healthy, most birds will make the attempt to breed, when the time comes— the instinctive drive to perpetuate the species will see to that. But a wise breeder will not rely on such a bird to produce youngsters, and a caring one will see that it is not allowed to exhaust itself making the attempt.

A hen who is not in tip-top shape may still lay eggs and sett on them, but she should be given fake eggs instead of real ones, so she will not have to go through the exhausting process of raising the young. If she has valuable bloodlines, she may be allowed to mate so her fertilized eggs may be fostered out to a stronger hen, but unless she is completely healthy, she should not be allowed to raise chicks herself.

by R C McDonald

In the end, conditioning your birds properly for breeding starts almost six months earlier, and stretches through the winter into the spring. But if it's done properly, your birds will reward you with plentiful nests full of bright, healthy, active youngsters, who in their turn will fill your life with their songs.

Pairing Canaries

Your canaries live in separate cages and have seen only the equivalent of natural daylight throughout the winter. You've paid special attention to their diet, and made sure they got plenty of exercise. Now the winter solstice is over, and the birds are beginning to act as if breeding season is here already, though you've increased their lights only a little.

Your hen has begun ripping paper and carrying it around, strewing little bits of it everywhere, while your male is in full song, singing constantly, a much louder, stronger song than his former tunes. He is eager to join the hen, and so restless that he is practically dancing on the perch when he sings. Like all new breeders, your question now is when and how to go about mating your birds.

The literal answer to this question really is, *"When they are ready."* But that's more than a little cryptic, so I'll add a little detail.

In general, the longer you can put off pairing your birds, the better chance you will have of getting fewer infertile eggs, especially in the first nest of the season. Firstly— since your birds are seeing only natural light, you need to be sure not to allow them to start breeding too early, because they are likely to want to keep breeding right up until midsummer's day, perhaps longer; sometimes a stubborn hen will try to keep laying eggs for a month past midsummer's day, or more.

That doesn't mean that allowing them to do so is good for them, though— wild songbirds will do the same if they can,

by R C McDonald

but their average lifespan is only a year or two— about what a canary's lifespan will be if it is if allowed to choose its own breeding schedule.

That's because repeated and successful breeding and rearing of chicks takes so much effort that when the moult starts, their bodies will have a difficult time providing the necessary energy to regrow their feathers, after expending so much effort rearing the chicks.

Unfortunately for canary breeders, this kind of physical exhaustion is not at all obvious; in fact it won't show at all until the hormonal effects of breeding have left the bird's system. This in turn creates a problem commonly found, especially with new breeders— they feel that because the birds *want* to continue to breed, that it's cruel to try to make them stop. Really though, exactly the opposite is the truth.

Just remember that if your hen lays some unexpected eggs too early or too late in the season, rather than taking them away you can and should simply switch them for a bunch of fake plastic canary eggs, and leave her peacefully incubating her 'eggs' for a couple of weeks or so, knowing that you are relatively secure in that plastic can't hatch.

It's a good idea to have plenty of fake canary eggs on hand during breeding season even if you only have one pair of canaries—you will find they come in *very* useful. You can easily find fake canary eggs online from several sources, usually listed under 'canary breeding supplies'.

Speaking of laying eggs, I've had canary hens lay fertile eggs up to two months after being separated from a male, so separating a pair won't necessarily cause the next-laid batch of eggs to be infertile. For that matter the opposite is also true; having a pair sharing a cage won't necessarily mean that you'll get fertile eggs.

Successfully mating a pair of canaries is seldom a simple matter of just putting the two into a single cage—there can be quite a lot of aggression on both sides, and injury may be done. Because of this it is best to allow a pair you plan to mate a short period when they can get to know each other, before being required to share a cage.

You may have noticed that most canary breeding cages come equipped with a removable divider, with which it is possible to separate the cage into two areas. Some cages have a simple wire divider, while the better ones will often come with two interchangeable dividers, a wire one and a solid one.

The wire divider allows you to introduce a pair to each other without harm to either, as will sometimes happen if they are just put into the same cage together. This is true especially if both birds are not equally ready to breed.

The idea is that they can get to know each other through the bars, but won't be able to do much (if any) harm to each other, should any arguments arise. The male can court the hen by feeding her through the bars, and the hen will have a choice about accepting this courtship without the need to worry about getting thrashed if she should turn down a too-eager male, as can happen if the birds are introduced to each other in an unpartitioned cage.

Once you've put your pair into the divided cage, it's best to wait until active feeding is going on between the two of them before considering removing the divider. Another sign of readiness for mating is when the hen begins to carry her nesting material in the back of her beak. About this time she will have begun to work more seriously on building her nest, not just 'playing house' by ripping and shredding her papers and scattering pieces of that and anything else she considers worthy to be nesting material all over the cage.

The solid cage dividers will sometimes be needed instead of the wire ones; they are used to separate birds who are actively hostile to each other, and fight through the bars. The idea is to remove all sight of the other bird for awhile, then slide the divider back just a little, so that there is only a small gap through with they can interact. In this way it is sometimes possible to encourage such an originally hostile pair to accept each other. When the birds are no longer trying to fight each other through the gap, the solid divider can be replaced with the wire one and the prospective pair can then be allowed to interact more equitably.

If you have two separate cages and neither has a divider, you may be able to get a similar effect by putting the cages closely enough together that the birds can reach each other through the bars well enough to be able to perform their courtship feeding. Once you see mutual feeding, and nest-building has begun, you can remove the divider and allow your pair the run of the nesting cage.

Mating is only the start of the process, though. Success at each step through breeding season entails knowing how to interpret how the birds are acting, and what response is necessary for any given series of actions.

Remember, any youngsters will require some rather intensive care until they are around six months or so old, and you will probably not be able to sell them until they are nine or ten months old. In other words, breeding and successfully raising young canaries to adulthood is a much more labour-intensive and drawn-out process than is the case when breeding many other avian species commonly kept as pets, who, unlike canaries and most other song-birds, can often be sold quite young.

Whichever resources you choose to guide you, I highly recommend that you do as much research as possible on everything breeding canaries entails, before you jump in and get your feet wet— it will save you a *lot* of confusion and maybe even some possible heartache too.

This in turn will allow you to spend more time enjoying your birds, instead of worrying about them. And after all, when it comes right down to it, isn't enjoying them what it's all about?

Egg-Binding

Please note that if you think your hen is egg-bound, you need to consult an avian vet A.S.A.P. in order to save her life. This article is intended to help you to gain an understanding of the entire egg-laying process, and to help you to prevent such occurrences from happening in your flock, or if it does, to offer assistance during the time it takes to get your hen to your vet. None of the measures mentioned are to be considered as a replacement for a consultation with a qualified avian vet.

Every springtime you'll hear them; stories about how a female pet bird suddenly looks to be at death's door, when the previous day she was happy, active, and building a nest. As often as not, the cause of such sudden 'illness' is not really a disease at all, but the result of her inability, for whatever reason, to lay her egg. This is most commonly known as 'egg-binding', and it can be deadly; if she is not able to lay her egg, she will die within 24 hours or so.

In order to understand egg-binding and how to prevent it, it's necessary to first know a little about how birds form and lay their eggs. There's some variance between species, but the process itself is similar in all birds.

The yolk develops in the ovary, as part of a group of immature yolks resembling a tiny cluster of grapes. Each yolk slowly matures until it is released in turn into the upper area of the oviduct, where it will meet the male sperm and hopefully become fertilized. The new egg then moves to an area known as the 'magnum', where a layer of albumen (egg white) envelopes the developing yolk. At each end of the yolk, thin strands of albumen twist together to form 'chalaza', rope-like strands which will act as support. These strands cradle the yolk in the center of the albumen as it continues down the oviduct, keeping it protected from bruises and bangs during the process of formation.

Once the chalaza forms, another layer of albumen is wrapped around the yolk, and the whole mass proceeds down the oviduct to the 'isthmus'. Here the egg is wrapped in two loosely-fitting membranes, before proceeding to the uterus, where the final stages of development occur. The shell membranes begin to tighten around the albumen-surrounded yolk while the eggshell is secreted over the entire mass. As the new shell hardens, the egg proceeds to the cloaca, and is laid.

This entire process can take from 24 hours or so for smaller species such as the canary, budgie, or parrotlet, to 48 hours or more for larger species such as a parrot or a macaw. Whatever the size of the hen, if she is not able to lay her egg, trouble is inevitable; with the egg in the way, the entire digestive system is fully blocked. Once the process of egg development has entered the final stage, a hen *has* to be able to lay her egg in order to survive.

There's several possible causes for disruption of this process, ranging from disease to lack of exercise, but the most frequently seen is due to a sudden shortage of calcium. Ironically, this can happen if there is *too much* dietary calcium being supplied regularly, as well as not enough.

If too much calcium is being supplied too regularly, the hen's body will begin to rely on the supplies of calcium carried in the blood for its day-to-day needs, and will temporarily lose the ability to regulate its own levels of calcium, including the normal ability to mobilize calcium from the bones at need.

When the need to form an eggshell creates a sudden demand for calcium, the bloodstream can't possibly supply enough, so ordinarily her body would simply take what it needs from her bones. But if she has been receiving calcium supplements daily in her feed or water, she may not be able to mobilize enough calcium from her bones quickly enough to cope with the sudden demand.

Once the blood supply of calcium runs out, with the bone mass inaccessible, her body will attempt to fill the need by removing calcium from her muscles and nerves. But there's a problem. These muscles require a minimal amount of calcium to be present in order to function properly, so once the calcium begins to be withdrawn, her muscles will no longer work normally.

The result? Though the body's drastic measures allowed the shell to be formed, without proper use of her muscles she won't be able to lay her egg. She has become a classic egg-bound hen.

Too much calcium is not the only cause of egg-binding, of course. In most species, a hen's bones can safely produce from two to three eggs, but without an outside source of digestible calcium, trouble can occur if an attempt is made to lay more eggs than her body can manage on its own.

What is needed is a large influx of calcium into the system at the right time, so that the body can quickly replace what it has withdrawn from the bones. Most hens, of whatever species, seem to know exactly when this needs to happen, and will take advantage of and use a supply of calcium in one or more of several forms, if presented in a fashion they find acceptable.

For hundreds of years now bird keepers have been giving their female birds access to supplies such as the bones of cuttlefish, crunched-up oyster or other shellfish shells, or even dry crunched-up eggshells from chicken eggs, which have been sterilized by baking. These may go untouched for long periods of time, but when the extra calcium will soon be needed, most hens will be found diligently chowing down their calcium in whatever form it is presented.

It should be noted that no hen cannot properly digest her

calcium without adequate vitamin D also being present, along with other needed trace elements. Lack of a necessary element in the proper proportions can render some or even all of the calcium indigestible, and cause it to instead be deposited in small painful crystals around the joints or in the organs.

Many of the required essential elements can be found in foods— but one important vitamin is often lacking. Vitamin D is *not* found in most foods, so most species of birds have a unique method of acquiring this essential vitamin—the vitamin D necessary for their health is produced by the action of unfiltered sunshine on healthy feathers.

Unfortunately for our pet birds though, most windows filter out the long-wave UV rays, which are the wavelengths essential to this process. If unfiltered sunshine is not available, then the missing elements need to be supplied. Most bird keepers do this through use of a dietary supplement made specifically for birds.

It should be noted that many avian suppliers can offer one or more of the specific supplements available intended to assist in the egg-laying process. Often these supplements offer a liquid form of quickly digestible calcium. The better ones include the associated trace minerals and vitamins needed to insure proper digestion, and if careful attention is paid to their labels, it will be noted that the instructions specify not to offer such a supplement daily, but instead to offer it once or twice a week.

This is because daily offerings will cause the problem mentioned above, where the body will temporarily 'forget' how to mobilize calcium from the bones, causing possible egg-binding problems.

Offering these supplies on an on-and-off basis avoids this problem, and allows the body the chance to exercise its ability to regulate calcium levels naturally. This in turn allows plenty of calcium to be available for maintaining high bone calcium levels, allowing the hen to be able to easily lay large clutches of eggs. The 'off' days offer opportunity for the body to remove excess calcium from the kidneys or other organs where it would otherwise be deposited, eventually causing damage.

So, now you have an idea how eggs are formed, and why egg-binding can sometimes happen, even in situations where plenty of calcium is available. But, what should you do if one of your hens suddenly becomes eggbound?

There is a lot of advice out there offering ideas on various procedures to try in order to assist the egg to pass. Unfortunately, unless judged necessary for use by trained and experienced persons, most of these procedures amount to nothing more nor less than the torture, however well-meant, of an already suffering creature.

One frequently heard recommendation is to apply grease or oil to try to help the egg slip out. This seems reasonable to a human, but in actuality is one of the worst things you can do to an eggbound hen. Oil or grease will chill the vent and cause the feathers surrounding the vent to lose their insulating ability, in turn causing more chill. Eggbinding is associated with extreme contraction of muscles that are not able to operate normally. This reduces blood flow, which itself causes a certain amount of chilling, but a greater rate of chilling will make matters even worse.

Another common piece of advice is to hold the bird's vent over steam. This is a *very* bad idea— steam burns! You'll not only stress the hen, you're liable to burn her vent—and your hands!

Yet another bit of frequently-heard advice, is to gently massage the area just above the vent in an attempt to assist in pushing the egg out. This too sounds reasonable, but is in fact a bad idea, unless, as noted above, it is performed by a trained and experienced individual.

That's because even a *little* bit too much pressure on the abdomen could cause the egg to break while still inside her. If that should happen the shards could cut her internally, in which case you would be almost certain to lose her.

Instead, call your avian vet and arrange for your bird to be seen as soon as possible. Then remove her from her nest and put her into a separate cage with a thick layer of soft towelling on the floor. Don't add any perches—if she falls off a perch, she could break the egg inside her. The towelling will help to provide traction as well as comfort.

Warmth makes it easier to relax, so it's a good idea to offer her some extra warmth. Do be careful, though, not to offer her too much heat. She needs to be able to cool off if she gets too hot. A good way to meet this need is to put a heating pad underneath one end of the cage, so she can choose her own comfort zone. Put water, greens and a little dry food at the cooler end of the cage. Now she is ready to be carried in to see the vet, whenever she can be seen. But there's still help you can offer her, in the meantime.

Cover the back and sides of the cage to offer her some privacy if you wish, but be careful not to cover the entire cage. More than one well-meaning owner has lost a sick canary simply by covering the cage so thoroughly that it could not see to eat or drink! Many avian species, including canaries, have no black-and-white vision, but can see only colour. This gives them incredible eyesight during the day, but it also means that they can't see much if anything in the dark, so remember to keep even a sick hen's area fairly bright.

The next step is to get some calcium into her. Any form of liquid calcium will hit her bloodstream quite quickly, and help to smooth the muscle action that caused the egg to bind. Usually an eggbound hen will not easily eat or drink, so it may be necessary to administer the calcium orally. This is not as difficult as it seems, if you have a plastic-tipped syringe such as dentists use. You can also use a dropper or the tip of a small spoon, whatever you have that will fit the need for the moment.

Be careful to avoid placing any pressure on her abdomen. Get some liquid calcium into the syringe or dropper, and see if she will open her beak. If she will, place a few drops on her tongue. Be careful to not to give her too much at once, as you don't want her to accidentally breathe in liquid —in her weakened condition, such an accident could kill.

If she won't open her beak, as is often the case, turn her head sideways, and place the liquid calcium a drop at a time on the 'hinge' of the beak. Make these drops as tiny as you can, and most should be drawn into the beak, rather than running off.

If you don't have any liquid calcium handy, you need to come up with a substitute. Don't even bother with milk! It doesn't have enough calcium in it to make a difference, and it is indigestible to birds anyways. If she is still eating, sesame seeds are high in calcium, and may help, but too often we don't realize a hen is eggbound until she is already too weak to eat or drink. In a pinch, you can grind up a calcium tablet with a little water, and place the mix a bit at a time into her beak, then stroke her neck to encourage her to swallow— whatever it takes to get that necessary extra calcium into her.

I like to try to keep some Calci-Boost on hand, myself. This is a liquid calcium supplement made by the Bird Care Co in Britain. It offers highly bio-available calcium, includes all the trace elements needed for proper digestion, and is readily available through many retailers or online.

Whatever form you use, once you've given her warmth and some calcium, leave her be for a half hour or so, then check how she is doing. If she still looks miserable, 'disturb' her gently, forcing her to move a little. Her tendency will be to huddle in a miserable heap, but you want her to keep moving every now and again. This will help her circulatory system deliver the calcium to her muscles, and the movement may assist her in expelling the egg.

Continue checking her every half an hour or so, and every time you do, give her a few more drops of liquid calcium; something like Calci-Boost, that also includes vitamin D, magnesium, etc, is best. But in a pinch, any kind of liquid calcium will do.

If you've caught it in time, the assistance you and your vet can provide should help to her lay her egg, and in most cases, she will be seen to bounce back to health and vigour with remarkable rapidity, once the problem-causing egg has been laid.

Egg-binding can be very scary, especially if you've never dealt with it before. But once you know and understand the root causes, prevention really is quite simple.

Learn that, and with any luck neither you nor your birds will ever have to deal with a bound egg ever again!

Infertile Eggs

It's an odd fact that the 'common' canary is one of the most difficult of all the more commonly kept pet birds to learn to breed reliably and successfully. They *are* the easiest of the songbirds to breed— but that is about the only light in which you could call most canaries 'easy breeders'.

Of all the problems that can arise when learning about breeding canaries, one of the most confusing can be that of constantly getting infertile eggs from your pairs.

Even when both birds involved are in tip-top shape and full breeding condition, there are a number of possible causes for infertile eggs. Some of the more common causes are relatively simple to fix— for example, if the hen doesn't have a solid, stable, easy-to-grip surface to perch on while mating, infertile eggs are almost a certainty. In such a case, all that's needed is to see that the perches provided in the breeding cage are solid, not bouncy, not slippery, and of a size and shape that is easy for a canary to grip firmly.

Other causes for infertile eggs can be more difficult to diagnose. Possibilities include a diet low in sufficient trace elements and essential nutrients, or a lack of compatibility between the birds. Age is often cited, too, and it is true that once a hen passes three years old, her fertility can drop quite drastically. This can happen with the males as well, although generally it will not occur until they are somewhat older— say, 5 or 6 years of age or more. But age is a factor rather less often than many think.

As ever when it comes to canaries, another important factor involved in breeding canaries is the amount of light

by R C McDonald

they receive. Canaries are photosensitive, which means the increasing light of spring days triggers a desire to breed. This also means that lighting that simulates longer days can trigger breeding activity outside of the normal breeding season. Unfortunately, unless all the other conditions necessary to breeding are also simulated successfully, this can mean too many problems such as egg-binding, infertile eggs, mate or chick aggression, irregular egg-laying, or more. Because of this I use a chart such as the one posted at *robirda.com/sunset.html* as a guideline. While it is not essential to follow such a schedule exactly, adopting something similar makes everything much easier over the year, and can definitely impact fertility.

Diet plays an important role, too. For example, Vitamin E provides a powerful breeding stimulus. It is found in quite high concentrations in fresh wheat germ oil, wheat or sunflower sprouts, and some vitamin supplements— yet I have rarely seen good results from including more than a very tiny amount of a concentrated supplement of vitamin E in a breeder canary's diet.

Too much dietary E tends to make the hens try to breed too soon and too often, favouring egg production over care of the chicks. A hen who has been receiving large doses of Vitamin E in her diet will not care well for any young she produces, and in fact will often abandon the nest, either before or shortly after the eggs hatch, often just to turn around and begin building a new nest right on top of the dying youngsters.

Usually not only will the quantity of eggs laid rise, but often, so will the occurrence of infertile eggs, if too much of this stimulating nutrient is given. Worse, too much dietary E tends to make the mates more aggressive towards each other and any chicks. Destroyed eggs and mate or chick injury or even death is not uncommon in such cases.

Another common cause of infertile canary eggs is due to improper pairing; either pairing too early, or pairing too late. It is generally not a great idea to allow any pair of canaries you intend to breed to share a cage until they are both in full breeding condition— unless they are in a large cage with at least two visually separated areas, with food and water available in each area. Such a set-up will allow each bird to claim one area for themselves, and in turn provide somewhere safer to retreat to if a cage-mate should get testy.

Some hens may try to dominate the males, and have been known to get fairly abusive if a male in the same cage wants to mate. The reverse can be true as well, of course, and either way, problems are almost certain to arise if both birds are not at the same level of breeding condition. Aggression from one will in turn cause the other to retaliate — *not* a situation conducive to eventual successful breeding!

It is quite rare for two canaries sharing the same cage to both achieve full breeding condition at the same time, and this is especially true if they have been kept together all along. Usually one will come into condition several weeks sooner, and proceed to harass the other. This can quite effectively prevent the other bird from achieving any kind of breeding condition at all, or instead it may mean that only partial condition is achieved by the second bird, resulting in— among other things— infertile eggs.

So if you want successful mating, it is important not to attempt to pair the birds too soon. Instead, you want both birds to be fully ready and in tip-top breeding condition, *before* being introduced to each other. This will be of great help to you, as a breeder, in reducing aggressive tendencies and personality squabbles.

How can you tell when your birds are in full breeding condition? You will know they are ready by the way they are acting, and you can also examine their vents.

When adult canaries are in breeding condition, their vents and lower abdomen will become a little more red in both genders, and will swell a little. The vents themselves will be raised, and the area around them slightly swollen in

by R C McDonald

appearance. The male's vent will be sharper-looking, having almost a point at the end, while the hen's will be flatter but broader. They are both surrounded by a ring of small feathers that will be standing almost erect— at other times of the year these tiny feathers lay a bit flatter to the skin.

The male will be singing strongly, and when she hears his song, the hen will crouch and twitter, calling to him. She will be actively building a nest, rather than just scattering nest material all over the cage, and often there will be a lot of mutual feeding going on through the bars of their cages (assuming they can reach each other through the bars, that is...)

Having this period of introduction and courtship where they can feed each other but not pursue or harass each other, is quite important to canaries—and it's why dividable breeding cages are so popular with canary breeders.

If you don't have a dividable cage to introduce your birds to each other, you can try putting two separate pet canary cages together with a make-shift 'pop-hole' between them. Depending on the cage design, sometimes you can just set the cages together door-to-door, with one door closed and a perch on either side so they can get acquainted through the bars. Then, when they are getting along, you can leave both doors open and let them choose which cage they prefer, eventually removing the other cage.

Others breeders simply cut their own pop-holes— you can easily cut a piece of wire slightly larger than the hole you've cut (or had cut) into the cage, and make a flap to cover it when the pop-hole is not in use. Some cages even come with their own built-in 'pop-holes'; extra doors that can be used as just described, or to hold a nest, or bath, or for some other such arrangement.

Another method for introducing two different birds to the same cage is to take both and put them together into a cage new to them both, so that neither bird 'owns' the space. (If you plan to breed them, note that it is still very important that both birds be in full breeding condition before you try this.) You will sometimes find that one bird in a pair will be a little more aggressive, and in these cases it may help to take some of the 'starch' out if you introduce it into a cage already familiar to the intended mate.

Hens in particular benefit from having a large cage with lots of flying room, as it helps to keep them fit enough to be able to more easily lay their eggs, but breeder males can benefit from extra flying room as well.

A hen's eggs are very large in relation to the size of her body, with each egg totalling as much as 25% of her body's mass. Laying such an egg requires strength, which she gains from flying; but remember to consider that the male is required to hover almost motionless over her during mating— even if only for a split second— and you will realize that successful mating requires strength, skill, and coordination— from him as well as her. Physical fitness is a must on both sides, for canary mating to prove successful.

Finally, familiarity with the surrounding environment and a reliable and regular schedule of care is necessary in order for any canary to be able to successfully come into— and remain in— full breeding condition.

Moving a canary who is already in breeding condition to a new situation will often result in a set-back, where some time must pass before the bird is able to return to full breeding condition. In the males, this period can vary from a few hours to a few weeks, but for the hens, the more usual adjustment period ranges from two or three weeks to a few months or more.

This is why most breeders will recommend that if you plan to buy new hens for your next breeding season, you should purchase your new stock at least several months before breeding season is actually due. You can plan on a new hen taking from at least six weeks to three months to adapt to her new environment and become comfortable and familiar enough with it to be willing and able to breed, even with all other conditions optimal.

This is especially true if her new home is quite different from the environment she came from. Allowing your hens plenty of time to adapt to your home and system of care can make a world of difference, when it comes time to breed. It also means that you can ensure that your canaries are properly prepared to meet breeding season, with plenty of time for you to attend to their physical fitness, along with seeing to it that they have a properly balanced schedule of lighting, a complete and varied diet, and more-than-just-adequate housing.

If you do it right, you just may find your pairs will be *so* fertile that you're having difficulty keeping up with caring for all the babies they have given you! How do you go about doing that? Well, that's the topic for another chapter...

Non-Feeding Issues

It's one of the oldest problems in the book, if you have ever tried breeding canaries; parent birds (particularly hens) who successfully fertilize and hatch eggs, but who refuse to feed their young. Learning to understand why this can happen, and just what can be done about it, is an ongoing education every time a canary breeder encounters this kind of problem.

There's lots of reasons why an adult canary hen might refuse to feed her newly-hatched chick(s), but most of them are rooted in one of two causes.

1) (Apparent or real) lack of adequate food for the babies, or

2) Fear. Fear of any number of things can make a hen nervous, which in turn will cause her to sit tightly on the nest, rather than relaxing enough to feed.

Let's consider these two issues in a little more detail.

The first issue, food, is more important than you might at first think. Not only must the breeding diet provide a complete and properly balanced source of nutrition, to ensure proper fulfilment of the youngsters' potential, but it must also appeal to the hen's taste. All the nutrition in the world will not do your chicks the least bit of good if the hen turns up her beak at your offerings!

One common reason for refusing food is due to the hen's unfamiliarity with the food being offered. For this reason,

by R C McDonald

many breeders offer their canaries— males as well as hens — small portions of nestling food (also known as 'egg food', whether it contains any egg or not), prior to the start of breeding season, during the weeks when the birds are still slowly beginning to come into breeding condition.

Gradually the size and frequency of the portions offered are increased as each member of the flock comes closer to being in full breeding condition. This familiarizes them with one of the most important staple foods that will be needed when the chicks hatch.

Canaries will also often refuse to eat foods that do not taste good to them, or that look different from what they are used to receiving, so making sure that they are familiar with a wide variety of foods *before* breeding season starts is a very good idea.

Commercially made nestling foods often contain enough sugars to be dangerous to a newly hatched canary chick, and most such foods will carry the recommendation that they not be offered to the parent birds until the chicks have reached three days of age. This being the case, you must also be careful about just which foods you offer your hens to feed their newly hatched chicks,

In general, you want to keep the diet plain and bland while the hen is actually incubating her eggs. Too much rich food during this time can cause her to lose her incubating heat, and can even make her sick, which in turn can cause her to abandon the eggs. This is one reason why it is so important that she become acquainted with the nestling food you plan to offer, *before* she begins to nest. Once she has begun to brood, you need to *stop* offering her any such nestling food, until just before the eggs are due. Then, once they have begun to hatch, everything changes.

Hatching chicks require a sudden rise in humidity at just the right moment, in order to soften the shell and assist them in chipping their way out. As long as the hen has a bath she is used to available to her, she will provide them with the right amount of moisture, at just the right time. All you need to do is make sure she has the bath available all day every day from at least her twelfth day of incubation on.

Once you know that the eggs are hatching (if you listen closely you will hear a tiny high peeping as the hatching chicks and their parents 'talk' to each other), you can begin to offer some extra foods.

You'll want to be sure to offer a variety, and keep them constantly available as soon as the chicks begin to hatch out, so the hen will be tempted to eat. This in turn will encourage her to feed the chicks, who will instinctively raise their heads for her when they feel her return to the nest. Small amounts of sugar-free or low-sugar nestling foods may be provided, along with the usual food sources such as seed or pellets, and a generous supply of fresh foods that the bird is used to eating. Dark leafy greens such as kale or rapini are a great choice, as most canaries will eat them readily, and these power-packed greens contain enough nutrition to make an excellent first food for a new canary hatchling.

If you prefer, you can make your own healthy and effective nestling food mixes using any number of recipes used by other canary breeders; there is often a wide variety of recipes available at club meetings or through discussion groups and forums online. One such easily made nestling food is described in the book *'Brats in Feathers, Keeping Canaries'*, or (in a little less detail) can be found online at *www.robirda.com/faqs.html#nestfood*

Many nestling foods come with instructions to moisten with water before feeding. This tends to make these foods more palatable to the birds, but also means that they will go sour quite quickly, especially if the weather is warm and/or there is a lot of humidity present. So if you are not going to be able to replace moist foods every few hours (or less, if the weather gets hotter), it's a good idea to leave a dish of dry nestling food out as well.

Many breeders recommend feeding egg to any breeding pairs who have or are expecting young. I myself don't tend to use eggs much for my canaries though, and they do very well without them. My reason for avoiding use of egg in a nestling food, even though so many others have and continue to use them successfully, is based on the simple fact that eggs can sometimes begin to incubate some rather dangerous bacteria, yet not smell at all bad until some time later.

Especially if the parent birds have no other soft foods present to choose from, this can make it all too easy for a case of sour crop to occur. An adult canary who has a sour crop will feel poorly and will not be able to feed, while a chick with sour crop will be hungry, but not able to eat.

If, as can happen, the crop becomes further impacted with yet more food that has also been rendered indigestible due to the overly acidic condition of the ventriculus, sour crop can kill, if left untreated.

That is why many canary breeders, particularly if they have a job which takes them away from home for several hours during the day, will see to it that there's a variety of foods available to any birds with youngsters. Items such as dry nestling food, fresh greens, rolled oats, crushed corn flakes or or wheat biscuits, etc, will help to ensure that there will always be *something* available for the parent birds to feed their babies.

One thing to remember, and that is that if a hen will feed anything, she will feed greens. If possible, try to always have plenty of nutritious dark, rich greens available to a hen with new chicks, to help get her in the mood to feed.

Any of the kales are a good choice, and so are collards and leafy broccolis, especially broccoli raba, or rapini. The leafy endives and chicories are also appreciated by most canaries, and they are almost as nutritious as the kales, so you can let the birds eat all they like.

I don't recommend that anybody try it because it's not really an adequate diet, but kale is actually nutritious enough that it is possible to raise healthy canary chicks with the parents being offered a diet consisting solely of a standard canary seed mix and a continuous supply of organically grown kale! (Yes, I have seen this done).

Such a diet lacks protein, and so the youngsters mature more slowly, but the fact that it is possible at all points out just how rich in nutrients this lowly green vegetable really is. Another advantage to feeding plenty of greens, is the fact that even if some of the foods the birds are eating are getting a little off, the presence of the greens in the bird's crop will act to prevent the impaction that can be such a severe consequence of a soured crop.

But what if the non-feeding issue is not being caused by foods?

One fairly common problem tends to happen most often with a younger hen on her first nest. She's not experienced enough yet to know exactly what is going on, but knows her eggs are precious and must be guarded. If she suspects that her humans or her mate are interested in her eggs, she may feel that they want to harm them, and so will feel she must remain on the nest to guard them.

New breeders in particular can have problems with this, as they tend to want to hover over parent birds with eggs or newly-hatched chicks, anxious to know if the youngsters are hatching, or wondering if they are being fed. Especially if they are trying to closely watch the nest while being as quiet as possible, the bird's instincts will make her think that they really want to *eat* her babies, and she will become more nervous, and guard her babies even more closely.

Occasionally a new breeder will go so far as to use their hand to push the hen a little way off the nest so they can see how the chicks are. Doing this is *never* a good idea, as it will simply reinforce the hen's suspicions about you.

Instead, be very careful to never disturb *any* of your hens while they are on their nest, but most especially the more nervous ones. Always be sure to make some noise when you enter their area, especially while you are looking at them—since in the wild, a hunt is always conducted silently, this will tell your hens in the most basic terms possible that you are *not* hunting their babies.

Sometimes the hen is afraid of the male, rather than her human associates, but whatever the reason for her fear, the results are the same; she will stay on her nest as if her life depends on it, and will not get off until she thinks the danger has passed. If it doesn't pass soon enough, she will continue to follow her instincts, which will tell her that it has become unsafe to raise her babies, and that she must allow them to die, and abandon the nest.

This means that it is wise to keep an eye on your pairs while the hen is still incubating the eggs. Watch the male's activities in particular; is he feeding her on the nest and tending her caringly, or is he restless and 'antsy', disturbing her at every turn?

Especially if he has not been feeding the hen while she is on her nest, the best way to remove him is to simply allow him to fly out of the cage. Sure, you could catch him in the cage, but that will upset her, and an upset hen may decide to abandon her eggs. So just open the cage door and let him fly out, then catch him in the breeding room rather than risking catching him in the cage and disturbing her.

Alternatively, if you have a dividable breeding cage and you think there's a chance he might resume feeding her, instead of removing him you can just use the wire divider to keep him in the other half of the cage.

Then, once the youngsters have hatched out, all you need to do is make made certain a good food supply is available. You know the hen is familiar with it, so after providing it the next thing is to remove yourself from the picture. Don't hover, don't watch her, don't even peer around the corner of the door! You can come into the room to check how her chicks are doing, only if she is off the nest.

If she has been sharing her cage with her mate and you suspect he is the one who is making her nervous, even though they were getting along during incubation, you can temporarily remove him. Since you already know that he was feeding her while she was on her nest, it's best to leave him in the same cage but keep a wire divider between them, so she can still be fed by him through the wire partition. Don't forget to see that he gets some nestling food too!

This solves a few problems. Firstly, it makes the hen feel more secure; she can still see her mate, but she knows that he cannot access her nest, and so he can't (inadvertently or otherwise) harm her chicks. Secondly, it means that she will now have to get off the nest whenever she is hungry; either to eat some food on her own, or to go to the wire divider to be fed by her mate.

This does not seem like a big deal, but it means that when she has finished eating and returns to the nest, the 'thump' of her landing on the nest edge will cause the chicks to raise their heads and beg to be fed. This sight (combined with her new feeling of security and a crop full of nutrition-laden food) is often all it takes to convince a hen to start to feed.

As long as he was feeding her on the nest it's not usually necessary to separate the male for more than a few days or so, in such a case. By then, the chicks will have begun to grow rapidly enough that the hen will be noticing that her youngsters require quite a lot of work to keep fed, and in most cases, she will welcome the aid provided by the return of her mate. As long as the chicks are still in the nest when the divider is removed, usually there will be no problem with his providing any assistance he can to his mate.

Some hens won't allow the males to feed the chicks until they have begun developing feathers, but will instead require him to feed her, then she will turn around and feed the youngsters. Like us, each of these little birds has his or her own personality, and like us, each tends to have his or her own way of doing things. Bottom line; if it is working for you, don't change your system trying to 'improve' anything— not in this breeding season, at least.

by R C McDonald

If you *must* introduce changes in your care system during breeding season, make sure that you introduce the changes slowly enough to give the birds plenty of time to adapt to the new system. Remember, our birds are not as adaptable as we humans are! Too many changes, especially if they are introduced too quickly, can destroy their sense of security and in turn affect their willingness to breed or feed.

It is up to us, their caretakers, to provide our birds with an environment in which they feel safe, and comfortable enough to feel encouraged to raise babies. If we haven't succeeded at that, they will let us know by either not trying to breed at all, or by not feeding. More often than not I will find that a non-feeding hen's problem is a reaction to something in her environment that is making her feel threatened. Once this is corrected she generally will do just fine.

It is easier to blame 'age', or 'bad genes', or even to simply write a bird off as a 'bad breeder' than it is to do a systemic analysis and endure the problem-solving process; but if you wish to be successful in the longer term with your canaries, you will learn to practice such a routine, solve the problem at the root of the matter, and let the canaries take care of the rest.

Banding Babies

'Banding' is the name given to the process of putting a small unique 'ring' on a bird's foot, so as to be able to identify it individually.

There is a variety of different kind of rings or bands used for this purpose. Many are 'closed' bands— in other words, a simple, solid ring that can't be changed in size, and must be put on the bird while it is still in the nest. Usually these bands are put on when the bird is about a week old, though the timing will vary, not only between species, but between individuals, depending on, not just the species, but also the breed and the rate of growth.

Closed bands may or may not be coloured, depending on the issuing organization, but will usually be stamped with the year and a unique code, allowing it to be used as proof of the year the bird was hatched. Usually, too, each band will be registered by the selling club to the name of the buyer. This allows these bands to act as proof of breeding. Many shows require any birds entered in the show to be wearing such a closed band, in order to be eligible for the current-year classes.

Other bands are 'open' or 'split'; these are most often made of coloured plastic, but may also be made of aluminum. An open band can be put on any bird at any age. These bands are usually used by breeders to help them to identify individual birds at a glance. Sometimes a split band will be used as an indicator of gender, or it may be used as a 'family' band, where all related individuals will wear a plastic band of the same colour, making it easier,

by R C McDonald

when planning matings, to prevent the accidental breeding of closely related birds.

The decision of whether or not to band your birds rests on a number of variables. Would you like to show your birds? Then you should always close-band all your young canaries, while they are still in the nest. Do you raise a specific breed of canaries, such as the American Singer? Then you should purchase your bands from a club that issues bands specifically for that breed. This makes the banding records much easier to trace, should the need ever arise.

Perhaps you don't ever plan to show, nor do you breed very many birds. You believe that you will always be able to remember each and every chick hatched in your household. But what will you do if a youngster should turn out to look exactly like his or her parent? Banding the youngsters in the nest with the bands for that year will give you visual proof of the year of hatch, for the rest of that bird's life, and, once you have more than one canary, such bands can be of invaluable assistance in preventing confusion.

Occasionally a nestling will manage to wriggle its way out of its band (or a parent has removed it from the chick's leg). If this is discovered in time a new band can be put on in its place, but sometimes the lost band isn't discovered until the hatchling is too big to re-band.

This situation is one where the open or split bands can be particularly useful. Placing a coloured band on the leg of such a youngster can help to ensure that you never get that particular bird confused with another, similar-looking canary. In fact, using a coloured split band can help solve a number of potential problems at any stage of life.

So now that you've decided to band your baby birds, where do you get your bands, and how to you use them?

There's several possible sources for closed or open bands, depending on where you live. Often the easiest source is your local bird club; once you've joined, you'll

Canary Crazy

have the right to purchase registered closed bands from them, sized for the breed you keep.

Most clubs also sell a variety of 'open' plastic split bands, often available in a wide choice of colours. You may have already noticed that some breeders use both open and closed bands on their youngsters; many a canary is seen with a closed band on one foot, and a coloured plastic split band on the other, usually indicating either the bird's family, or its gender. These 'open' bands come with a tool that makes it easy to put onto a bird's leg at any age.

There are plenty of other sources for bird bands, but if you think you would like to show your birds, it is usually to your advantage to purchase your bands from the local club that will be hosting the shows you'll want to attend. For one thing, some clubs will not allow birds to be exhibited at their shows unless they are wearing the bands issued by that specific club.

If there is no such club anywhere near you, you may need to join a national organization, or you can purchase your bands online; some sources are listed in the 'links' area of *robirda.com;* look for them under 'supplies'.

Wherever you get your bands, be sure to obtain the right size for your youngsters' breed. It's no fun discovering that you've used bands that have become too small for the bird as it grows. This might not sound like much, but it means that the band becomes embedded in the skin of the leg as the chick matures. Needless to say, this kind of thing can cause all sorts of problems if the band is not cut off as soon as possible, once the problem's discovered.

That raises another issue; if you're going to be close-banding your babies, it's a *very* good idea to also purchase a good pair of band-cutters. You never know when an unexpected problem might arise, and you'll suddenly find yourself having to cut a band off a canary leg. You need to know how to do something like this safely, without harming the bird or it's leg, *before* the need arises. There are a number of good bird supply houses who will be happy to sell you a

by R C McDonald

good pair of band cutters. I strongly recommend buying some extra bands at the same time, then use them to practice using your band cutter.

I don't, though, recommend that you put these extra bands on a canary leg and then try to cut them off! Instead, find yourself a willow tree, and cut some small green twigs, making sure they are about the same size as a canary leg.

Slip one band after another onto a twig, and practice cutting them off the twig until you can do it without leaving any marks on the tender green bark of the twig. Once you can do that, you should have no problems removing a band from a bird's leg, if you should need to.

Now that you have your bands and know how to use your band cutters, the next question is, how and when to put the closed bands onto your young canaries?

Occasionally I am asked if there is such a thing as a 'banding machine' to assist in the chore. No, there is no such invention available, nor is there ever likely to be— baby canaries, like most other close-banded birds, are banded by hand.

Basically, getting a closed band onto a young chick's leg involves slipping the band over the first three toes, then over the joint of the foot almost to the end of the back toe near the ankle joint. The back toe is then gently pulled through, and, the band is on.

Just when to put the band on is a good question— it can vary from bird to bird, and from breed to breed, and also depends on just how fast the chick is growing, which in turn has a lot with how well and often it's being fed by its parents.

In general, the idea is to put the band onto the chick just before the leg reaches its full adult size; this allows the band to be slipped over the joint of the foot onto the leg. Within a day or two after this is done, the foot joint will have become too large to allow the band to be removed, leaving it in place permanently unless it is cut off.

Canary Crazy

With canaries, the right time to close-band the youngsters averages about seven days or so of age, but that can vary by some days, depending on the genetics of the breed and the rate of growth. Also, since canary hens will usually clean the nests of all foreign materials until the babies are about a week or so old, if you band the youngsters too soon you risk the chance of the hen noticing the addition of something strange on her chick's leg, and trying to 'clean' the band out of the nest. Usually she will try to pull the band off the baby's foot, but if she is not able to do this, too often she will just toss the whole works, baby, band, and all!

Because of this, I usually wait to band my youngsters until I see a dropping on the edge of the nest that has not been cleaned up by the hen. This tells me she has stopped paying such close attention to keeping the nest clean, and that she will not be as likely to take as extreme an objection to bands on her babies' legs as she would have even a day or so earlier.

There's yet another preventative step that can be taken too, but this one starts before the eggs are laid, back when the hen is building her nest. Many clubs vary the colour of the bands they are offering year by year. When I am making nesting material for the year, I take into account the colour of that year's bands, and buy some embroidery floss of the same colour.

It is cut, sterilized and pre-shrunk along with the rest of the nesting material I offer my hens; this is always a good idea, since the heat of an incubating hen's body can cause any unshrunken natural fibres to begin to shrink and curl around her feet as she incubates her eggs. If they shrink enough to cut off her foot's blood circulation, she could lose one or even both feet before all is said and done.

Prevent such accidents by always pre-shrinking and sterilizing all nesting materials offered to your hens. This is easily done by simply heaping the prepared, cut-up nesting material into a bowl and pouring boiling hot water over it. Stir it about, to ensure that all the fibres get thoroughly hot

by R C McDonald

and wet, then let it sit until it is cool enough to handle. Pull the shrunken, sterilized heap of fibre out of the bowl, wring it out, and let it dry on a heap of newspaper or towelling before storing it or using it.

Each year I cut some short strands of floss of the same colour as the year's bands, into the nesting material I offer the hen. She becomes used to seeing this colour in her nest, and when the bands appear, they won't tend to startle her as much.

Before banding your babies, always be sure to examine the inside of all the bands closely, and make sure they are smooth, with no tiny sharp cutting edges, and no tiny beads or pieces of scrap metal to act as an irritant or cause damage to the skin. Such irritants can cause a bird to fuss with his band, and may eventually cause problems such as infections or worse, perhaps to the point of necessitating removal of the band. If necessary use a tiny file to smooth any roughness you've found.

Even though I've waited for droppings to begin to show on the edge of the nest, I take yet another step of precaution to make sure that the hen doesn't take an objection to the new bands on her youngsters legs, and plan to band the babies in the evening, shortly before the lights go out for the day.

I prepare the area where I'll be banding, then wait until the babies have had their evening feed, so their crops are full for the night. Then I lift the entire nest full of youngsters off the hook and take the whole thing away, out of the birdroom and out of sight of the youngsters' mother.

I recommend banding baby canaries sitting down at a table, with a warmed towel spread out before you. If your nest has a flat bottom, just put it down on the towel, but if the nestpan instead has a rounded bottom, use something like an empty tuna tin to act as a stand. Put the nest and stand onto the towel, then gently remove the babies and place each one individually on the warmed towel.

Plant both elbows firmly on the table, and gently pick up

the first youngster. It will probably produce a dropping, in its surprise at being picked up; it won't harm you, just ignore it, until you have a chance to shake it off. Remember, it's encased in a special sac that prevents it from sticking, so it will shake off easily. Wiping, on the other hand, will just smear it in.

If you're right-handed, hold the baby in your left hand, and gently grasp the youngster's right foot. Take the band you're going to put on the baby, and wet it with a little saliva from your mouth— it will help the band slide on more easily. Some use vaseline, mineral oil or some other kind of salve or cream instead, but this is *not* a good idea, since it can cause chilling, particularly if it gets onto the hen's feathers.

If you're lucky, the baby will stick the three front toes straight out, and it will be easy to slide the band onto them. Sometimes they insist on holding their foot with the toes curled up tightly, in which case you may have to gently rearrange them, until you can get the band over the front three toes.

Slide the band up the toes and over the joint or 'ball' of the foot. You may have to wriggle it about a little to get it over the joint of the foot, but you should not have to force it too strongly. If you do, you could put the back toe out of joint; this is called a 'slipped claw', and while it can be fixed, it takes some time and trouble to do so. Worse, it's painful for the bird, so it's easier on both you and the youngsters if you avoid forcing a band on.

Sometimes the band just won't go on, whatever you do, and the baby stays unbanded. Such a bird can still be shown in the open classes or sold as a pet, but will not qualify to be shown in current year classes. If some such event occurs in your flock, make a note of the parents, and the next time they have babies, try banding a day earlier.

If the babies are at the right age for banding, you should be able to *just* get the band over the ball of the foot, with a little extra push and wriggle, but without having to use too much force. Once the band is over the 'hump' of the joint, continue sliding it up the leg until the back toe is free. If necessary, use the tip of a toothpick to pull the tip of the back toe free. Tah-dah! You've banded your first baby canary!

Once the baby is banded, put it back into the nest, and proceed with the next youngster. They might wriggle some, but take your time and be patient and gentle, and you should have no real problems— and remember, *don't* try to rush yourself! After all, it's not urgent that it be done fast, just that it be done well.

Once you've banded all the youngsters, return the nest to the hen just before the lights go out for the night— that way she won't have enough time to examine the nest and notice the presence of the bands. You want her to barely have time to cover the nest before it's time to sleep. This way, when she wakes in the morning, she will be far more likely to accept the bands as belonging in the nest, even if she does spot them.

Banding the youngsters is one of those chores that can seem terribly difficult, when you first consider it, but it really takes very little practice to get the hang of it. And once you do, you may just find yourself wondering why you ever thought it was such a big deal in the first place!

What Now?

It happens to so many new canary owners; their first canary seemed lonely, so they bought him a mate. The birds quickly became more than just friends, and before you quite knew what was happening, they began nesting, and all of a sudden you've gone from owning two birds, to owning a dozen. For now, they're all sharing a large flight cage, but the question seems inevitable... what now?

The problem really is, that canaries by nature are not very social. We humans, who are so very sociable, find it difficult to imagine, but canaries are *very* territorial, and most will usually see other birds in their cage (especially other canaries) as unwanted intruders rather than welcome company, as we tend to fondly imagine.

Putting two canaries into the same cage at any time of year other than spring more often than not simply results in some serious fighting. But as many new canary owners have accidentally discovered, if it is springtime and both canaries are in good physical health and in the mood for breeding, putting them together can achieve quite different results.

If both canaries are in good condition, the pair will be able to mate and raise babies, rather than going into the more common 'territorial contest' routine. Territorial issues between two canaries will often end with the weaker of the two dead, in the long run. This is the most common scenario, in fact, when two canaries (of whatever gender) are expected to share a cage over a longer term.

Younger canaries tend to be a good bit less territorial

than the adults, and most can usually share a flight cage in relative safety until midwinter or so, perhaps a little longer if their owner is careful with the lighting.

One of the biggest problems with territoriality is that the birds almost never display their issues while their people are around to see— ninety-nine percent of the aggression is liable to happen privately.

Even so, we humans just don't tend to recognize canary aggression for what it is even when we *do* see it. It is far more common for a new canary owner to think the birds are playing, when what is *really* going on will eventually mean life or death for one or more of the birds involved. Some breeds or strains of canaries are less aggressive than others— but even so, they are still canaries, and can still be fairly territorial.

Even if everybody gets along fairly well up until midwinter, if they are like most canaries, your youngsters will need to be separated each to his or her own cage by mid-December or so. There they will stay until a new home is found for them, or they become ready to breed and are paired with a suitable mate.

Of course, pairing will occur only if you decide you want them raising more youngsters. Other owners may prefer to keep the genders separated, so that the hens cannot lay fertilized eggs— usually a hen in the mood for breeding will still lay and incubate her eggs, but if they haven't been fertilized nothing will hatch.

If you don't plan to keep your youngsters, you will need to sell them. Many hobby breeders will simply sell the youngsters to other prospective pet owners, but there's another option available that is all too often over-looked, and that's showing your birds.

Especially if you have pure-bred birds, this can be a great way to meet other bird keepers, and better yet, it offers another option for selling your youngsters; any bird who's shown well will sell for a much better price than it would

Canary Crazy

otherwise, and it will be much more likely to sell to somebody able to appreciate it's qualities, and willing to provide a high level of care.

Requirements for showing vary from breed to breed, so the best way to find out the details you need in order to go about showing your particular bird(s), is to look up and join a club specializing in your favourite breed of canary. If you can't find a local club, join a national one, and you may even consider starting a local chapter.

So how do you go about finding the right bird club to join? One good place to start is the list of links we've posted at *robirda.com* under the category "Clubs & Organizations", which you'll find at *www.robirda.com/links1.html* . (this is by no means a complete list though.)

If you decide not to show, your next task will be to begin to attempt to separate your youngsters by gender, before setting about finding them new homes. Understanding canary territoriality is important when trying to discern the gender of younger canaries, because if the youngsters are living together in the same cage, often only the more dominant birds will sing. The 'dangling needle' method that some breeders use, works on the same principles as dowsing for water. For some folks, it seems it can work fairly well— but for most of us, it's rather unreliable. After all, even guesswork has a fifty-fifty chance of being right!

The old saw about 'only male canaries sing', is another misconception that is not too dependable; mostly because it is *not* true that canary hens don't sing. *Some* canary hens don't sing at all, of course—but a great many of them do sing somewhat. Most are not capable of singing as well as the males, but a few are capable of singing equally as well as any male, and do.

I have owned several such canary hens over the years, and I have a friend who had a young waterslager hen who sang so well that 'he' won a ribbon for 'his' high-quality song, at a show! It's difficult to imagine what she felt and thought when her prized show-winning 'male' canary turned around the next spring and began laying eggs!

Some canary people will tell you that a singing hen can be artificially manufactured, by giving her male hormones— this is true, but those same male hormones will prevent egg-laying, so a singing hen who allows a male to court her, lays her eggs and then commences to sing while incubating her eggs, as some of my hens have done, certainly does not have too many male hormones, or she would not be able to successfully breed and lay her eggs while continuing to sing.

Generally though, it must be said that often the more freely singing young canaries will turn out to be male; but as mentioned above, often only the more dominant birds in a shared-cage situation will sing. If your youngsters are all sharing the same large cage, it's possible that some of the non-singing youngsters might actually be males, but being less dominant, they are not comfortable singing out.

Generally, any canary will sing best if caged alone. That means that the best way to find the probable gender of your youngsters is to place each in a cage by itself, and then wait a few weeks to see who sings, and how much. The birds that sing a lot, and who have the longer, more complex songs, are more likely to be males. The birds who sing less often, or who have shorter, less complex songs, or who don't sing at all, are more likely to be hens. Just remember, all such methods involve guesswork, and in the end there's still no guarantee of gender.

What it really comes down to, is that, with few exceptions, there is only *one* time during the year when it is possible to tell the gender of an adult canary by visual inspection at all reliably, and that is when it is in full breeding condition. Then, if you have some experience at it, it is possible to examine the birds' vents and find out their gender fairly accurately.

But canary genders can look similar even then, so you must know and be able to see the subtle differences between the genders. Note too, that this only works if the birds are fully ready to breed— otherwise, with most

Canary Crazy

breeds, there will be no visible difference whatsoever.

The best way to learn to tell the visual gender differences in a canary who is ready to breed, is to examine a known female, and compare her with a known male. As with any skill, this gets easier with a little practice. But since this method only works when the birds are fully ready to breed, the rest of the year you will still be left guessing.

The birds themselves are luckier; if they are provided with full-spectrum lighting, they can tell at a glance who is who, using a method that so far, we humans have been unable to duplicate.

That's because the feathers of the male and female canary refract ultraviolet light differently. Other canaries can easily see these differences— like most birds, canaries have extra colour cones in their eyes that allow them to see well into the ultraviolet range of wavelengths, light and colours we can't see at all.

To our birds, the different refraction of the UV light off the feathers of a male or a female makes each bird's gender very clear. Eventually we may be able to use this fact to develop a truly reliable method of telling canary gender for ourselves, but for now, since we humans can't see far into the UV range, nor have we yet developed an inexpensive means to allow us to do this artificially, this method is unfortunately not available to canary breeders. Yet.

Two things I *can* tell you. The first is that figuring out the gender of the youngsters is one of (if not *the*) toughest chores of the year faced by any canary breeder. The second is that the person or people who manage to come up with an easy way for us to reliably tell the difference, is likely to make a small fortune. Until then though, we are stuck with a series of rather round-about trial-and-error methods.

This can be a fairly tough chore, and it's why many canary breeders will sell you a guaranteed singer— but they will *not* guarantee that the bird is a male. That's because they know that there is a chance that any such singer could

by R C McDonald

turn around and begin to lay eggs during the next spring. Many longer-term canary keepers will tell you that there's only one thing that's relatively certain, when it comes to telling canary gender; if it lays an egg, it's a hen, if it has filled a hen's egg, it's a male.

For now at least, all else is guesswork; but one guarantee still remains, when it comes to working with canaries—chances are quite good that all this will keep you busy enough, that you really won't have much (if any!) time left to wonder, *"What now?"*

Unseasonal Breeding

Canaries are photosensitive; that is, their bodies react to the changing length of days and their physical systems adjust in accordance to the perceived season. This generally means breeding season will occur during the lengthening days of the spring, slowing as the season moves into high summer, when the annual moult is soon due for an adult canary.

This is only true of adult canaries; youngsters will begin to swap out their nest feathers for adult body feathers at around six to eight weeks or so of age, moulting until they are around twelve weeks or so old. However their wing and tail feathers are not usually replaced until the following year, when the youngster has become fully adult, at a bit older than a year of age.

Territories are established and songs developed during the fall and shorter days of winter, when days are short and energy must be conserved and food sources protected. The hens listen to the males closely, learning their songs and studying their survival skills; in spring each will compete with the other hens to attract the strongest, most successful male with the best song, to sire her chicks and help her to raise them.

Since this is the case nature intended for canaries, why then are there reports every year of canary breeders who encounter problems with their canaries wanting to breed as

by R C McDonald

early in the season as fall or winter?

Hearing of canaries attempting to breed outside of their normal season is nothing new; every year stories are told of canaries who continue to try to breed right through the summer months into fall, putting off their moult until into the late fall, or even well into the winter. Other stories tell of canaries who suddenly, for no apparent reason their owners can decipher, decide to begin breeding sometime during the fall or winter.

These attempts are frequently blamed on mismanaged lighting, and indeed, lighting (specifically, the length of days the canaries are experiencing) *is* an important factor. It's well documented that when the length of the days begin to increase, any canary in good physical condition who is not too old, will begin preparing for the attempt to breed.

But what about those cases where the lighting has been managed properly and daylengths are decreasing, yet a male canary continues to feed and breed his mate, or a hen canary eagerly continues to make nests, lay eggs, and incubate them?

The fact is, canaries do not breed strictly by day length alone. While length of day is of primary importance to the canary body as an indicator of season, several secondary seasonal indicators (or 'triggers') exist as well. These secondary indicators act in conjunction with the primary stimulus of lengthening days; together, they provide an unmistakable signal to the wild canaries of the arrival of spring, and breeding season.

While none of these secondary triggers tend to act as strongly on the canary body as does photo-periodicity, still, such stimuli *can* have the effect, alone or in combination, of 'pushing' the canary to attempt (or continue to attempt) to breed, no matter what the lengths of the days actually are.

One of the most important of these secondary triggers is the availability of water. This has strong significance to the canary's instincts in several ways. Plentiful water means easy access to water for bathing; most canary breeders acknowledge that free access to bathing can help to bring a canary (hens in particular, but also the males) into breeding condition, as well as aiding in fertility and providing timely essential assistance to a hatching chick.

In the wild, however, availability of plentiful water is also an unmistakable indicator of the presence (or imminent arrival) of foods suitable for raising chicks; soft-bodied, high-protein insects, and soft, easy-to-eat, vitamin-loaded sprouting seeds, especially those of grasses and other similar plants.

Both the insects and the sprouting seeds are quite high in moisture as well as protein and other essential nutrients to raising chicks, and they generally can not be found unless the weather is damp enough to encourage their presence.

Thus, several thousand years of evolution tells the canary's instincts that the plentiful availability of water means that plentiful quantities of good quality foods perfect for feeding young hatchlings will be available soon, even if there is not much currently on hand.

Another strong stimulus to canary breeding instincts is the diet; if the diet being provided to domestic canaries is rich in protein, fats, and/or vitamins, particularly if some or all of these foods are softer or high in moisture, canary instincts will try to push the bird's body into breeding. If this is the case yet plentiful water is *not* being supplied, canary instincts will begin to suspect the coming of mid-summer, when the environment canaries evolved in becomes dry and hot, and food supplies become less reliable. This in turn can increase the metabolic pressure to breed *now*, before everything dries up and food supplies begin to run out.

So, either a plentiful water supply or a protein and/or fat-rich diet can act to trigger unseasonal breeding attempts no matter what the length of day the canary is experiencing— or, for that matter, can have the effect of pushing a canary to put off their normal moult, in favour of continuing to breed.

by R C McDonald

Warmth is another secondary trigger which can help to encourage canaries to breed, but this particular stimulus seems to be of less importance than the availability of water and proper foods for rearing young; no matter how warm the weather, if protein-rich foods and a reliable supply of fresh water are not present, few if any attempts to breed will be made.

The healthy canary's rapid response to these physical triggers is the result of the instinct to try to perpetuate the species whenever the opportunity arises. This instinct is very strong, and is present in most (and probably all) avian species living on our planet.

After all, birds in the wild encounter heavy predation; if their species is to be successful, they must raise enough babies each year so that, no matter how many youngsters (or adults) are lost, there will be enough individuals remaining to carry on and hopefully increase the overall species population.

Many avian species pay little to no attention to the length of their days, instead keeping their breeding attempts to those times when the climate and available food supply will support producing and feeding youngsters. These species are known as 'opportunistic'— when they realize conditions seem right for successful breeding, they will seize the opportunity and attempt to produce and raise young.

Species such as canaries, who react primarily to the changing length of their days, are known as 'photosensitive', but that doesn't mean that their instincts to perpetuate the species are any weaker! It simply means these particular birds require more complex changes in their surroundings and diet, in order to convince them it's time to breed.

So what's to be done with a canary (or canaries) who persists in attempting to breed unseasonally?

As you have probably already guessed, the first step in solving such a riddle requires a thorough understanding of the pressures environmental conditions put on a canary, during the attempt to breed. Once these 'breeding triggers' are understood through and through it should no longer be difficult to tell which element or elements necessary to breeding are impacting the bird's perception.

From there it will usually be a fairly simple step to figure out just what changes will need to be made in the bird's lighting schedule, environment or diet, in order to restrict any further breeding attempts to the proper time of year, and foster a return to balance with the seasons.

It's important to remember, during the process of actually achieving this balance, that any eggs laid should *not* be thrown away! This will simply encourage her to lay more. You might as well leave her a nest, too, since otherwise she will choose some place else to lay her eggs; perhaps a seed cup, or a corner of the cage floor. Either position will make cage maintenance more of a chore for you, so leave her the nest— for now.

Meanwhile, continue to adjust her environment to reflect the end of breeding season by removing bathing water, and at the same time reducing or eliminating all soft foods, particularly any that are rich in proteins or fats.

Give any egg-laying hens a nestful of the fake eggs sold by many suppliers of canary breeding accessories. These can't hatch, dry out, or go bad, and so the broody canary hen can proceed to incubate her 'eggs' to her heart's content. This will in turn help to make her less likely to succumb to the urge to lay more eggs, which will help her to conserve her physical resources.

Those same physical resources will be needed, once she has stopped trying to breed unseasonally; she will need all her strength to assist her through her annual moult, in order to transit the winter with enough energy to allow her to come into breeding condition properly, when springtime and breeding season finally arrive for real.

Older canary breeders may be heard to offer some rather unusual nuggets of wisdom such as, "Show them the season!" when asked about how to deal with a problem entailing unseasonable breeding. While such a statement may sound cryptic, it actually indicates a depth of understanding achieved by years of trial-and-error experiences. It is a literal, if brief, explanation of what that breeder has learned to accomplish with his or her canaries.

Learn to observe your canaries carefully, and within a few seasons you may just find that you too have learned how to make those few seasonal adjustments each year, to help make life easier and better for both you and your canaries. You'll easily be able to show your canaries spring, summer, fall, or winter, using the appropriate foods, lighting, and care for the season. In fact, some day you may even be surprised to find yourself wondering why you ever thought that it was difficult to keep your canaries from breeding unseasonally!

Canary Crazy

To Breed or Not?

Sometimes it happens that, even though you'd planned to breed your canaries, a situation arises that makes it clear you won't be able to devote the time and attention you'd planned on to increasing your flock, for one breeding season at least. The inevitable decision follows; should you go ahead and breed your canaries, trying to keep up with everything that needs doing, or should you instead try to delay breeding and perhaps even prevent it for the year?

If not done carefully, deliberate changes to the canary breeding cycle can affect the moult, which in turn can affect canary health. This means that a clear understanding of the canary life and breeding cycle is necessary before you begin trying to apply any changes.

Whether you decide to proceed with breeding but not allow any youngsters to hatch, or choose instead to try to prevent any attempts to breed, each method has its own advantages and drawbacks. Each approach requires some work to achieve the desired results, and both methods work best if begun well before breeding season is due, so it's a good idea to consider your options well ahead of time, carefully and thoroughly.

Lots has been written about what's necessary to be successful with breeding canaries, and if you decide to proceed with breeding but not to allow any hatching, then the procedure is quite simple— you'll keep to a normal breeding schedule. All that's necessary is to switch any eggs produced with fake eggs, then let the hens 'incubate' them as long as they wish. They will usually incubate fake eggs longer than they would infertile eggs, because infertile eggs slowly lose moisture as the incubation period advances, becoming gradually lighter in weight. Eventually they grow light enough to alert the hen that there is no chick inside; the egg is empty. When this happens she is apt to throw out the old eggs and begin laying a new clutch all over again.

On the other hand, the fake eggs have no moisture to lose and so will not lose weight. The hen's instincts will tell her that this egg is fertile, and so she will tend to sett it for longer than she otherwise might. Eventually, when nothing hatches, she should abandon her nest, at which time you can give her a week or two in a flight cage. Then you will need to decide whether you will have to allow her to repeat a nesting cycle, or, if the season is at midsummer or later, leave her in the flight and encourage her to advance into her annual moult.

Some hens, instead of abandoning their nests, will simply lay more eggs and continue incubating, so a close eye needs to be kept on all nests to ensure that each egg is replaced soon after being laid, particularly if it could be fertile.

But what if you would prefer not to allow any breeding at all?

This is trickier, since it goes against the instinct for species survival. This method has more potential for problems, too, because if you adversely affect the moult, you will also be adversely affecting your canary's health. Canaries *need* to be able to achieve a successful moult, to stay healthy.

There are other problems that can arise too. If you prevent young canaries from breeding in their first year, it's possible that they may never learn properly how to breed successfully. Young, newly-adult canaries learn with everything they do, and if they decide that all breeding season is about is 'playing house', they may never properly learn how to actually produce and raise chicks.

Older canaries, who have successfully raised chicks in the past, will know better, and even if they aren't allowed to produce chicks during the current year, will often prove to be reliable in a following year— although they are also more likely to resent being prevented from breeding in the first place.

Older birds with positive experience can help to teach younger, inexperienced birds the finer points of successful mating and hatching, so if you decide you will need to put off breeding for a year, but plan to keep breeding canaries in the long run, you will want to be sure to keep as many experienced breeding birds as you can manage. When the time to breed finally does roll around, they will prove to be worth their weight in gold, for their ability to teach the less experienced birds 'the ropes'.

Alternatively, if you want to keep several canaries but plan to never breed at all, you might be better to start out with stock that has never been bred, so they will have less of an idea just what spring is all about. This way they may be less likely to become frustrated and upset with you over your lack of cooperation in helping them to produce babies.

I personally find it easier to let them go through the motions, whether I plan to let them raise babies or not. This allows me to keep them in pairs, rather than having to cage them singly, and seems to help lower the frustration levels, by allowing them to 'play house'. Of course, you need to be sure that all your pairs all get along well! They don't seem to experience much (if any) frustration over the eggs not hatching, but they can and *do* experience quite a lot of frustration if they are caged singly throughout the whole season, and can see and/or hear other birds of the opposite gender who want mating.

Keeping canaries in pairs gives you less cages to clean, which is always nice, especially if you are busier than usual. If you're trying to discourage breeding activity, you can try housing the canary hens together in a large flight cage, but watch for arguments— even the usually more peaceable canary hens can get quite territorial when in the mood to nest.

I don't recommend ever keeping male canaries grouped together in flight cages during the late winter or spring, because there is apt to be some serious fighting, even when the birds are not yet in full breeding condition.

An important factor in preventing attempts to breed involves maintaining the nutritional levels high enough for good health, but not so high as to encourage breeding. This means being careful not to offer much in the way of protein and oil-rich supplements, and keeping all soft foods down to a scant minimum.

It also means not offering water-rich greens such as lettuces and endives, instead offering only denser greens such as kale or collards, and only in amounts that will be completely cleaned up within a few hours. If you offer vitamin supplements in a mix such as soaked seed with nestling food, increase the amount of vitamins included so you can reduce the amount of mixture offered to a small amount given no more than once weekly.

Lighting is important too of course. Part of preparing for breeding season involves spending some time during the winter with reduced hours of lighting. If you know that you will not be able to breed the following spring and wish to try to prevent breeding, then don't reduce your winter lights as much as usual; instead of reducing the winter hours to 10 1/2 hours, reduce them only to 12 hours, then leave the lights set at 12 hours on and 12 hours off throughout the entire winter and spring.

The decreasing winter lighting pattern tells the birds that now is the time to fly and get strong and healthy, so as to be in good shape when the days again start to get longer. The fact that the lights don't decrease so much means that there will be less competition for food during the winter daylight hours. This in turn will allow all the birds to eat their fill before the lights go out. Plus, thanks to the shorter nights, they will have less time to wait before the next day and their next meal, all of which helps keep them healthy without alerting their bodies to the fact that it is actually midwinter.

Generally, breeding behaviour begins as soon as the days begin to lengthen, and becomes stronger until the days are long enough for the birds to achieve full breeding condition. But since you won't be advancing the lights until close to time for the moult, there will be no signal for breeding behaviour to start, nor will the birds be primed by shorter winter days to jump into spring as days begin to lengthen.

This should keep them relatively healthy, without encouraging the almost frantic preparations for breeding that you would more normally see. As long as they are unaware that the season is advancing towards spring outdoors, your canaries should remain fairly healthy and happy.

Of course, you can't allow this to go on for the entire year, or the birds will never move properly into their moult. So instead, you can resort to offering them a shorter, later spring, which does not include the time or nutrition to breed. Close to midsummer, in or around the first or second week in June, suddenly jump your lights from 12 hours a day up to 16 hours a day. Be sure to keep a close watch on the diet you are offering, and be certain that it doesn't offer any extra nutrition to encourage breeding activity.

The idea here is to see that the birds get approximately two to three weeks of the longer days before you begin to gradually reducing the day lengths again, by about a half an hour every week or so. So, near the end of June you will reduce the day lengths to 15 1/2 hours, then throughout July, you'll gradually reduce the day lengths by a 1/2 hour per week, until by early to mid-August, the birds are getting 13 hours of daylight, and have started to moult.

This is when you have to make your decision— do you continue to reduce your lights to the normal winter low of

10 1/2 hours, or will you instead leave them at 12 hours? It all depends on if you think you will want to breed your canaries during the following spring or not.

This method is a bit trickier to follow than the simpler 'replace the eggs with fakes' method... but if done properly, it can mean less frustration for your birds, and overall, less work for you.

Hopefully the need to skip a breeding season will not happen to many of us very often, but as with everything in life, it's always a good idea to be prepared for whatever possibility might arise. And besides, as the old saying goes, if you're prepared for the worst, anything else is a pleasant surprise. And who doesn't like pleasant surprises?

Shipping Birds

Of all the controversies that have arisen in the world of pet birds over the last few decades, few have been fought over so much or had such an impact as the rules and regulations about shipping birds. The US Post office has recently changed their rules yet again, and for now at least, US bird keepers can again ship their birds 'Express' via the post office. (See the Legislation area of *www.nfss.org* for more details).

But the original ban on shipping birds by mail was because so many studies showed that for a great many species, shipping by mail was extremely strenuous and could seriously impact their health. Has that changed, or did the US post office give in to popular demand?

Like the rest of us, you will have to make up your own mind where you stand on this issue. But since it helps to have as much information as possible in order to do that, I decided to share with you some of what I know and some of what I've been able to find out about shipping birds.

My first acquaintance with shipping birds was when a friend of mine decided to get some Colourbred canaries shipped to him from Ontario. The particular colour he wanted was not available in our area of British Columbia. He decided that the cost of having new stock shipped to him would be well worth it, and went ahead and ordered four pairs of birds, to be shipped to him by air.

It was late August, and the weather had been pretty good. Ordinarily there would have been no problem— the birds were taken to the express delivery counter just before the plane left, and he'd been told when the flight was due to arrive. He was promised that his birds would be among the first items offloaded, and that he would be able to pick them up immediately.

Then the weather threw in an unexpected twist. Over the prairies, the plane encountered a sudden storm, and was forced to land in Edmonton. The wings required de-icing, and for whatever reason, the cargo had to be temporarily offloaded.

As a result, my friend's birds sat out on the tarmac in a cold pounding rain for almost 3 hours, in a specially-made cardboard box inside a nylon-mesh pet-carrier. This small 'travel-cage' arrangement was *not* waterproof. Intended only as a temporary carrier, it offered only partial shelter at first, and none at all once the cardboard became wet through. Once everything was done and it was time to continue the flight, the whole affair was put— still soaking wet— back into the plane with the rest of the luggage.

By the time they arrived a few hours later, five of the eight birds were dead, and the other three were seriously ill. Of the eight birds originally shipped, only two hens survived. Of these two, only one ever bred successfully.

Total cost? Well over three thousand Canadian dollars. My friend was devastated. No insurance would ever cover such losses, and to this day he will have nothing to do with shipping birds.

True, it was a simple accident, and events could very well have turned out differently— but to me a story like this emphasizes the risks involved in shipping, something very often glossed over. The fact is, no matter how careful you are, successful shipping of birds still requires a rather large component of sheer luck.

American Singer Club, Inc webmaster Ginger Wolnick, a well-known breeder of American Singer canaries, says of the recent change in the rules about shipping; "Regardless of what is 'official', you are at the mercy of your local post office, and the post office at the receiving end. There are just too many unknowns and things out of your control. I am still not going to ship my birds."

Ginger also says, "I believe the safest way to transport canaries is to hand carry in your own car or with you on a plane in a pet carrier that you take on board with you. I recommend people try to find local breeders. With the resources now available online, most people should be able to find a canary breeder within driving distance. If someone just *has* to have some special type of bird, well, if they want it badly enough, they can wait for an airfare war, buy a discounted ticket and visit a breeder near a major city.

"When you compare the total setup costs of breeding a good line of quality birds, spending a couple hundred dollars to visit the seller and pick out your birds instead of letting them ship you what they want to get rid of may actually be to your advantage. So, my recommendation is to not ship, but to hand-carry instead."

She further points out that many people miss an annual chance at one of the best opportunities around to get good quality birds; attend the National Cage-Bird Show. Many exhibitors will be happy to make arrangements for you to visit them and buy the birds you need.

Some years American Airlines has been known to offer a show discount, allowing birds on board if they are travelling to the show. No quarantine was needed even for Canadian visitors, as a vet was at the show to issue health certificates for those who need them.

If you feel you absolutely must ship, please be sure to consider everything that's involved before-hand. The American Singer Club website that Ginger manages has some excellent US shipping information posted, including a thorough outline of what's involved in shipping canaries internationally. Everybody should read this information before considering shipping any bird (or birds), especially to or from another country.

by R C McDonald

Others feel very strongly about this issue too. Parrot rehabilitator Wilhelm Kiesselbach says, "Neither the airlines nor the postal service are absolutely reliable. Flight cancellations, delays and the 'people factor' can spell a real danger to the physical and emotional health of the bird. Horror stories about birds left in the heat on the tarmac, missing flights and being roughly handled abound. I see ads all the time with statements such as, 'Parrot Chicks For Sale! Fully weaned, raised with lots of love, healthy— will ship.'

"These ads make me ill. They include the word 'love', but really they are all about money. Many airlines now offer unaccompanied shipping for animals, since the US Post Office has announced it will resume this service as well. There's a number of reasons why I consider this an unethical, cruel and potentially very dangerous practice.

"I know of the fate of an African Grey chick which was shipped from Florida to Minneapolis. The breeder assured the buyer that this would be no problem, and that she did it 'all the time'.

"Unbeknownst to the shipper, the airline cancelled the outbound flight. The chick was then put into a holding area for 6 hours, and when it was loaded the container was roughly handled—the baby Grey arrived in Minneapolis traumatized and in shock, and died three days later.

"I know of another occasion where a Macaw was shipped from the west coast to the east coast. It was summer, the weather was hot, and the bird was left in its container on the tarmac in the sun for an unknown period of time. It was dead by the time it arrived in New York.

"Buying a pet bird should be a well considered decision. The buyer should meet the breeder and the youngster before the 'big day'. He or she should make sure that the bird is properly reared in a healthy, clean environment and that the breeder is the person he or she claims.

"The importance of proper rearing, weaning and most especially proper socializing cannot be over-emphasized.

Canary Crazy

Apart from the purely ethical considerations of subjecting a living creature to so much physical and emotional stress, there are also realistic concerns: a bird that's been shipped is close kin to the 'cat in a bag'. Parrots and many other species of birds are not cheap— this in turn means that shysters abound, and anyone investing this much money should be *very* careful.

"An ethical breeder will not ship his or her birds under any circumstances. In my opinion anyone who advertises a willingness to ship birds automatically disqualifies him or herself as a responsible, loving and caring breeder. Someone once said: 'If you would not do it to your child, don't do it to your bird.'"

As our birds have taught so many of us so well by now, there's always something new to learn. Fascinating though it can be to keep and learn about species, colours, or breeds of birds new to us— if obtaining those birds means having them shipped, you might want to be sure you've considered all the possibilities before committing yourself one way or another.

After all— the life and health of both your birds and your pocketbook could be seriously affected. Isn't it a better idea to be sure you have learned everything you need to know about what you could get into, first?

by R C McDonald

Sharing the Dream

Over the years, there's been a great many people who have taught more me about my birds, one way or another. Most had kept birds for several decades or more at the time I first encountered them, and all generously and willingly shared their knowledge and experiences with me whenever they could. I will always be grateful to all of them, but thinking back, I find that one man in particular stands out from the rest.

It was late afternoon, and I'd just finished caring for my birds after returning home from a long day's work. I was planning to settle down with a freshly-made cup of coffee and browse through the paper for awhile, when the phone rang.

Grabbing for my coffee with one hand and the headset with the other, I heard, "Is this Robirda? I just read your story in Newsbeak (our local bird-club's newsletter), and I *love* it! I'm the editor for the Okanagan Bird Club, and I'd like to use your story in our newsletter, is that okay?"

Of course it was, but that was only the start. Over the next few hours, our conversation ranged through all the vagaries of keeping birds of any kind; feeding, breeding, taming, training, healing, judging, selling, showing, and more. By the time I hung up the phone almost four hours later, I felt that I had learned more about keeping canaries in those few hours, than I had in the previous decade.

Canary Crazy

It wasn't until that moment that it dawned on me that I had no idea who I'd been talking to! We'd been so busy talking about our birds that he'd forgotten to introduce himself, and I'd not even noticed.

Luckily, the same fact dawned on him that same evening, and the next afternoon he called again. This time we made sure to first exchange contact info before settling down to another lengthy, wide-ranging, inspiring discussion, and before the evening was out, I knew I'd found a kindred spirit.

His name was Jack Merkens, and he had a lot to share. He was 78 at the time, and had been keeping birds since his childhood in Bandoeng, on the Indonesian island of Java, where he'd been born.

As a member of a Dutch family, at that time he was considered one of the ruling elite, and was not allowed to work. Born with a naturally restless spirit and an endless drive to learn, by the age of six Jack had turned to keeping birds as an outlet for some of his energy. In a way, it was a natural enough choice, since his father was a veterinarian. (Luckily for both of them, working with birds or animals was not considered 'work' at the time.)

He started with budgies, finches, and canaries, and a single large aviary. It wasn't long before he began building (at first, with help) more cages, and almost before he knew it he was keeping several more species.

Considered by most to be just a hobby, Jack told me that bird-keeping was to be responsible for driving him to gain experience in a wide range of fields. Among them were a keen interest in nutrition and food values, along with an interest in the plants from which foods came. He became an accomplished carpenter, and went on to learn cabinetry too, so he could build his own cages, show-cages, and aviaries.

He learned to weld, braise and paint, not just passably, but well enough to have made his living at any of those trades, if he'd wanted. But perhaps the best thing Jack excelled in? Communication. He seemed to have an almost instinctive understanding of and interest in people of all kinds and walks of life, and was always able to draw them out.

When he retired in 1983 from his job in Calgary as a draftsman for an engineering firm to move to Kelowna, his station wagon was packed full of birds.

"There wasn't enough room to keep all of them, so I decided that canaries were my first love," he told a reporter from a local newspaper during an interview a decade later. Eventually his birdroom grew to include several breeds of canaries, but his first and biggest love was always the petite Gloster canary.

He was not impressed by the trend to increase the size of the Gloster Canary; the standards, he maintained, stated that one of the key traits of a Gloster was that it be a diminutive bird. To Jack, that meant as tiny as possible, and in order to remain in his aviary as a breeding bird, a Gloster had to be just that.

Jack also had a keen awareness of each and every canary's personality and pet potential. He insisted that young birds required plenty of stimulation as they matured, and that this apparently small element was actually key to their ability to develop their personality to its maximum potential.

To Jack, this meant providing them a variety of toys, as well as allowing them to become used to changing cages, a varied and changing diet, even changing the environments around them, all with the goal of getting them used to as many different experiences as possible.

Sometimes he would pack several youngsters into show cages and take them for rides in his car, driving slowly, and allowing them to see out the car windows while he was driving. He told me that before each show season began, he would be sure to wear different clothing, hats, and even on occasion different wigs or a fake beard, while in the birdroom doing chores.

This led them to develop to their full potential, he felt, and he stated unequivocally that these experiences allowed them to become far more adaptable than the usual cage-raised canary. This in turn would allow them to become almost complacent in a situation that would drive another, more nervous bird, into fits. Such a canary, he said, made for both outstanding pets, and top-notch show-birds.

Although he didn't raise any of the canary breeds bred specifically for song, a male canary's singing style was another important factor to consider when breeding, according to Jack. He required his birds to be free in offering their song, and made sure that those he chose to use for breeding sang no harsh tones. Even if everything else about them matched his requirements in all other ways, if he didn't like the song a particular canary sang, he would not use it for breeding.

Although he loved red canaries for their colour, he found them frustrating. Most red canaries are bred with complete disregard for the quality of their song, and Jack found their songs far too harsh or even shrill, too often degenerating into stridency. When he heard that I had some red canaries descended from an old line of siskin-roller canary crosses, he was thrilled, and decided on the spot that he just had to come to visit, and acquire a few.

At that time, we lived almost four hundred miles apart, and my clunky old rattletrap of a car was not at all reliable, especially when it came to distances over ten miles or so. Jack, on the other hand, was involved in community, bird club, and family activities, and his life generally had a very full schedule. As a result, it was over three years before he had a chance to visit, and although neither of us knew it at the time, it was to be both our first and our last face-to-face meeting.

We had arranged to trade birds one on one, equally. I had chosen several of my best birds, and put them together into a convenient flight, to make it easier for him to choose. He, in turn, would bring some of his best Glosters along. Each of us would choose the birds we liked best, then the rest of the evening would be devoted to visiting. I could hardly wait.

I was practically dancing with excitement by the time he pulled into the driveway— it's not every day you get to meet somebody who excels in an art you admire! When he turned to the car and began to unpack the group of birds he'd brought along, my admiration grew. I've never before or since seen a more practical, useable, or efficient travelling case for canaries.

It had several unique points, fitting a rather remarkable number of show-cages into a compact and easy-to-handle space while still allowing the birds light and air. Perhaps the most unusual and (to me, at least) attractive point about the whole affair was the way it unfolded into a small but effective show-stand, once he'd brought the case into the house. Without moving the cages it contained, he simply unfastened a couple of clips on either side, folded out a couple of braces, and unfolded the box so that the two parts stood side-by-side, instead of back-to-back as they had travelled.

Within a few short minutes, he'd assembled a display stand for his canaries, modelled after the display stands seen at any bird show. His canaries were ranked on three shelves, each of which held six show cages side by side. It stood on fold-out legs, to bring the birds to a height easy to look at, for a person standing in front of the birds. I slowly realized that in the space of that one carrying case, which even fully loaded was still light enough for him to haul into and out of his station wagon, he now had a small show stand in which to display the eighteen birds he'd brought along with him. I shook my head in wonder, and looked at him.

He was gazing fondly at me, wearing a grin as broad as the Mississippi while he watched my reaction.

"Where on earth did you come up with that design?" I

asked, although I was sure, from the size of his grin, that it had to be an original.

"Oh, it just seemed the logical thing to do," he demurred, then demanded to see the birds I'd set aside for him to choose from.

We both took our time choosing the birds we wanted, and then spent several hours talking. All too soon, our time had passed, and he had to leave. I wandered out to the car with him, to see him off, but before getting in, he turned and fixed me with a serious gaze.

"I want you to promise me you'll keep writing about your birds," he insisted. "Never stop, okay?"

I was a little surprised at the strength of his insistence, but willingly promised, and he climbed into his car and drove away. I don't think either of us knew that those were the last words we were ever to share.

Two weeks later, worried that I hadn't heard from him, I phoned his home and talked to his son-in-law, who shocked me to my toes when he told me Jack was in the hospital; he had suffered a serious heart attack only a few days ago. I was charmed to learn that he'd insisted on having at least one canary in the hospital room with him, and that he'd chosen one of my canaries for the honor.

Apparently he'd been telling the whole family how much he enjoyed the song, and insisting that he was going to be okay, because he *finally* had some good red singers for the next breeding season. But it was not to be—shortly afterwards, he suffered yet another heart attack, and soon after that, he left this life behind. But the legacy Jack left behind lives as strongly as ever, in the hearts of every bird lover his life touched over the years.

I, for one, plan to keep his last request to me, and keep writing about my birds. It just seems to be the best possible way to honour his courage, generosity, and caring.

Thanks, Jack. For everything.

by R C McDonald

About the author:

Robirda has been living and working with animals & birds, as well as writing stories about them, all her life. Her first literary publication, a poem about the family's pet beagle's quirkier side, occurred at age six, much to her parents' surprise. An entry into a story-writing contest at eight was disqualified on the grounds that it was *too good* to have been written by a child of that age!

But Robirda didn't let hardship and rejection stop her; in the coming years she would have a number of stories, articles and poems published in a variety of newspapers, books, and magazines.

These days Robirda continues to run the website 'A Place For Canaries' at *robirda.com*. She works and lives in Westbank, in British Columbia's heartland, the Okanagan valley, (although she's yet to see the lake's mythical inhabitant, Ogo-Pogo). Robirda shares her home with her husband David and an ever-changing number of pets, always including, of course, her beloved canaries.

If you like this book, you might be interested in Robirda's other books, 'Brats in Feathers, Keeping Canaries', and, 'The Canary Angel'. Both are available from libraries or bookstores, online at Amazon.com, or from Robirda's website at www.robirda.com

Canary Crazy

Made in the USA
San Bernardino, CA
08 July 2018